THE
FUTURE
OF
AMERICAN
BANKING

COLUMBIA UNIVERSITY SEMINAR SERIES

THE FUTURE OF AMERICAN BANKING
James R. Barth, R. Dan Brumbaugh, Jr., and
Robert E. Litan

DEBT, CRISIS, AND RECOVERY
The 1930s And The 1990s
Albert Gailord Hart

THE
FUTURE
OF
AMERICAN
BANKING

James R. Barth
R. Dan Brumbaugh, Jr.
Robert E. Litan

M. E. Sharpe, Inc.
Armonk, New York ■ London, England

Available in the United Kingdom and Europe from M. E. Sharpe, Publishers,
3 Henriettta Street, London WC2E 8LU.

First printing 1992

Library of Congress Cataloguing-in-Publication Data

Barth, James R.
  The future of American banking / by James R. Barth, R. Dan Brumbaugh,
Jr., and Robert E. Litan.

        p. cm. — (Columbia University seminars)
    Includes bibliographical references and index
    ISBN 1-56324-034-3: $49.95
    1. Banks and banking—United States. 2. Bank failures—United States.
    3. Banking law—United States. I. Brumbaugh, R. Dan, II. Litan,
    Robert E., 1950-   . III. Title. IV. Series.

    332.1'0973—dc20   91-42825
                                                               CIP

For
Mary and Rachel Barth

Mary Adele and Robert Dan Brumbaugh

and
Avivah, Ariel, and Alisa Litan

Table of Contents

List of Tables xi
List of Figures xv
Foreword xvii
Introduction xxi

ONE: Framing the Issues 1
**The Bank Insurance Fund: Repeating the Sins
of the S&L Debacle 1**
The BIF's Projected Resources 1
The BIF's Closure Costs: Baseline, Mild Recession, and Worse 2
Our Conservative Estimate: Insufficient BIF Cash Resources in 1990 4
**The Debate About Recapitalizing the BIF:
Insolvency versus Illiquidity 5**
Who Can and Should Pay: Banks, Taxpayers, or Both? 6
Minimizing the Risks While Waiting for Funding 8
How to Avoid a Disaster for Healthy Banks and Taxpayers 8
Balancing Opportunities and Risk in Banking Reform 9
Notes to Chapter 1 11

TWO: The Banking Industry in Decline 13
**Hiding Decline Behind Industry Averages and
Accounting Techniques 13**
A Bifurcated Industry Based on Income and Capital 15
Growing Portfolio Risk 18
Savings Bank Bifurcation 18
Rising Bank Failures and Soaring Problem Bank Assets 19 ✗

Growing Capital Inadequacy 21
Which Banks Are Healthy? Generally Smaller Banks 25 ✗
The Erosion of Taxpayer Protection 26
Large Banks Became the Big Problem In the 1980s 28 ✗
Special Problems at the Big Banks 29 ✗
Loan Losses, Now And In The Future 29
"High-Risk" Lending Concentration 33
Using Stock Prices to Evaluate Problems At Large Banks 37
Estimating the Put Option Value of Deposit
  Insurance and Forbearance for Big Banks 44
Updating the Put Option Analysis 45
Citicorp Case Study: "Technically Insolvent?" 54
Notes to Chapter 2 56

THREE: Banking In A Long Downward Spiral 59

Competition: Boon to Consumers, Bane of Depositories 59
Inflation Forces Deregulation of Interest Rates:
  Depository Costs Rise, Competitors Proliferate 61
Technology Spurs Securitization of Depository Assets,
  and Reduces Depository Revenues 62
How Securitization Squeezes Depository Revenue 63
Proliferating Indices of Bank Decline 64
Spread Income and Loan Quality Fall 65
From the Banks' Income Statement: Falling Aggregate Net Income 68
From the Banks' Balance Sheet: More Risk 72
Liabilities Also Reveal Risk-Taking 77
A Shrinking Share of U.S. Financial Assets in Depositories 79
Developing a Policy Perspective As Depositories'
Uniqueness Erodes 85
Notes to Chapter 3 86

FOUR: Déjà Vu All Over Again? The Condition of the Bank Insurance Fund 87

A Framework for Understanding Deposit-Insurance
Cost Estimates 87
An Almost Certain Understatement of Actual Losses
  with Most Estimates 88

Methodological Overview for Baseline and Recession Scenarios 90
Baseline Estimates of the Condition of the BIF 90
Estimating the Probability of Bank Failures 91
Factoring Big-Bank Problems into Consideration 94
Resolution Costs per Dollar of Failed-Bank Assets 94
Projected Three-Year Baseline Failure Costs 98
Implications of the Growing Problem Bank List 110
Higher Failure Rates 110
Evidence of Forbearance in Problem-Bank and Closure Data 111
Higher Estimated Costs Based on Problem-Bank Failures 113
The BIF's Net Cash Reserves: Increasing Insurance
Premiums Struggling to Keep Pace with Losses 117
GAO and CBO Income and Reserve Projections 117
A More Appropriate Framework 122
BIF Cash Reserve Shortage at Any Moment
   Even with Baseline Estimates 122
FDIC's Estimates: Wrong and Optimistic 127
Effects of Recession on Bank Failure Costs 127
Three Scenarios Based on Recent Regional Recessions 129
Baseline Estimates Adjusted to Reflect Recession's Effects 129
Conclusion: Effective Present-Value Insolvency for the BIF 131
Notes to Chapter 4 132

FIVE: Recapitalizing the Bank Insurance Fund 137
Charting a Course Between "Type 1" and "Type 2" Errors 137
Officials versus Some Experts: Whom to Believe? 138
The Big Difference Between the Savings and Loan Debacle
   and the Banks 139
How Much Is Needed and From Where Should it Come? 141
Calculating What the Banks May Be Able to Afford 141
A Modest Additional Increase in the Premium or a One Percent
   Capital Infusion 141
Meeting Higher Capital Requirements While Paying
   Higher Premiums 143
When Does it Become Counterproductive to Tax Banks? 144
Timing of Bank Failures and Who Should Pay 144
Notes to Chapter 5 146

SIX: Reducing the Taxpayer's Risk From Deposit Insurance 149

Preventing an Explosion of Future Deposit-Insurance Costs 149
The Problem with Higher Capital Requirements 150
Discipline Versus Opportunities 152
Enhanced Discipline 153
  Early Intervention 153
  Improved Financial Reporting 154
  A Role for Subordinated Debt and Private Reinsurance 155
  Automatic Regulatory Intervention Is Essential 156
Enhancing Profit Opportunities 157
  Nationwide Operations Are a Must 157
  Wider Asset Powers and Bank Affiliations
    with Other Firms Are a Must, Too 158
Dealing With the Big Troubled Banks 160
Hope and Pray, or Forbearance 160
Suspend Dividends 161
More Continentals 161
Aggressive Merger Policy Coupled with Financial Reform 162
Notes to Chapter 6 164

Postscript 167
**The BIF Revises Reserves Downward and
Borrows From the Treasury 167**
Not-So-Subtle Changes in the Legislative Focus 168
**The Proposed Big Bank Mergers of 1991: Cost Savings or
Dangerous Gamble? 169**
The Future of American Banking: Let the Banks Compete 170
Notes to Postscript 171

Bibliography 173
Appendix 179
Index 203

List of Tables

Table 1: Alternative Bank Failure Costs, Estimated 1990 3

Table 2: Federally Insured Commercial Banks: Size and
Condition Ratios, 1980–1990 14

Table 3: Bank Insurance Fund: Problem and Failed
Bank Statistics, 1980–1990 20

Table 4: Capital-to-Asset Ratios for Federally Insured
Commercial Bank Industry, 1980–1990 22

Table 5: Taxpayer Protection: Commercial Bank Capital
and Bank Insurance Fund Reserves, 1980–1990 27

Table 6: Loan Loss Exposure of Large Commercial Banks,
June 30, 1990 30

Table 7: Commercial Bank Nonaccrual Loans and Loan Loss
Reserves, June 30, 1990 32

Table 8: Banks with a Heavy Concentration of Construction
and Development Real Estate Loans, June 1990 33

Table 9: Metropolitan Office Vacancy Rates, 1980–1990 36

Table 10: Loan Risk Exposure of Largest 25 Bank Holding
Companies in the U.S., June 30, 1990 38

Table 11: Stock Price Perfomance of the 25 Largest Bank
Holding Companies, November 30, 1990 40

Table 12: Book and Estimated Market Equity Capital-to-Asset Ratios for the 25 Largest Banks, June 30, 1990 42

Table 13: Accounting and Market-Value Capitalization of Selected Commercial Banks and Value of Deposit Insurance, 1989 and 1990 46

Table 14: Accounting and Market-Value Capitalization of Selected Commercial Banks and Value of Deposit Insurance (Greater Forbearance), 1989 and 1990 50

Table 15: Income and Expense of Federally Insured Commercial Banks, 1980–1990 70

Table 16: Assets and Liabilities of Federally Insured Commercial Banks, 1980–1990 73

Table 17: Off-Balance-Sheet Items of Selected Large Bank Holding Companies, December 31, 1989 78

Table 18: Percentage Distribution of U.S. Financial Assets Held by All Financial Service Firms, 1950–1989 82

Table 19: Concentration Ratios for Federally Insured Commercial Banks, 1980–1990 84

Table 20: Bank Resolution Probabilities by Capital-to-Asset Categories, Banks with $0–500 Million in Assets, All Failures 1987–1989 Based on Year-End 1986–1988 Data 92

Table 21: Bank Resolution Probabilities by Capital-to-Asset Categories, Banks With Assets Above $500 Million, All Failures 1987–1989 Based on Year-End 1986–1988 Data 93

Table 22: Bank Losses by Type of Bank Charter and Size of Bank 1985–1989 95

Table 23: Largest Bank Failures By Estimated Loss, 1985–1989 99

Table 24: Alternative Three-Year Bank Resolution Probabilities 102

Table 25: Failed Bank Resolution Costs as a Percentage of Assets 103

Table 26: Banks and Assets, Two Different Capital-to-Asset Categories, June 30, 1990 104

Table 27: Estimated Three-Year Bank Failure Costs Under Alternative Assumptions Concerning Failure Probability and Resolution Costs 105

Table 28: Selected Characteristics of Reporting Insolvent Banks, June 30, 1990 106

Table 29: Weakly Capitalized Banks, June 30, 1990 108

Table 30: Cumulative Failure Probabilities of Problem Banks, 1985–1989 111

Table 31: Number of Consecutive Months Failed Banks Received Examination Ratings of 4 or 5 Before Closure, 1980–1989 113

Table 32: Correspondent Balances and Interbank Deposits of Selected Large Banks, June 30, 1990 116

Table 33: Insured Bank Deposits and the Bank Insurance Fund, 1934–1990 118

Table 34: GAO and CBO Income and Cash Flow Projection for the BIF, 1991–1995 121

Table 35: Bank Insurance Fund: Statements of Financial Position, 1980–1990 124

Table 36: Net Outlays for the Bank Insurance Fund of the Federal Deposit Insurance Corporation, Fiscal Years 1980–1990 126

Table 37: Estimated Three-Year Bank Failure Costs Based Upon Alternative Assumptions Concerning Recession Scenarios, Failure Probabilities, and Resolution Costs 128

Table 38:   Estimated Three-Year Incremental Bank Failure Costs   130

Table 39:   Number of Unprofitable Banks Paying Dividends   157

Table 40:   Equity Capital an Liquidity of Major Non-Bank
            Companies Already Engaged in Financial Services   163

Table 41:   Equity Capital of 10 Largest U.S. Banks   164

Appendix Tables

Table A-1:   Assets and Liabilities of FDIC-Insured Savings
             Banks, 1980–1990   180

Table A-2:   Income and Expense of FDIC-Insured Savings
             Banks, 1980–1990   182

Table A-3:   Federally Insured Mutual Savings Bank Industry   184

Table A-4:   Concentration Ratios for Federally Insured
             Mutual Savings Banks, 1984–1990   185

Table A-5:   Selected Information for Federally Insured
             Commercial Banks   186

Table A-6:   Selected Information For Federally Insured
             Commercial Banks   190

Table A-7:   Total Banks Rated 4 or 5 As of Each Year-End,
             and Such Banks Failing in Each Subsequent Year   196

Table A-8:   Total Banks Rated 4 or 5 As of Each Year-End,
             and Such Banks Failing in Each Subsequent Year   197

Table A-9:   Top 100 Bank Resolution Losses, 1985–1990   198

Table A-10: Total U.S. Assets of Foreign-Controlled U.S.
             Banking Offices, 1972–1989   201

List of Figures

Figure 1: Bank Equity Capital to Total Assets, 1980–1990 16

Figure 2: Returns on Assets for Banks, 1950–1990 60

Figure 3: Adjusted Net Interest Margin As a Percentage of Interest-Earning Assets, 1985–1990 66

Figure 4: Net Loan Charge-Offs to Average Total Loans for Banks, 1960–1990 67

Figure 5: Bank Equity Capital to Total Assets, 1934–1990 80

Figure 6: Number of Months Failed Banks Received the Lowest Regulation Examination Rating Before Closure, 1980–1989 112

Figure 7: Bank Insurance Fund Reserves Relative to Insured Deposits, 1934–1990 120

Foreword

The University Seminar movement has flourished for forty-six years, growing from the original five seminars in 1945 to over seventy-five seminars today. Each seminar acts as an autonomous and voluntary grouping of scholars and practitioners, brought together under the auspices of Columbia University by their dedication to a particular line of investigation. The movement is not only interdisciplinary, but inter-institutional, and involves members of the community who might not otherwise participate in university activity.

The seminars have as their central goal the integration of otherwise fragmented knowledge, a pulling together of the many threads of knowledge and experience through the stimulus of continuing discussion. Frank Tannenbaum, Professor of Latin American History at Columbia, founder of the University Seminars, and director until his death in 1969, was an ardent believer in the potential for enlightenment contained in meaningful dialogue. In an essay entitled "Implications of an Education Movement," Tannebaum wrote: "The primary aim of the University Seminar is the attempt to see things whole, to merge the disciplines for the purpose of getting a unified view. The aim is synthesis, insight, wisdom, the understanding of the full incidence of the ongoing phenomenon to which any collegium is devoted."

In this regard, the seminar movement may be viewed as the protagonist for the development of a new relationship among the various institutions that comprise our intellectual communities. However great the need forty-six years ago, when the seminar movement was founded, the subsequent explosion of knowledge and increasing fragmentation of disciplines make more urgent than ever the establishment of interdisciplinary forums for learning and communication. There is a manifest need for a structure which acts both to unite specialists, and to join the academy with other elements of society, into an "intellectual guild." The University Seminars embody such a dynamic structure, and will continue in the future, as they have in the past, to provide new perspectives on issues which are critical to the disciplines involved.

Members of the seminars are drawn from numerous departments in the faculties of Columbia University, from other colleges and universities, and from experts and specialists in nonacademic pursuits. Apart from the members, seminars attract authorities in many fields of scholarship as speakers and guests. Seminars range from small discussion groups to larger bodies that, in some cases, have become regional centers for intellectual exchange where such centers would not otherwise exist.

The current volume on *The Future of American Banking* has benefited from discussions in the University Seminar on U.S. Monetary-Financial Reform in a World Context. It is appropriate that the *Columbia University Seminar Series* should be inaugurated with this timely and provocative study of the contemporary U.S. banking and financial crisis that includes a longer-run prognosis for the banking industry, the financial service sector, and important suggestions for changes in the nation's banking laws. The consequences of this crisis for the U.S. economic system and its political and social implications are so profound that we find little precedent for it in American history except for the banking and financial collapse of the Great Depression in the 1930s.

Aaron W. Warner
Director of University Seminars
Joseph L. Buttenweiser Professor Emeritus of Economics
Columbia University

Acknowledgments

The authors thank the House Subcommittee on Financial Institutions Supervision, Regulation and Insurance for commissioning us in May 1990 to prepare a report on the condition of banks and the Bank Insurance Fund. This book updates the data and more fully discusses many of the issues considered in our report. We also gratefully acknowledge the collaboration of Daniel Page on a portion of this book. We thank Carl Hudson for assisting us in the preparation of the charts and tables as well as Don Inscoe for being so helpful in supplying us with most of the bank data. In addition we thank Gaston Acosta-Rua and Maya MacGuineas for their computational assistance on the bank failure projections. We especially thank Jennifer Byrd for assisting us in the preparation of the entire book and for making sure that the final draft was completed so promptly.

Introduction

This nation faces an almost unprecedented situation with many of its largest banks operating on—or conceivably, over—the edge of insolvency. Debating on which side of the line they currently fall is unproductive. The key fact is that by any reasonable standard many banks not only have weak balance sheets but they also are highly exposed to additional deterioration. Their already eroded capital is at risk due to their significant involvement in high-risk lending, the "kryptonite" of the banking system—generally loans for commercial real estate and corporate restructurings—that are so toxic that they threaten the biggest banks.

Perhaps most disturbing of all, the fundamental structural changes occurring in the banking industry will impel even those institutions that survive the current banking crisis and the nation's current economic sluggishness to take greater risks in the future. An expanding number of financial-service firms increasingly from around the globe are competing against U.S. banks with a wider menu of products. Yet, at the same time U.S. banks are excessively constrained in where they can locate, who can own them, and the products they can provide by outmoded laws that have been on the books since the 1930s. We can expect greater risk-taking and more failures unless the laws currently governing the banking business are substantially modified.

Not since the creation of deposit insurance in 1933 have the U.S. banking industry and its deposit insurer been as troubled as they are today. Indeed, the future of American banking is in doubt. The ingredients of the turmoil have been simmering in public view since at least the early 1980s when commercial-bank loans to lesser developed countries (LDCs) began to default. The difficulties began to boil at the end of the decade when it became conceivable that bank insolvency costs could rise so high that they would not only deplete the Bank Insurance Fund (BIF) that is administered by the Federal Deposit Insurance Corporation (FDIC) but also that the costs would exhaust the financial ability of healthy banks to pay for the insolvencies. The specter arose that taxpayer dollars might be needed to resolve bank failures as occurred in the savings and loan debacle.

Concerned about the condition and future of the banking industry and its insurance fund, the Subcommittee on Financial Institutions Supervision, Regulation and Insurance of the Committee on Banking, Finance, and Urban Affairs commissioned us in May 1990 to analyze the current and prospective condition of commercial and savings banks and the BIF. That month the FDIC Chairman predicted that the number of bank failures would remain the same as the year before and that the FDIC fund would not decline in 1990. On December 17, 1990 we delivered our report, which provided the basis for this book, and testified before the subcommittee.[1] The day before we testified, and six days after receiving a copy of our report, the FDIC Chairman announced that the BIF would need to borrow as much as $25 billion in order to close all the banks that the BIF and FDIC projected would become insolvent in the foreseeable future. Equally significant, shortly following our report, three major government watchdog agencies—the General Accounting Office (GAO), the Congressional Budget Office (CBO), and the Office of Management and Budget (OMB)—confirmed our key prediction that without additional resources, the BIF was headed for insolvency.

Thus, we began this book as the nation began to look upon the banking crisis as a possible extension of the savings and loan debacle. Chapter 1 frames the major economic and policy issues raised by the banking crisis; the resolution of these issues will largely determine the future of American banking. Chapter 2 focuses more specifically on the current reported condition of the banking industry, concentrating on large banks in particular. Chapter 3 presents our longer-run economic prognosis for the banking industry and the implications of our projections for the financial services sector and federal regulatory policy toward that sector. Chapter 4 presents our bank failure cost projections made at the time of our report. Chapter 5 presents and discusses alternative methods of financing the payment of these potential liabilities. Chapter 6 concludes with our suggestions for changes in the nation's deposit-insurance system and accompanying banking laws. As this book went to press, Congress had just completed legislation incorporating only a few of these suggestions. We believe future changes are still necessary to reduce the federal government's deposit insurance liabilities and to provide banks with potentially profitable future opportunities.

Notes

1. James R. Barth, R. Dan Brumbaugh, Jr., and Robert E. Litan, "Banking Industry in Turmoil: A Report on the Condition of the U.S. Banking Industry and the Bank Insurance Fund," Report of the Subcommittee on Financial Institutions Supervision, Regulation and Insurance of the Committee on Banking, Finance and Urban Affairs, House of Representatives, One Hundred First Congress, Second Session, Committee Print 101-8, Washington, D.C.: U.S. Government Printing Office, December 1990.

ONE

Framing the Issues

The Bank Insurance Fund: Repeating the Sins of the S&L Debacle

Since the establishment of federal deposit insurance in the 1930s, the federal government—first through the FDIC and the BIF, but ultimately through the U.S. Treasury Department and the taxpayer—has been exposed to losses from bank failures. Federal policymakers have a responsibility to limit this exposure. It is almost impossible for them to meet this responsibility, however, unless the deposit insurer has sufficient cash resources to close or reorganize insolvent depositories in a timely and cost-effective manner. This is perhaps the most important lesson of the savings and loan debacle: because the Federal Savings and Loan Insurance Corporation (FSLIC) had insufficient cash reserves to take prompt corrective action against insolvent savings and loans, policymakers permitted institutions with massive incentives to gamble for resurrection with federally insured funds to run up present-value losses exceeding $200 billion.

The BIF's Projected Resources

Substantial evidence indicated to us that by 1990 the BIF, like the FSLIC in the mid-1980s, lacked sufficient cash resources to pay for its expected caseload of failed commercial and savings banks. At the end of 1990 the

FDIC projected that the BIF would experience a net loss that year of $4 billion. Assuming this loss estimate was accurate, and that the deposit-insurance premium rate effective January 1, 1991 remained at 19.5 basis points for the indefinite future, we projected that the BIF would have at most $28 billion during the next three years to pay for the resolution of failed depositories. An increase in the premium rate to 23 basis points, as projected in the fall 1990 budget agreement and that took effect in July 1991, would raise this total to $31 billion.

We pointed out that the BIF's actual level of cash resources to handle future failures could even be considerably below either of these figures because of the nature of the transactions made by the FDIC in providing financial assistance to acquirers of already failed institutions. More specifically, by 1990 the FDIC had begun granting options to the acquirers of many failed banks, allowing the acquirers to put back to the FDIC certain problem assets under specified circumstances in exchange for cash. Although we accepted the FDIC's estimates of the costs of these options, they are nonetheless multibillion dollar contingencies that easily could cause the FDIC's cash outlays to soar and its cash reserves to evaporate if the FDIC's estimates prove too low and the options are exercised. This is only one of many examples of how highly volatile contingencies could adversely affect the FDIC's cash resources.

The BIF's Closure Costs: Baseline, Mild Recession, and Worse

We estimated the FDIC's future costs for resolving failed institutions by examining a wide range of financial data and other information about the commercial and savings banks insured by the BIF. The FDIC aided us in our task by providing much of the data. Even though we requested data in our role as advisers to a congressional subcommittee and were willing to sign appropriate confidentiality agreements, the FDIC denied us access to certain information it routinely collects about the failure risks of individual banks. In other cases, the FDIC did not respond in a timely fashion to our requests for nonconfidential data. We reported our cost estimates as ranges to reflect the substantial uncertainties involved in projecting bank failures and their resolution costs based on the available data. Had the FDIC provided all the data requested we believe we could have narrowed the range of our estimates.

Still, based on publicly available financial data as of the end of the second quarter of 1990, we estimated a baseline—which assumed no recession—that bank failure costs during the following three years would total at least $17 billion and could be as high as $36 billion. Thus, even without a recession, the FDIC's future costs could outstrip its resources. Of course, given the decline in economic activity since June 1990, we considered the baseline cost estimates too optimistic. Accordingly, we estimated the federal government's likely liabilities for bank failure costs under three alternative recession scenarios using June 30, 1990 financial data. These alternative cost estimates are presented in Table 1.

In the mildest of the recessions in which the nation (except for the Southwest where rising oil prices had stemmed a downward spiral) was assumed to experience a downturn roughly half as severe as the one that already plagued New England, the FDIC's projected three-year liability grew by as little as $2 billion to a minimum of $19 billion and by as much as $7 billion to a maximum of $43 billion. In the severest recession in which the nation (except for the Southwest) was assumed to be plagued with a downturn as severe as the one that rocked Texas in the mid-1980s, the estimated three-year liability ballooned to between $10 and $26 billion on the low side, to as much as $63 billion on the high side.

Table 1 Alternative Bank Failure Costs, Estimated 1990 ($ Billions)	
	Bank Resolution Costs
Baseline (No Recession)	17 - 36
Mild Recession	19 - 43
"New England" Style Recession	24 - 51
"Texas" Style Recession	27 - 63

Source: Authors' calculations based upon FDIC data.

The estimates at the lower end of our cost ranges, moreover, reflect the assumption that the FDIC will continue, as it has in the past, to resolve large troubled banks less frequently than similarly troubled smaller institutions. This pattern reflects either that there has been an implicit policy of forbearance for larger banks or, more doubtfully, that there have been proportionately fewer problems in the recent past among large banks. The estimates at the upper end of the different cost ranges assume that this pattern will change, such that both large and small banks will be resolved in the future with the same frequency.

Our Conservative Estimate: Insufficient BIF Cash Resources in 1990

Although we have presented our estimates as ranges, we believe the most likely costs fall between the middle and upper parts of our ranges. There is substantial evidence that current bank accounting data, on which we have based our estimates, can significantly overstate the true economic capital at depository institutions, especially those that report being weakly capitalized. Stated another way, our estimates assume that the past relationship between reported book-value capital and market-value capital in weak banks will continue to apply in the future, when in fact the discrepancy between these two accounting methods may have grown as the condition of some banks has deteriorated. In the savings and loan debacle, for example, ample evidence indicates that deteriorating savings and loans used accounting techniques to obscure their true economic deterioration.

In addition, as we have noted, our failure cost estimates are based on reported financial data as of June 30, 1990, the latest date for which comprehensive data were available at the time our original report was completed. Since preparing our report the FDIC has released bank statistics for three subsequent quarters that show significant additional loan losses and declines in aggregate bank profits. It is likely, therefore, that had we been able to calculate our failure cost estimates based on more recent data our loss estimates would be higher than those reported here.

In addition, we believe it is most likely that the historically lower resolution costs upon which we rely reflect regulatory forbearance for large banks. As a result, we believe that the lower bounds of our different cost ranges reflect this pattern and, given the longstanding difficulties of large banks, understate the true economic costs of resolving bank insolvencies. Finally, at the very least, the economy was in a mild reces-sion when we simulated the BIF's costs of resolving failed banks. At the end of 1990 then, we concluded, conservatively in our opinion, that the BIF was facing three-year bank failure costs of between $31 and $43 billion, the midpoint to upper end of the cost range for the mild recession.

At this level of costs, the BIF's current and projected cash resources during the next three years are exhausted. Moreover, we have simulated many other scenarios in which the BIF's potential liabilities would be substantially greater, and thus the magnitude of the BIF's resource shortfall correspondingly higher.

The Debate about Recapitalizing the BIF: Insolvency versus Illiquidity

Since 1989 the explicit full faith and credit of the U.S. government has stood behind the federal deposit-insurance funds. As a result, regardless of the depletion of cash resources or illiquidity and regardless of how long the depletion is tolerated, it is technically impossible for the BIF to be insolvent. The technical impossibility of insolvency has one big effect: it protects against runs. Because insured depositors know that the federal government has the financial resources to protect them, there is no incentive for insured depositors to run under any circumstances.

But the technical impossibility of insolvency does nothing, in and of itself, to ensure that the deposit insurer will behave appropriately with timely closure or reorganization of insolvent banks. The deposit insurer can act as if it is effectively insolvent. A deposit insurer without adequate cash resources may keep insolvent depositories open and operating rather than go to Congress for additional funding to close them. That is what the FSLIC did for several years—with disastrous consequences—and what the FDIC may have also been doing in recent years.[1] Indeed, in late November 1991, the new FDIC Chairman William Taylor warned that his agency had been slowing the pace of failed bank resolutions because of a shortage of liquid funds. In other words, a deposit insurer without cash resources can and probably will fail to engage in prompt corrective action just as it would if it were technically insolvent.

In a perverse way, placing the full faith and credit of the U.S. government behind the deposit-insurance funds can actually encourage inappropriate closure policies by the deposit insurer. By completely removing any possibility of runs by insured depositors, the full faith guarantee removes any potential pressure from insured depositors on the deposit insurer to close troubled banks in a timely fashion. The most important point in the context of the BIF's current fiscal woes is that whenever the deposit insurer lacks the cash resources to close insolvent depositories, a chain of events develops that in the past has always led to higher costs: closures of troubled depositories are delayed; incentives to take great risks soar; containment of risk-taking is flawed; and the excessive risk-taking almost always fails.

Who Can and Should Pay: Banks, Taxpayers, or Both?

To correct the BIF's current financial woes three potential financial remedies that rely exclusively on the banking industry itself are on the table: (1) further increases in annual deposit-insurance premiums, (2) a large injection of capital by banks into the BIF, such as the one percent of insured deposits that credit unions deposit with the National Credit Union Share Insurance Fund, and (3) a substantial increase in the BIF's line of credit at the U.S. Treasury Department, from the current $5 billion to something like $70 billion, with later repayment by banks over an extended period.

Option (1) may be counterproductive. As recently as the mid-1980s the bank insurance premium was 8.3 basis points, half of which was rebated. The effective premium was therefore approximately 4.2 basis points. This means that the 23-basis-point increase in the July 1991 premium represented a five-fold total increase in only a few years. The new premium, moreover, equals approximately one-third of the average profitability of all commercial banks in the past few years and is one-half the average profitability of the nation's largest banks. In order to raise funds to cover the costs that we estimate are necessary to resolve failed banks, an additional premium increase would be needed that, if it could not be passed on, would adversely affect the profitability of banks.

Both options (2) and (3) would gain the BIF quick access to substantial additional resources to resolve failed banks. The additional advantage of option (3)—the line of credit—is that only it can realistically provide sufficient cash resources to cover the costs implied by our worst-case cost scenarios. The proposed borrowing plan would have the banks obligated to pay back the borrowings over time—primarily through the deposit-insurance premium. Although this approach relies most heavily on the banks for repayment, it nonetheless entails an indirect taxpayer contribution. Borrowing through the U.S. Treasury Department rather than borrowing in purely private markets conveys a subsidy to the banks approximately equal to the differential between federal government and private borrowing rates.

There are additional factors to consider regarding these options. A contribution from capital or the obligation to pay back federal borrowing is really no different than a reduction of income via a permanent increase in the insurance premium. To further compound matters, many banks appear to have positive or adequate capital only because current accounting conventions allow them to obscure economic deterioration, making it quite difficult to calculate actual owner-contributed equity capital.

Whether recapitalization of the BIF comes from premium income immediately or from future premium income to repay an immediate borrowing, however, changes the timing of the payment. An unexpected future economic development, for the better or worse, would affect the ability of the banks to make future payments. The effectively cash-deficient BIF and banks at or near economic insolvency have an incentive to hope for "better times" or to take excessive risk. Stated another way, they have an incentive to bet on a future unexpected or lower probability economic bonanza to bail themselves out of their current difficulties.

One way the BIF and banks have manifested the incentive to take risk is by encouraging the federal government to borrow now and to promise that banks will pay back the borrowing later. If no economic bonanza develops or if deterioration is worse than expected, the banks can default and taxpayers will become responsible for the borrowing. The burden to pay and the likelihood of closure are shifted to the future. The borrow-now-pay-back-later approach may therefore actually increase the contingent taxpayer liability besides shifting it to the future.

Any further financing from banks also raises the issue of whether it is fair for healthy banks to bear yet another deposit-insurance "tax." Whether additional payments of any kind can be assessed without sending even more weak banks into insolvency, and whether the resulting closure costs will exceed the proceeds from the capital contribution or premiums, are also legitimate issues.

Another funding option is to use general revenues, which would explicitly commit taxpayer dollars to the BIF (as has been done with the now defunct FSLIC). The advantage of this approach is that it could guarantee adequate funding without requiring any adverse affects on the banks. If the funds were borrowed, they would be borrowed at the lowest cost. If funding is necessary beyond what banks can reasonably pay, then this is the least costly funding method. This option implicitly assumes that banks should not or cannot pay an additional part of the cost.

There also may be hidden costs if taxpayer funds are explicitly used to buttress the BIF. When tax dollars were made available to the FSLIC, for example, costly asset restrictions were imposed by Congress on healthy savings and loans. In addition, if taxpayer dollars are used for the BIF, intense political opposition could delay their use. Such a delay drastically increased the cost of the savings and loan debacle.

Minimizing the Risks While Waiting for Funding

Regardless of the source of additional BIF financing, the Congress can and should minimize future bank failure costs both by enhancing regulatory and market discipline against excessive risk-taking and by creating new opportunities for cost reductions and profits in the banking industry. The core feature of additional discipline should be a more automatic system of regulatory intervention.[2] In particular, banks that are not yet economically insolvent but are nevertheless weakly capitalized must be closely supervised to ensure that they do not take additional gambles that can push them over the edge with insured funds. In addition, if weakly capitalized banks do not choose to or cannot raise additional equity capital, regulators must suspend their dividends as a means of building capital. This has not happened in the recent past. Finally, banks near insolvency should be closely supervised or placed in conservatorship pending recapitalization by existing owners or sale to new owners, or liquidation.

How to Avoid a Disaster for Healthy Banks and Taxpayers

The commercial banking industry, like the savings and loan industry, is bifurcated. One sizable segment consists of unprofitable and poorly capitalized banks, while the other segment consists of the majority of well-capitalized and profitable banks. As we have said, however, some banks that report themselves to be in the second, or "healthy" category, in fact are there only because of accounting practices that hide their true condition. A reflection of the exaggerated capital occurs frequently when the BIF closes or reorganizes troubled banks and suffers substantial losses, indicating that by the time the regulators take action, the banks are deeply insolvent on a market-value, or economic, basis. Because the BIF relies on accounting practices to determine solvency, this pattern of reporting sizable losses only upon closure confirms that historical accounting principles lead to substantial overstatements of a bank's economic capital.

Intense competition is replacing the intermediation functions traditionally provided by banks. Securities markets, for example, through the flight of high-quality bank borrowers to the commercial paper market and the "securitization" of increasing types of loans, are eroding bank assets. Mutual money market funds are providing alternatives to bank deposits. Because of an explosion in information technology all of this is taking place in an increasingly international market. As a result, banks–especially big banks–are taking more risks to maintain income.

We anticipate even further complications ahead given the clear and unmistakable trends we highlight in this book. Net interest margins earned by banks, adjusted for loan losses, have been falling. Apparently healthy banks are seeking profitability by increasingly investing in the kryptonite of the banking industry: high-risk loans and other assets. Erratic and inadequate provisioning for loan losses has propped up the earnings and capital of many banks but has not been able to obscure the downward trend in both financial statistics. Barring some unexpected beneficial economic development, we believe that many more banks—including perhaps some major banks—will become insolvent, even by historical accounting standards. Some may be economically insolvent already.

Balancing Opportunities and Risk in Banking Reform

Ultimately, the government's deposit-insurance liabilities can only be contained if the banking business promises sufficient opportunities for profits without excessive risk to attract and retain equity capital. The nation's current banking laws, however, frustrate this objective. In particular, restrictions against interstate expansion by banks and their holding companies, for example, lower industrywide profitability and raise overall risk by preventing efficient consolidation and geographic diversification. Limitations on the ability of banks to affiliate with, or to be owned by, nonbanking organizations prevent banks from realizing any "economies of scope" from the joint provision of numerous financial products and services offered by affiliates. Furthermore, nonbanks— industrial as well as financial firms—might bring additional capital to the banking industry that could help reduce the BIF funding requirements.

We know it has been tempting for the Congress in any debate over recapitalizing the BIF to avoid the structural questions of interstate branching, bank and nonbank affiliation and ownership, and additional powers for healthy banks. Indeed, shortly before this book went to press, that is what the Congress has done. We believe this was a significant mistake. The fundamental structural changes in the banking industry we outline below will impel many banks to take greater risks in the future unless the laws currently governing the banking business are substantially modified.

Regulators should also be more aggressive in promoting mergers between troubled banks and healthy nonbank partners. Current banking laws, however, severely limit the pool of potential acquirers to healthy banks, of which there are just a few with sufficient capital to absorb any of the major troubled institutions and none, for example, large enough to acquire troubled behemoths like Citicorp. It is for this reason that the Congress should permit nonbanks, including nonfinancial companies, to acquire banks under the appropriate safeguards so as to insulate the BIF from risks posed by the nonbanking operations. To some extent the failure of Congress to do so ignores that such combinations already exist in many forms and compete with banks. A large number of commercial firms already own financial firms that provide nearly all of the functions that federally insured depositories provide. More than 21 percent of all domestic commercial-bank assets are in foreign-controlled banks, whose home countries in many cases allow nonfinancial firm ownership and wide access to nonbank activities. Moreover, a large number of states permit state-chartered banks to engage in securities brokerage, general securities underwriting, real estate equity participation, real estate development, real estate brokerage, insurance underwriting, and insurance brokerage.

At the very least, Congress should permit commercial firms to bring their capital to troubled or failing banks in particular. In the savings and loan debacle such major nonfinancial firms as Ford and Sears acquired troubled savings and loans. As far as we know, there have been no cases where the affiliation *per se* between a troubled savings and loan and a nonfinancial firm has caused a problem. Certainly the great savings and loan debacle was not caused by commercial ownership of these institutions. We know there may be risks in permitting affiliations between banks and commercial firms. Indeed, that is the reason two of us (Brumbaugh and Litan) in the past have urged that such affiliations be allowed under only the condition that the banks in such combinations narrow their assets to safe, marketable securities.[3] In addition, it is not clear that if allowed to enter the banking business—and specifically to purchase interests in troubled major banks—many large commercial and industrial concerns would take advantage of the opportunity. Nevertheless, the condition of the largest banks as a group is sufficiently serious that we recommend that commercial firms be allowed to acquire such banks under appropriate conditions.

Notes

1. For a description of the savings and loan crisis and how the FSLIC handled its funding shortage, see R. Dan Brumbaugh, Jr., *Thrifts Under Siege: Restoring Order to American Banking*, Ballinger, 1988; James R. Barth, *The Great Savings and Loan Debacle*, American Enterprise Institute, 1991; R. Dan Brumbaugh, Jr., *The Demise of the Savings and Loan Industry: Explaining the Collapse and the Taxpayer Bailout*, Garland Publishing Inc., New York, 1992; and, James R. Barth and R. Dan Brumbaugh, Jr., "Thrifts," in *The New Palgrave: The Dictionary of Banking and Finance*, Peter Newman, Murray Milgate, and John Eatwell, eds., Stockton Press, New York, June 1992.

2. For a description of early intervention, see George J. Benston, R. Dan Brumbaugh, Jr., Jack M. Guttentag, Richard J. Herring, George G. Kaufman, Robert E. Litan, and Kenneth Scott, "Blueprint for Restructuring America's Financial Institutions: Report of a Task Force," Brookings Institution, Washington, D.C., 1989. In support of early intervention or prompt corrective action, two of the authors (Barth and Brumbaugh) argued in 1985 that not closing insolvent institutions increases the eventual cost to the insurer. (See James R. Barth, R. Dan Brumbaugh, Daniel Sauerhaft, and George H.K. Wang, "Insolvency and Risk-Taking in the Thrift Industry: Implications for the Future," *Contemporary Policy Issues*, Volume III, Number 8, Fall 1985.) In 1986 they presented the first empirical evidence to our knowledge confirming that delay in closing troubled institutions does indeed increase the costs of closure. (See James R. Barth, R. Dan Brumbaugh, and Daniel Sauerhaft, "Failure Costs of Government-Regulated Financial Firms: The Case of Thrift Institutions," Federal Home Loan Bank Board Working Paper No. 123, October 1986.)

3. *Ibid.*

TWO

The Banking Industry in Decline

Hiding Decline Behind Industry Averages and Accounting Techniques

In evaluating the condition of federally insured depositories, it is important to look beyond industry averages and to scrutinize accounting techniques that are often used by deteriorating depositories to obscure troubles. The primary reasons are that the risk to the desposit-insurance system generally comes from the poorly performing institutions within the industry, and these institutions have the greatest incentives to use historical, or book-value, accounting techniques to cover up market-value deterioration.

For years in the early part of the savings and loan debacle, for example, regulators and industry trade associations pointed to the industry's average capital levels and other indices to deflect criticism of the FSLIC's closure policies. Yet the industry was bifurcated with a large segment of deteriorated savings and loans. These savings and loans ultimately bankrupted the FSLIC because their market-value losses far exceeded reported accounting capital. Whether the same process has occurred within commercial banking is an important issue.

Table 2
Federally Insured Commercial Banks: Size and Condition Ratios, 1980 - 1990
(As a Percentage of Total Assets)

	1980	1981	1982	1983	1984	1985	1986	1987	1988	1989	1990
Number of Institutions	14,435	14,415	14,453	14,467	14,472	14,393	14,188	13,694	13,120	12,705	12,338
Total Assets ($ Billions)	1,856	2,029	2,194	2,342	2,508	2,731	2,941	2,999	3,131	3,299	3,389
Net Income After Taxes (%)	0.75	0.73	0.68	0.64	0.62	0.66	0.59	0.09	0.79	0.47	0.50
Net Operating Income Before Taxes (%)	0.78	0.77	0.71	0.63	0.61	0.59	0.45	0.04	0.76	0.44	0.46
Equity Capital (%)	5.79	5.83	5.87	6.00	6.14	6.19	6.19	6.02	6.28	6.21	6.46
Gross Loans and Leases (%)	55.14	56.01	55.98	56.31	60.87	60.34	60.28	61.48	62.23	62.83	62.33
Loans & Leases Past Due > 90 Days (%)	N/A	N/A	0.54	0.49	0.37	0.34	0.33	0.29	0.28	0.29	0.31[1]
Nonaccrual Loans (%)	N/A	N/A	1.11	1.26	1.37	1.26	1.31	1.82	1.52	1.59	1.66[1]
Reserve for Loan Losses (%)	0.54	0.56	0.61	0.66	0.74	0.85	0.98	1.66	1.48	1.62	1.64

Source: FDIC.

[1] June 1990.

A Bifurcated Industry Based on Income and Capital

By looking at industry averages alone, American banks can appear relatively healthy. As shown in Table 2, reported industrywide accounting net income as a percent of total assets generally has been stable throughout the past decade.

There were, nonetheless, dismal performances in 1987 and 1989 when major banks made substantial additions to their loan loss reserves, primarily for loans to developing countries or LDC debt. Similarly, the reported industrywide equity capital-to-asset ratio for the banking industry has been essentially stable during this period, growing slightly from less than 5.8 percent in 1980 to barely over 6.4 percent in 1990.

Throughout the 1980s and still today, some point to these average capital-to-asset ratios as signs of health in the banks. However, by historical standards they are low, substantially lower than levels that exceeded 20 percent after the Great Depression and exceeded 10 percent as recently as years in the 1970s.[1] Only by using relatively contemporaneous comparisons do the reported levels seem substantial. More important, the aggregate capital-to-asset ratio for banks is relatively low as a buffer protecting the BIF. In 1989, for example, the task force of economists assembled by the Brookings Institution to evaluate the deposit-insurance system concluded that depositories with capital between 6 and 8 percent were "weakly capitalized" and those with capital between 3 and 6 percent were "inadequately capitalized."[2] Moreover, these economists would base capital on market values rather than accounting historical cost or book values.

Figure 1 illustrates dramatically that the averages hide big problems as well. Capital-to-asset ratios are presented for all banks and for banks by size. What jumps out from the figure is that throughout the 1980s the capital ratios of small banks significantly exceeded the capital ratios of large banks. Thus, the reason that overall capital levels are as high as they are is that the capital ratios of the small banks have pulled up the ratios of the large banks.

The low level of capital for the larger banks is a major reason for concern. As Figure 1 shows, the capital of the largest banks in 1980 was 4 percent and rose to only five percent by 1990. Since those ratios are themselves averages, some of the banks in that size category were below average. In 1990, the forty-six banks comprising the largest bank category

Figure 1. Bank Equity Capital to Total Assets 1980-1990.

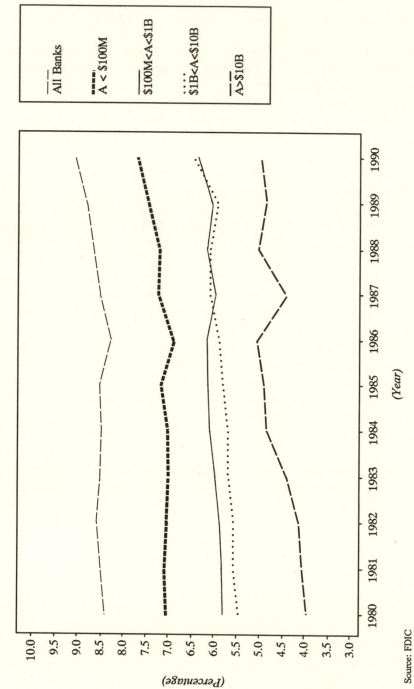

held $1.3 trillion in assets, the same size as the entire savings and loan industry at its peak. For perspective, the minimum regulatory capital level for savings and loans in 1980 was 5 percent, measured in approximately the same way as the capital levels presented in Figure 1. In other words, a relatively few banks combined equal the size of the entire savings and loan industry and as a group these banks fail the minimum requirements that proved inadequate to prevent the disaster that struck the savings and loan industry.

These averages, moreover, are reported using accounting conventions that allow assets whose market value has fallen below their original or historical cost to be reported at that inaccurate level nonetheless. Our judgment is that troubled savings and loans and banks use these conventions to conceal deterioration, and as a result, the reported averages overstate the true financial condition. In general, the reported capital levels are relatively reliable for demonstrably healthy institutions; but the reliability deteriorates as the condition of the depository deteriorates. Thus, the reported capital levels of the nation's largest banks in the most trouble should be viewed as potentially significant overstatements of true economic health.

One of the most important ramifications of this phenomenon is that the BIF, like the FSLIC before it, closes a bank based on an accounting measure of insolvency that invariably leaves the BIF with large market-value losses. When the Bank of New England was closed in early 1991, for example, it was reporting positive accounting capital of about 1 percent. But within days of the closure the BIF estimated that the cost to the BIF in financial assistance to an acquirer was going to be about $2.5 billion, approximately 10 percent of the bank's total assets and equal to the BIF's average cost to close a bank in 1989. This is one of the major reasons why the Brookings Institution task force and others have recommended both that depositories report the market value of their assets and liabilities and that the deposit-insurance agencies close or reorganize depositories before book-value insolvency is reached.

Even the way the FDIC accounts for the banks it closes in public releases has helped overstate the industry's actual performance in the 1980s. When the FDIC closes a bank, the FDIC removes its income and other financial data from the industry's overall database for the entire year in which the closure occurs. In contrast, when a federally insured savings and loan institution fails, it has until recently remained in the savings and loan industry's aggregate database throughout the reporting year. With annual closures of between one hundred and two hundred banks, including banks with $20 billion or more in assets, the effect on the reported aggregates can be significant.

Growing Portfolio Risk

As the industry's income and capital have dwindled, the industry's asset portfolio has become riskier. As Table 2 shows, gross loans and leases as a percentage of total assets has grown from approximately 55 percent in 1980 to 62 percent in 1990. This means that nonrisk assets like cash and short-term Treasury securities have declined as a percentage of assets. It appears that as income has fallen and capital eroded, banks have been seeking greater return from higher-earning, higher-risk assets.

As Table 2 also shows, indices of deterioration have risen along with the risk. Nonaccrual loans (past due loans for which banks are no longer allowed to book accrued but unpaid interest payments) rose from 1.1 percent of assets in 1982 to more than 1.6 percent in 1990. Reserves for loan losses rose from approximately 0.5 percent of assets in 1980 to over 1.6 percent in 1990. Although reserves for loan losses are estimates of future losses on loans made by banks based upon accounting conventions, these reserves are allowed to be counted in selected capital-to-asset ratios.

Savings Bank Bifurcation

Table 2 and Figure 1 present data for commercial banks only, excluding the 469 savings banks with $259 billion in assets as of December 31, 1990, whose deposits are also insured by the FDIC. More complete data for savings banks alone are shown in Appendix Tables A-1 to A-4. Again on the surface, these institutions appear relatively healthy, displaying capital-to-asset ratios in the 7 percent range throughout the 1980s.[3]

Savings banks, however, have had to make staggering provisions for loan losses beginning in 1989 that have imposed dramatic declines on income thereafter. In 1990, the overall return on equity was a negative 13 percent.[4] Indeed, in 1990 the savings bank industry lost $2.5 billion, or about a forty basis point reduction in the aggregate capital-to-asset ratio (for many individual institutions, of course, the reduction in capital-to-asset ratios has been far worse). Savings banks with assets greater than

$1 billion reported a return on equity of negative 16 percent while those savings banks with assets less than $100 million reported a return on equity of negative 6 percent. In order to achieve an overall equity capital-to-asset ratio of 6.6 percent in 1990, the large savings banks' ratio of 6 percent was pulled up by the small savings banks' higher ratio of 8 percent.

It is particularly ironic that the bank regulators have emphasized aggregate measures of bank performance and allow the proliferation of accounting techniques that inflate the averages because they have so little relevance to the federal government as guarantor of federally insured deposits. Instead, the government should care mostly about banks at the "tail of the distribution," those that become insolvent or are likely to do so in the foreseeable future, and the costs of resolving them. Unfortunately for the BIF, the tail of the banking industry has been growing longer and fatter through most of the last decade while the quality of assets held by these banks has been deteriorating.

Rising Bank Failures and Soaring Problem Bank Assets

Table 3 shows the rising trend of FDIC reported annual bank failures throughout the 1980s. Failures rose from 10 in 1980 to 206 by 1989. In addition, Table 3 shows that the number of problem banks (those receiving one of the two worst ratings by bank examiners) also rose, from 212 in 1980 to a peak of 1,575 in 1987.

In preparation of our report for the House Subcommittee on Financial Institutions Supervision, Regulation, and Insurance, we asked the FDIC to supply us with the names of the banks currently on the problem list to enable us to make a more precise assessment of the failure risks of these banks. Our request was never answered. We also requested the asset size of the banks on the problem list. That request was denied. We were, however, given data on the deposits in problem banks as reported in Appendix Tables A-7 and A-8.

To our knowledge, these data in our Congressional report were the first public indication of the size of the problem banks. The data given us by the FDIC indicated that deposits at problem banks were $211 billion in 1987 and fell to $185 billion in 1988. Because deposits are almost always less than total liabilities or assets, however, these figures are necessarily underestimates. This appeared to be confirmed when for the first time the

Table 3
Bank Insurance Fund: Problem and Failed Bank Statistics, 1980 - 1990

	1980	1981	1982	1983	1984	1985	1986	1987	1988	1989	1990
Number of Insured Institutions[1]	14,758	14,766	14,767	14,759	14,825	14,906	14,837	14,289	13,606	13,239	12,807
Problem Banks	212	223	369	642	848	1,140	1,484	1,575	1,406	1,109	1,046
Problem Bank Assets ($ Mil)	N/A	N/A	N/A	N/A	228,000	238,000	336,000	359,000	352,000	236,000	409,000
Bank Failures	10	10	42	48	79	120	138	184	200	206	169
Assisted Banking Organizations	0	3	9	3	2	4	7	19	21	1	0
Failed Banks in Receivership	N/A	N/A	N/A	N/A	N/A	N/A	N/A	684	848	964	1,023[2]
Assets Held in Liquidation ($M)	1,800	1,900	N/A	4,100	10,000	9,600	10,900	11,000	9,300	11,500	14,900[2]
Number of Assets In Liquidation	N/A	N/A	N/A	N/A	N/A	N/A	N/A	179,000	119,000	159,000	175,000[2]

Source: FDIC.

[1] Includes both commercial banks and those savings banks insured by the BIF.
[2] June 1990.

FDIC reported the assets in problem commercial and savings banks in 1991.[5] As shown in Table 3, although the number of problem banks has declined since 1987, their assets have jumped from $359 billion in 1987 to $409 billion in 1990. In 1984, the first year for which data have been made available, the assets in problem banks were $228 billion.

Growing Capital Inadequacy

The average capital-to-asset ratios for the industry as a whole and for banks of certain sizes conceal the sizable number of weakly capitalized banks. As shown in Table 4, at the end of June 1990, 35 banks with $1.5 billion in assets were still open, but reporting insolvency, and another 148 banks with aggregate assets of $28 billion had equity capital-to-asset ratios below 3 percent, the minimum so-called leverage requirement for the best-rated banks under the federal regulators' new capital standards.[6]

The number and aggregate assets of insolvent and weakly capitalized banks (those with equity capital-to-asset ratios below 3 percent) in mid-1990 nevertheless were substantially below the corresponding figures for year-end 1989, suggesting improvement in the industry. There were 67 banks in mid 1990 with aggregate assets of $80 billion that were reporting capital-to-asset ratios slightly above 3 percent, or between 3 percent and 3.5 percent.[7] Significantly, the capital-to-asset ratios of 48 of these banks, about 70 percent, fell between year-end 1989 and mid-year 1990.

More broadly, we find it disturbing that many of the largest banks fail to meet the risk-based capital standards adopted by U.S. bank regulators and other major industrialized countries (the so-called Basel Accord standards). According to a recent Federal Reserve Board analysis, by year-end 1989, 591 banks with a total of almost 28 percent of the nation's banking assets—including assets in 20 of the largest banks in the country—did not meet the risk-adjusted capital standards that will be fully effective January 1, 1993.[8] Similarly, in the fall 1989 Senate testimony, the Comptroller of the Currency reported that almost 700 banks holding over 40 percent of all bank assets did not meet the new risk-adjusted standards.[9]

These figures are important because although the new standards will not be totally phased in until 1993, presumably they reflect the regulators' collective judgment about the minimum amounts of capital banks should have today to protect the BIF and to prevent their managements from taking excessive risks.

Table 4
Capital-to-Asset Ratios for Federally Insured Commercial Bank Industry, 1980 - 1990

	1980	1981	1982	1983	1984	1985	1986	1987	1988	1989	1990
Number of Institutions	14,435	14,415	14,453	14,467	14,472	14,393	14,188	13,694	13,120	12,705	12,338
Number of Branches	38,736	40,786	39,784	40,857	41,907	43,347	44,356	45,701	47,063	50,224	51,225
Multi-bank BHC's	284	302	315	396	513	639	821	886	872	853	831
Banks Owned by MBHC's	2,269	2,427	2,783	2,935	3,299	3,583	4,053	4,346	4,153	3,886	3,780
Total Assets ($ Millions)	1,855,715	2,029,461	2,194,153	2,342,161	2,508,488	2,730,539	2,940,675	2,999,187	3,130,888	3,299,035	3,388,914
Capital ($ Millions)	107,526	118,282	128,765	140,486	154,008	169,085	182,138	180,536	196,507	204,840	218,862
Net Income ($ Millions)	13,974	14,737	14,881	14,932	15,499	17,981	17,412	2,806	24,817	15,647	16,378
Net Operating Income ($ Millions)	14,443	15,542	15,475	14,867	15,414	16,182	13,194	1,176	23,722	14,541	15,273
Provision for Loan Losses ($ Millions)	4,479	5,131	8,507	10,802	13,813	17,717	22,027	36,999	17,071	30,990	31,904
Taxes ($ Millions)	4,657	3,873	2,980	4,017	4,721	5,643	5,304	5,424	9,991	9,658	7,839

Table 4 (continued)
Capital-to-Asset Ratio Categories

	1980	1981	1982	1983	1984	1985	1986	1987	1988	1989	June 1990
< 0.0 %											
No. of Institutions	1	2	4	13	11	28	72	76	103	80	35
Net Income ($M)	0	(2)	(10)	(61)	(28)	(118)	(417)	(1,118)	(1,865)	(709)	(74)
Capital ($M)	(1)	(1)	(1)	(12)	(6)	(32)	(174)	(773)	(855)	(978)	(54)
Total Assets ($M)	17	37	156	746	414	1,485	3,596	9,923	21,163	11,160	1,485
0.0 % to 1.5 %											
No. of Institutions	2	5	13	22	23	37	88	108	97	70	56
Net Income ($M)	(3)	(3)	(37)	(58)	(40)	(103)	(306)	(250)	(402)	(989)	(204)
Capital ($M)	1	0	5	10	7	17	48	39	78	271	243
Total Assets ($M)	86	72	759	1,682	847	2,115	5,523	5,247	9,801	37,859	18,938
1.5 % to 3.0 %											
No. of Institutions	12	16	27	53	62	85	124	165	157	109	92
Net Income ($M)	(12)	(26)	(53)	(87)	(170)	(213)	(616)	(2,676)	(509)	(1,869)	(166)
Capital ($M)	29	95	71	90	173	169	346	2,740	1,028	2,049	238
Total Assets ($M)	1,583	3,982	3,204	3,778	7,279	6,970	14,137	111,474	38,607	75,610	9,747

Table 4 (continued)

	1980	1981	1982	1983	1984	1985	1986	1987	1988	1989	June
3.0 % to 6.0 %											
No. of Institutions	1,038	1,041	1,141	1,426	1,508	1,569	2,030	1,604	1,402	1,289	1,138
Net Income ($M)	6,475	6,926	6,990	6,542	7,702	8,605	8,826	(4,146)	13,947	3,069	3,760
Capital ($M)	50,193	56,062	62,279	67,665	74,321	81,906	90,706	75,540	86,610	77,036	81,472
Total Assets ($M)	1,141,363	1,259,599	1,375,203	1,431,948	1,498,606	1,632,547	1,776,650	1,588,148	1,679,702	1,570,391	1,667,774
6.0 % to 8.0 %											
No. of Institutions	5,401	5,411	5,292	5,280	5,439	5,340	5,168	4,944	4,705	4,401	4,395
Net Income ($M)	4,069	4,115	4,149	4,571	4,156	5,834	6,214	6,882	8,956	10,747	4,915
Capital ($M)	30,141	32,312	34,225	38,156	43,861	48,163	51,236	57,770	64,184	75,442	75,566
Total Assets ($M)	434,181	465,971	494,451	560,480	647,749	709,610	755,911	846,055	944,191	1,114,623	1,107,011
> 8.0 %											
No. of Institutions	7,981	7,940	7,976	7,673	7,429	7,334	6,706	6,797	6,656	6,756	6,785
Net Income ($M)	3,444	3,726	3,842	4,024	3,878	3,977	3,710	4,114	4,690	5,399	3,364
Capital ($M)	27,163	29,813	32,186	34,577	35,652	38,864	39,977	45,220	45,462	51,021	58,769
Total Assets ($M)	278,485	299,801	320,380	343,527	353,592	377,812	384,858	438,341	437,424	489,392	556,001
Resolutions: Commercial and Savings Banks											
No. of Institutions	10	10	42	48	79	120	145	203	221	207	103
Total Assets ($M)	N/A	N/A	N/A	N/A	N/A	8,337	6,830	9,198	52,623	29,538	8,932
Est. Cost: Nominal and Nondisc. ($M)	N/A	N/A	N/A	N/A	N/A	850	1,732	2,017	5,530	5,998	1,864

Source: FDIC.

Which Banks Are Healthy? Generally Smaller Banks

As Table 3 shows, there are approximately $1.7 trillion in assets in banks whose capital-to-asset ratios are between 3 and 6 percent and, as the preceding discussion indicates, some of them are undoubtedly using dubious accounting techniques to bolster their capital. Given the ability of deteriorated banks to use accounting techniques to obscure problems, we think that many of the banks in this category should be viewed with suspicion: many of them may be economically insolvent.

Our suspicion is buttressed by the net income and capital data presented in Table 4. The volatility in net income since 1986 for this group of banks is noteworthy as is the low income for the most recent periods. Significant losses occurred in 1987 followed by significant income for this group of banks in 1988 and relatively anemic income thereafter.

This group of banks is dominated in terms of assets by the largest banks in the country, many of which are struggling. The reported capital in banks in this group has fallen significantly as well: from approximately $91 billion to $81 billion from 1986 to 1990, respectively, which represents a drop of 11 percent.

It is highly disturbing to contemplate the potential for enormous taxpayer expenditures posed by this picture of a large, debilitated segment of the banking industry. Approximately 50 percent of the banking industry's assets in 1990 were in banks whose reported income and capital suggest that they are weak and declining.

The remaining half of the banking industry was reporting capital-to-asset ratios above 6 percent in 1990. As Table 4 shows, the income and capital for these banks has grown consistently over the decade of the 1980s. It appears that reported capital-to-asset ratios at or above 6 percent is currently a line of capital demarcation separating the demonstrably healthy banks from those that show signs of significant stress. These banks hold approximately half of the banking industry assets but represent 89 percent of the total number of banks. This disparity provides yet another indication that the current problems tend to be concentrated in the larger banks.

Appendix Table A-5 confirms this by showing that capital and income for smaller banks were higher than for larger banks when expressed as a percentage of assets.

The Erosion of Taxpayer Protection

Table 5 shows the erosion of taxpayer protection as the numbers of weakly capitalized and problem banks have increased, the costs of resolving failed institutions have risen, and the reserves of the BIF have fallen.

As the table shows, the reported reserves of the BIF have dropped from approximately $18.3 billion in 1987 to $8.5 billion in 1990. The decline in reported reserves reflects the increased number of resolutions, shown in Table 4, that have risen from 10 in 1980 to over 200 per year in 1987, 1988, and 1989.

The size of the BIF reserves, like bank income and capital, is in doubt and probably inflated due to accounting conventions. As we have described above, there are banks that are open and operating although they are reporting insolvency. Beginning in 1985, due primarily to the insistence of the General Accounting Office (GAO), the FSLIC reduced its reserves by an amount equal to the probable and estimable losses associated with deeply troubled savings and loans. The FDIC as administrator of the BIF has resisted attempts by the GAO to require the BIF to reduce its reserves more than it wished in 1990. The dispute is unresolved as we are writing this book, but if the BIF were to report as the FSLIC eventually did in the late 1980s, it would significantly reduce the BIF's reported reserves for 1990 below $8.5 billion. Indeed, at this writing, the GAO is reporting that the FDIC's reserves, when properly accounted for, will be exhausted by year-end 1991.

Although the fund has declined and resolutions have increased, the number of problem banks remained high in 1990 at 1,046 while assets in these banks totaled more than $400 billion. Table 5 also shows the dramatic rise in assets in banks with capital-to-asset ratios below 3 percent beginning in 1986. The huge difference between the number and deposit figures for problem banks and the corresponding figures for poorly capitalized banks apparently reflects a perception, which we share, on the part of examiners that many banks with capital-to-asset ratios above 3 percent are seriously troubled institutions.

The combination of decreasing BIF reserves, accounting disputes with the GAO, growing assets at problem banks, and open but insolvent banks suggests that a disturbing pattern has developed at the BIF similar to an earlier pattern at the FSLIC. When the FSLIC's reserves were depleted,

Table 5

Taxpayer Protection: Commercial Bank Capital and Bank Insurance Fund Reserves, 1980 - 1990 ($ Millions)

	Commercial Banks				BIF-FDIC				Problem Banks		Commercial Banks with Capital-to-Asset Ratio < 3 %		% Resolu- tion Cost
	Number	Assets	Insured Deposits	Capital	Insurance Fd. Balance	Net Income	Provision for Ins. Losses	Contingent Liability[1]	Number	Assets	Number	Assets	
1980	14,435	1,855,715	948,717	107,526	10,020	1,227	(38)	582	212	N/A	16	1,686	N/A
1981	14,415	2,029,461	988,898	118,282	12,246	1,226	320	960	223	N/A	23	4,091	N/A
1982	14,453	2,194,153	1,134,221	128,765	13,771	1,525	126	1,187	369	N/A	44	4,119	N/A
1983	14,467	2,342,161	1,260,332	140,406	15,429	1,658	675	1,418	642	N/A	88	5,460	N/A
1984	14,472	2,508,488	1,389,874	154,008	16,529	1,100	1,633	0	848	228,300	96	8,540	N/A
1985	14,393	2,730,539	1,503,393	169,085	17,957	1,428	1,569	4,021	1,140	237,800	150	8,670	10.2
1986	14,188	2,940,675	1,634,302	182,138	18,253	296	2,828	4,031	1,484	335,500	284	23,256	25.4
1987	13,694	2,999,187	1,658,802	180,536	18,302	49	2,997	4,069	1,575	358,500	349	126,644	21.9
1988	13,120	3,130,888	1,750,259	196,507	14,061	(4,241)	6,298	8,528	1,406	252,200	357	69,571	10.6
1989	12,705	3,299,035	1,872,953	204,840	13,210	(851)	3,811	6,232	1,109	235,500	359	124,629	20.3
1990	12,338	3,388,910	1,976,744	218,862	8,500	(4,700)	N/A	N/A	1,046	408,800	183[2]	30,170[2]	N/A

Source: FDIC.

[1] Liabilities for estimated bank assistance and incurred from bank assistance and failures.
[2] June 1990.

the FSLIC and its head, the Federal Home Loan Bank Board, denied that the depletion presented a serious problem and understated the magnitude of its future resource needs. It resisted all attempts by the GAO and others to write down more fully its reserves as deeply troubled savings and loans multiplied. It abetted attempts by savings and loans to obscure deterioration with accounting techniques. Finally, it reduced the number or altered the types of closures in order not to reduce the FSLIC's cash reserves to a point where it would be impossible to deny that it was overwhelmed. Every part of this pattern has existed at the FDIC and the BIF for some time.

Large Banks Became the Big Problem in the 1980s

The vast majority of failed banks since the Great Depression have been small in size. Only in recent years have we seen the demise of major banks: Continental Illinois in 1984; First Republic Bank and MCorp Banks of Texas in 1988; and the Bank of New England in 1991. Although this pattern is relatively new, it is not likely to end shortly. Data in Appendix Table A-5, presenting key financial data for banks of different sizes, demonstrate that the largest banks have had the lowest ratios of reported income to assets of any size category since 1980. As Figure 1 shows, the capital-to-asset ratios of the largest banks, those with assets above $10 billion, have also been the lowest of all size categories throughout the 1980s.

Appendix Table A-5 also shows that throughout the 1980s and into the 1990s the indices of distress for large banks—loans and leases past due, nonaccrual loans and leases, and reserves for loan losses—have soared relative to smaller banks.

With the current weakness in the United States banking system centered in the largest banks a significant number of unprecedented problems arise. A single large bank closure, for example, could eliminate all the BIF's cash resources and possibly even trigger direct taxpayer expenditures.

Worse yet, it is unlikely that if one large bank is closed or reorganized it will be the only one so treated because the deterioration extends to several large banks, the deterioration is longstanding, and the deteriorated assets of the large banks are similar.

Special Problems at the Big Banks

The immediate problems of the big banks center on bad loans. Recent increases in charge-offs, loan-loss reserves, and provisions due to poorly performing loans have reduced big-bank capital and income. Yet there are indications that reluctance by the banks to reveal fully their difficulties combined with regulatory forbearance and the use of accounting conventions have resulted in lower provisions, reserves, and charge-offs than would seem to be justified by reported deterioration in loans. Furthermore, the continued sluggishness of the economy appears to promise more deterioration in the loans that particularly bedevil the big banks—construction loans and other commercial real estate loans. As a result, our empirical evaluation of the market value of the big banks show substantial declines that are being validated by subsequent closures, reluctant but bearish bank equity analysts, and at least one major congressman.

Loan Losses, Now and in the Future

The weak market valuations of many major banks, of course, reflect the substantial increase in actual and anticipated loan losses suffered by these institutions. Table 6 provides information on nonaccrual real estate and commercial and industrial (C&I) loans, as well as total loans, for the largest U.S. banks as of the end of the second quarter of 1990.

In addition, the table illustrates the extent to which these banks had established loss reserves for these loans. Table 6 shows that many of the largest banks had substantial fractions of their overall loan portfolios—above 5 percent—in nonaccrual status. Even higher nonaccrual ratios were present in real estate and C&I lending.

In addition, with the exception of a few banks, most of the banks listed had loss reserve levels below the levels of their nonaccrual loans.[10] Although there is no magic reason why the ratio of loss reserves to nonaccrual loans should equal at least 100 percent, the fact that the loss reserves of most banks were not at this level at the end of June 1990—before the recession—provides a strong indication of the minimum extent to which these banks may be forced later into increasing their loss reserves, and thus depleting their capital. Indeed, for some of the banks

Table 6
Loan Loss Exposure of Large Commercial Banks, June 30, 1990

	Assets ($ Billions)	Nonaccrual Loans as Percent of Loans in Relevant Category			Nonaccrual Loans as % of Equity Capital	Loan Loss Reserves as % of Equity Capital	Unreserved Nonaccrual Loans as % of Equity Capital
		Real Estate	C & I	Total			
Citibank	164.2	10.5	20.8	7.0	98	39	59
Bank of America	90.7	0.8	8.1	2.9	43	55	(12)
The Chase Manhattan Bank	81.1	7.9	9.8	5.8	85	60	24
Morgan Guaranty Trust Co.	72.0	4.6	10.0	3.4	27	63	(36)
Security Pacific National Bank	64.1	1.0	6.0	2.3	36	25	11
Bankers Trust Co.	61.0	14.4	12.5	6.5	63	119	(56)
Manufacturers Hanover Trust Co.	56.5	6.0	6.1	5.6	82	70	13
Wells Fargo Co.	48.6	1.4	3.4	1.9	25	25	0
Chemical Bank	48.4	3.7	8.2	5.9	78	63	15
The Bank of New York	45.7	8.5	3.8	3.4	52	39	13
The First National Bank of Chicago	37.7	6.8	2.7	3.2	42	34	9
NCNB Texas National Bank	34.1	0.9	0.8	0.6	5	11	(6)
The First National Bank of Boston	30.2	9.9	4.2	5.1	64	50	15
Continental Bank	29.3	1.8	4.7	4.3	40	17	23
NCNB National Bank of North Carolina	22.0	4.1	1.6	2.6	31	18	13
Republic National Bank of New York	21.9	0.8	1.1	1.1	3	12	(9)

Table 6 (continued)

Marine Midland Bank	21.8	9.6	5.9	6.1	97	64	32
First Interstate Bank of California	20.5	1.1	4.5	1.6	21	23	(2)
Pittsburg National Bank	18.8	2.5	4.5	2.1	22	24	(1)
National Bank of Detroit	18.7	1.1	1.0	0.9	9	14	(5)
Mellon Bank	18.3	10.0	1.1	2.5	34	34	0
First Union Bank of North Carolina	17.4	1.1	1.5	1.0	13	11	2
First Union National Bank of Florida	16.1	4.9	2.1	3.2	21	16	5
Union Bank	16.0	1.2	2.7	1.9	23	31	(8)
Maryland National Bank	15.6	3.9	4.1	3.5	49	42	7
Wachovia Bank and Trust Co.	15.5	0.5	0.7	0.4	4	10	(6)
Southeast Bank	15.5	6.5	7.4	5.1	71	38	33
National Westminster Bank	15.0	10.3	3.0	3.7	77	50	27
Sovran Bank	14.6	2.0	0.7	1.0	11	17	(6)
Bank of New England	13.3	22.8	10.6	13.8	828	542	287
Bank One Texas	13.1	1.2	3.4	1.3	10	12	(2)
Citizens & Southern National Bank	13.1	2.0	1.4	1.1	11	17	(6)
Connecticut National Bank	12.5	5.8	6.9	5.5	70	42	27
Seafirst Bank	12.3	3.3	1.7	2.1	24	22	2

Source: *Bank Source*, W.C. Ferguson and Co.

shown in Table 6, an increase in loss reserves to just the level of nonaccrual loans as of June 30, 1990 would significantly reduce their capital.

Many banks, of course, have recognized still additional lending problems since mid-1990. But still, such large banks as Citibank, Chase, Chemical, Manufacturers Hanover, and the Bank of New York had reserve levels as of September 30, 1990 well below the levels of nonperforming assets.[11] Loan loss reserves appear to be especially insufficient at banks in New England, despite the recent well-known additions these banks made to reserves at the behest of federal bank regulators. Thus, while problem loans at New England banks represented 5.5 percent of total assets in the third quarter—far above the national average of 2.6 percent—loan loss reserves at New England banks averaged just 49 percent of their nonaccrual loans.[12] In short, we expect further deterioration in the capital of many large banks in the quarters ahead.

Table 7, developed from data in Appendix Table A-5, shows that as of mid-1990 the larger the bank, the higher its ratio of nonaccrual to total loans and the smaller its reserve coverage.

Table 7 Commercial Bank Nonaccrual Loans and Loan Loss Reserves, June 1990		
Bank Size (Assets)	Nonaccrual Loans/ Total Loans (%)	Loan Loss Reserves/ Nonaccrual Loans (%)
Below $100 Million	.72	124
Between $100 Million and $1 Billion	.91	109
Between $1 - 10 Billion	1.39	97
Over $10 Billion	2.49	80

Source: FDIC.

In fact, even these figures may understate the severity of the current problems banks are having with nonperforming loans. Recently, a controversy has arisen over the practice followed by some banks of labeling their restructured loans as performing assets, even though the interest rates on those loans may be lowered to below-market rates.[13] This accounting treatment hides the fact that in the process of restructuring loans, banks may end up eventually suffering a loss over the lifetime of the loan (since the restructured loans may be earning "negative spreads").

"High-Risk" Lending Concentration

Given the likelihood that many large banks will experience a further increase in their nonperforming loan ratios, a more revealing way to assess the exposure of the major banks to additional losses is to examine the concentration of their lending portfolios in high-risk loans.

Table 8, for example, lists the 37 large banks holding a total of $175 billion in assets that have heavy commitments (above 15 percent of total loans) to construction and development real estate loans, or the loans that recently have suffered perhaps the most significant problems in various regions of the country and especially New England.

Table 8
Banks with a Heavy Concentration of Construction & Development Real Estate Loans, June 1990

Name of Institution	State	Total Assets ($ Millions)	Nonaccrual Loans (as a % of) Primary Capital	Nonaccrual Loans (as a % of) Loan Loss Reserves	C & D Loans (as % of) Total Loans
Union Bank	CA	15,960	17.38	74.17	16.36
Maryland National Bank	MD	15,630	32.50	118.37	24.11
Sovran Bank	VA	14,638	9.28	64.97	16.37
Bank of New England	MA	13,265	120.25	152.91	17.53
Midlantic National Bank	NJ	10,101	49.64	128.19	21.20
Signet Bank	VA	9,174	5.18	47.24	15.70
The Bank of California	CA	8,426	32.68	136.84	16.64
Riggs National Bank	DC	6,409	17.90	145.91	18.19
American Security Bank	DC	6,374	43.05	148.01	22.26

			Nonaccrual Loans (as a % of)		C & D Loans (as % of)
Name of Institution	State	Total Assets ($ Millions)	Primary Capital	Loan Loss Reserves	Total Loans
European American Bank	NY	5,117	70.49	225.54	18.04
The Howard Savings Bank	NJ	4,905	98.09	292.62	32.45
First Union National Bank	GA	4,655	15.75	80.70	22.14
Continental Bank	PA	4,528	20.89	140.66	15.40
Security Pacific Bank	AZ	4,315	36.89	213.47	16.68
Sovran Bank	MD	4,177	8.54	67.92	18.60
First American Bank	VA	3,831	17.29	100.12	25.43
Merchants National Bank & Trust	IN	3,697	23.54	140.39	18.00
Signet Bank	MD	3,617	9.78	55.46	19.36
Valley Bank	NV	2,992	6.83	44.10	17.23
Imperial Bank	CA	2,888	6.72	52.58	21.67
River Bank America	NY	2,819	64.65	503.80	27.92
Bank of Boston	CT	2,397	72.22	153.03	16.66
First American Bank	DC	1,955	18.90	84.97	19.82
First American Bank	GA	1,895	34.12	171.82	19.25
Mercantile-Safe Deposit and Trust	MD	1,774	3.77	35.20	17.87
First American Bank	MD	1,557	12.18	78.18	20.42
Maine Savings Bank	ME	1,497	495.14	306.59	20.13
Mark Twain Bank	MO	1,434	8.33	69.49	15.36
Pacific Western Bank	CA	1,288	9.92	71.86	24.20
Connecticut Savings Bank	CT	1,200	100.88	124.53	18.02

Table 8 (continued)

Table 8 (continued)					
Name of Institution	State	Total Assets ($ Millions)	Nonaccrual Loans (as a % of) Primary Capital	Nonaccrual Loans (as a % of) Loan Loss Reserves	C & D Loans (as % of) Total Loans
Peoples Bank & Trust Co.	NC	1,160	1.88	19.47	15.86
LTCB Trust Co.	NY	1,123	0.00	0.00	22.38
The North Fork Bank and Trust Co.	NY	1,083	39.13	325.02	19.57
Capital Bank	FL	1,039	38.50	203.03	18.85
Sovran Bank	DC	1,001	14.79	82.64	22.08

Source: *Bank Source*, W. C. Ferguson & Co.

Significantly, a number of these banks not only have high ratios of total nonaccrual loans to primary capital, which includes loan loss reserves, but also appear to be under-reserved, with ratios of total nonaccrual loans to total loan loss reserves above 100 percent. These banks include: Connecticut Savings Bank; Bank of New England; Maine Savings Bank; The Howard Savings Bank of Newark; River Bank America of New Rochelle; and European American Bank of New York.

The growing weakness in real estate markets throughout the country raises all kinds of red flags for the banking industry since real estate loans were the fastest growing asset category in banks during the last several years. Table 9 highlights the fact that in many major metropolitan areas the office building vacancy rate in mid-1990 was well above the 1985 level, let alone the level in 1980.

With such substantial unused capacity on the market, not only will commercial building remain depressed for some time to come, but the value of much collateral held by the banks that helped finance the excess construction is substantially below the value of the loans the banks may be showing on their financial statements.

The sizable volume of real estate properties held by the Resolution Trust Corporation (RTC), coupled with the expectation that even more real estate will fall into the RTC's balance sheet in the near future, further

Table 9
Metropolitan Office Vacancy Rates, 1980 - 1990
(Percent)

City	1980	1985	1990
Atlanta	12.0	16.4	18.8
Baltimore	8.5	9.5	18.4
Boston	3.2	14.1	15.7
Chicago	4.8	13.6	16.8
Cincinnati	6.9	19.6	16.6
Cleveland	9.8	13.9	15.3
Columbus	3.6	18.1	16.0
Dallas	6.7	22.4	25.6
Denver	3.1	25.0	23.1
Detroit	7.4	9.5	18.4
Hartford	4.9	19.7	25.0
Houston	9.3	27.4	25.9
Indianapolis	9.5	12.6	22.0
Jacksonville	5.9	16.5	17.4
Kansas City	9.7	14.9	15.8
Los Angeles	2.6	17.0	16.8
Miami	1.5	19.2	22.5
Minneapolis	1.5	15.5	19.2
Nashville	6.3	20.1	21.8
New York	1.6	8.4	14.3
Oklahoma City	2.3	22.3	26.5
Philadelphia	4.2	12.7	15.1
Phoenix	6.0	24.5	28.4
Portland	2.9	19.6	16.5
Salt Lake City	9.0	20.1	19.7
San Antonio	10.2	22.0	29.5
San Diego	4.2	21.0	21.0
Seattle	4.4	16.5	14.7
San Francisco	2.5	15.4	14.9
St. Louis	6.1	10.4	18.1
Tampa	9.5	23.9	22.0
Washington, DC	1.8	13.1	15.4

Source: Coldwell Banker.

depresses real estate prices. Even residential mortgage lending, long viewed as much safer than commercial mortgage lending, has been showing cracks. Indeed, housing starts in October 1990 were at the lowest level since the 1981–1982 recession. Building permits fell almost 7 percent that month, to the lowest rate since June 1982. Furthermore, as of the third quarter of 1990, borrowers accounting for 4.5 percent of all U.S. home mortgages (held by banks, savings and loans, and other institutions) were at least 30 days delinquent in their payments, not far from the 6.1 percent record set in 1985 when many homeowners in the Southwest walked away from their homes rather than continuing their mortgage payment.[14]

Table 10 provides a more comprehensive indication of large banks' exposure to all types of "high-risk" loans—notably the combination of LDC debt, loans for highly leveraged transactions (HLT loans), and commercial real estate—as of the end of the second quarter of 1990.

The last column provides the most important information: ratios of high-risk loans outstanding to these banks' adjusted tangible capital.[15] For example, a banking organization with a ratio of 200 percent of high-risk loans to adjusted capital would face potential insolvency if it suffered a loss of 50 percent of the value of its high-risk loan portfolio; the margin for error is reduced if the ratio stands at 400 percent, indicating that a 25 percent loss in the high-risk loan portfolio potentially would wipe out all of the capital and loan loss reserves held by the bank. We are not making any predictions of the extent to which high-risk loans will deteriorate in value in the months ahead. Nevertheless, we believe that any banking organization with high-risk loans outstanding that amount to four times the level of current capital and loan loss reserves (combined) is highly exposed to substantial impairment of its capital. Significantly, Table 10 indicates that in fact, as of June 30, 1990, six of the nation's top banking organizations with aggregate assets of $282 billion in assets—Wells Fargo, First Union, Bank of Boston, Barnett Banks, Security Pacific, and Continental Bank—had ratios of high-risk loans to adjusted tangible capital in this neighborhood or even higher.[16]

Using Stock Prices to Evaluate Problems at Large Banks

Thus far, we have relied heavily on standard accounting techniques to measure the problems of the banking industry in general and the large banks in particular. There exist, however, several more market-based measures of the condition of banks. Some of the measures are indirect

Table 10

Loan Risk Exposure of Largest 25 Bank Holding Companies in the U.S.
Ranked by High Risk Loans to Adjusted Tangible Common Equity Capital, June 30, 1990

Rank	Name of Institution	Assets ($ Millions)	Tangible Common Equity/ Assets[1] (%)	Non-performing Assets/Assets[2] (%)	Allowance for Loan Losses/ Non-performing Assets (%)	High Risk Loans/Tangible Common Equity[3] (%)	High Risk Loans /Adjusted Tangible Common Equity[4] (%)
1	Wells Fargo & Co.	51.7	4.03	2.67	58.8	8.09	6.83
2	First Union Corp.	38.3	3.38	1.81	59.2	5.27	4.69
3	Bank of Boston Corp.	37.2	4.17	5.30	45.1	5.75	4.00
4	Barnett Banks, Inc.	31.1	4.22	1.57	67.8	4.29	3.99
5	Security Pacific Corp.	94.5	4.05	3.06	40.1	4.42	3.88
6	Continental Bank Corp.	29.5	4.18	2.55	37.3	4.23	3.82
7	NCNB Corp.	66.1	3.57	1.16	68.2	3.79	3.53
8	First Chicago Corp.	50.3	3.73	2.43	70.9	4.62	3.53
9	Citicorp	227.7	3.03	4.10	42.5	4.42	3.25
10	Chase Manhattan Corp.	102.3	3.42	4.86	53.3	5.03	3.22
11	Chemical Banking Corp.	75.2	3.02	4.26	66.0	5.47	3.11
12	First Fidelity Bancorp.	29.8	3.32	3.09	57.9	3.84	2.83
13	C & S/Sovran Corp.	50.3	5.20	1.36	74.4	2.85	2.65
14	SunTrust Banks, Inc.	31.2	6.48	1.73	66.3	2.76	2.57

Table 10 (continued)

Rank	Name of Institution	Assets ($ Millions)	Tangible Common Equity/Assets[1] (%)	Non-performing Assets/Assets[2] (%)	Allowance for Loan Losses/Non-performing Assets (%)	High Risk Loans/Tangible Common Equity[3] (%)	High Risk Loans/Adjusted Tangible Common Equity[4] (%)
15	Fleet/Norstar Financial	34.1	3.93	3.33	54.3	3.34	2.54
16	Mellon Bank Corp.	31.6	3.93	2.00	68.5	2.09	2.49
17	Bank of N.Y. Co.	48.9	3.36	3.49	54.9	3.19	2.33
18	PNC Financial Corp.	47.8	5.54	1.94	56.3	2.39	2.18
19	First Interstate Bancorp.	55.0	3.53	3.63	59.3	3.06	2.13
20	BankAmerica Corp.	103.9	4.97	2.91	94.8	2.96	2.11
21	Manufacturers Hanover	63.5	4.23	4.50	68.4	2.88	1.81
22	Republic N.Y. Corp.	29.1	4.46	0.59	145.7	1.60	1.42
23	Bankers Trust N.Y. Corp.	57.3	4.03	3.69	110.8	2.50	1.29
24	Banc One Corp.	27.9	8.60	1.54	63.4	1.10	1.07
25	J.P. Morgan & Co., Inc.	93.1	4.77	0.94	238.6	0.99	0.70

Source: A Major New York Investment Bank.

[1] Deducts all intangibles as of March 31, 1990 or June 30, 1990 where available.
[2] Nonperforming assets are defined as the sum of nonaccrual and renegotiated loans, loans 90 days past due and other real estate owned.
[3] High risk loans are defined as the sum of HLT loans, medium and long-term loans to LDC's and commercial real estate loans.
[4] Adjusted tangible common equity is defined as tangible common equity plus the allowance for loan losses less 1.0% of all performing loans.

Table 11

Stock Price Performance of the 25 Largest Bank Holding Companies, November 30, 1990

Name of Institution	Assets June 30, 1990	Stock Prices November 30, 1990	Previous 52 Week High	% Drop
Citicorp	227.7	12 3/4	30 1/8	57.7
BankAmerica Corp.	103.9	22 5/8	33 1/8	31.7
Chase Manhattan Corp.	102.3	10 7/8	37 3/8	70.9
Security Pacific Corp.	94.5	21 3/4	43 3/8	49.9
J.P. Morgan & Co., Inc.	93.1	40 5/8	44 5/8	9.0
Chemical Banking Corp.	75.2	11 3/8	32 3/4	65.3
NCNB Corp.	66.1	24	47	48.9
Manufacturers Hanover Corp.	63.5	18 7/8	38	50.3
Bankers Trust N.Y. Corp.	57.3	38	47 1/4	19.6
First Interstate Bancorp	55.0	20 5/8	53 3/4	61.6
Wells Fargo & Co.	51.7	51 5/8	84 1/2	38.9
C & S/ Sovran Corp.	50.3	17 1/8	21	18.5
First Chicago Corp.	50.3	17 5/8	38 7/8	54.7
Bank of N.Y. Co.	48.9	18	42 3/8	57.5
PNC Financial Corp.	47.8	22 1/2	44	48.9
First Union Corp.	38.3	14 7/8	22 3/4	34.6
Bank of Boston Corp.	37.2	6 7/8	19 7/8	65.4
Fleet/Norstar Financial Group	34.1	10 5/8	27 5/8	61.5
Mellon Bank Corp.	31.6	23 3/4	30 1/8	21.2
SunTrust Banks, Inc.	31.2	21	24 1/4	13.4
Barnett Banks, Inc.	31.1	20 1/2	37 1/8	44.8
First Fidelity Bancorp.	29.8	17 3/8	25 7/8	32.9
Continental Bank Corp.	29.5	9 1/8	21 5/8	57.8
Republic N.Y. Corp.	29.1	45 1/8	52 1/4	13.6
Banc One Corp.	27.9.	24 5/8	32 7/8	25.1

and partial; for example, rates paid on uninsured deposits and rates paid on subordinated debt. Debt ratings by Moody's and Standard and Poors, among others, also exist. The most direct and comprehensive measure is based on stock market prices. At the time of our report, stock market prices reflected the weakened condition of the largest banks. As shown in Table 11, the share prices of the nation's twenty-five largest bank holding companies dropped during 1990, most by substantial amounts.

The stock prices of eighteen of the twenty-five largest companies fell by 30 percent or more from the previous fifty-two-week high. Citicorp, Chase, Chemical, and Manufactures Hanover fell 58 percent, 71 percent, 65 percent, and 50 percent, respectively. Using the ratio of market-to--book valuations for these banking organizations at the end of November 1990, we have estimated the implied market equity-to-capital ratio for their subsidiary banks at that time, based on their reported book-value ratios as of June 30, 1990. Table 12 displays the results, showing many of the largest banks to have very thin capital margins.[17]

As the table shows, the fall in Citicorp's share price suggests that Citicorp's market equity was only 49.2 percent of the reported level, which means a capital-to-asset ratio of 2.38 percent instead of 4.84 percent. These estimates are conservative since the book-value capital ratios of a number of the large banks declined further in the third quarter due to additional provisioning for loan losses.

In contrast to Citicorp, the market value of Morgan Guaranty, for example, was approximately 164 percent of book value suggesting that its reported book equity understated its true economic equity. In total, for five of the twenty-five largest banks the market-value measure of equity exceeded the book-value measure, indicating that stock prices do signal significant differences among banks.

Unlike the share prices of any other firms in the country, however, bank stocks incorporate the value of deposit insurance. Perhaps the easiest way to understand how deposit insurance creates value for a bank is to understand that it allows a bank with a given amount of capital to gather funds more cheaply than if a large portion of the liabilities were not federally insured. The issue is far deeper than this and is crucial to understanding the movement in bank stock prices.

Deposit insurance effectively conveys a put option to shareholders allowing them to put the bank back to the FDIC in the event the owner-contributed equity value falls to zero. Shareholders in fact never exercise their put. Instead, when a bank is closed due to insolvency, the

Table 12
Book and Estimated Market Equity Capital-to-Asset Ratios
for the 25 Largest Banks, June 1990

Name of Institution	Equity Capital-to-Asset Ratio June 30, 1990	Market-to-Book Ratio of Holding Company	Estimated Market Equity Capital-to-Asset Ratio Nov. 30, 1990[1]
Citibank	4.84	49.2	2.38
Bank of America	5.09	86.4	4.40
The Chase Manhattan Bank	4.33	37.8	1.64
Morgan Guaranty Trust Co.	4.21	163.9	6.90
Security Pacific National Bank	4.66	58.8	2.74
Bankers Trust Co.	3.33	126.3	4.21
Manufacturers Hanover Trust Co.	4.71	45.9	2.16
Wells Fargo Bank	6.52	92.9	6.06
Chemical Bank	4.59	34.7	1.59
The Bank of New York	4.59	51.2	2.35
The First National Bank of Chicago	4.29	49.2	2.11
NCNB Texas National Bank	5.15	83.2	4.28
The First National Bank of Boston	4.75	30.7	1.46
Continental Bank	5.57	39.0	2.17
NCNB National Bank of North Carolina	4.78	83.2	3.98
Republic National Bank Of New York	6.88	116.1	7.99
Marine Midland Bank	4.89	120.2	5.88
First Interstate Bank of California	5.50	52.4	2.88
Pittsburg National Bank	4.33	77.5	3.36
National Bank of Detroit	5.76	119.6	6.89
Mellon Bank	4.15	75.9	3.15
First Union National Bank of North Carolina	5.29	72.4	3.83
First Union National Bank of Florida	9.01	48.3	4.35
Union Bank	6.29	62.7	3.94
Maryland National Bank	4.54	31.0	1.41

Source: *Bank Source*, W. C. Ferguson & Co. and *American Banker*, Dec. 3, 1990.
[1] Based on June 30, 1990 book value equity capital-to-asset ratio.

deposit-insurance agency seizes control of the bank. When an insolvent bank is not seized by the deposit insurer, it continues to be run by management and directors representing the shareholders. The availability of this option when an insolvent bank is not closed promptly can encourage institutions to gamble for resurrection by making high-risk (and seemingly high-return) loans and pursuing other risky activities because there is no longer any owner-contributed equity at risk.

Because the value of any option increases with volatility, it is rational to take excessive risk if a bank is not seized at insolvency. Accordingly, it is essential that the regulatory authorities either properly charge for that option—which the current flat-rate premium structure does not do—or cap its value through appropriate capital requirements and regulatory or supervisory constraints on risk-taking behavior. This, of course, includes closure or reorganization at or before insolvency.

The actual value of a bank stock, then, is the sum of the put option value of deposit insurance and the intrinsic value of its other assets and liabilities. Since the time we made our report to the House Subcommittee on Financial Institutions Supervision, Regulation, and Insurance, with some exceptions, bank stock prices in general and the large banks in particular have risen. The put option embedded in deposit insurance helps explain how banks with obvious signs of intrinsic deterioration can nonetheless experience rising stock prices.

As we were writing this, for example, the proposed merger between Chemical and Manufacturers Hanover banks was announced. Based on reported tangible equity capital, these banks once merged would have a 3.65 percent capital-to-asset ratio and yet it is conceivable, given their troubled assets, that the marked-to-market value of the capital of the combined bank is far lower. Yet, the stock prices of these two banks rose on the announcement of the proposed merger.

The press accounts of the rise attributed it to the prospect, highlighted in the announcement, that the merger would result in cost savings of about $650 million per year that would allow the new bank to raise $1.25 billion in capital based on the resulting higher earnings. It was also reported that investment banks were highly confident that such a capital increase could be achieved.

Another explanation can also plausibly describe why the stock prices increased. If they are allowed to merge, these clearly troubled banks may be the beneficiaries of regulatory forbearance, which increases the put option value. A merger approval, for example, may convey additional time to operate without greater regulatory interference to reduce costs individually, to retain all earnings, and to shrink or not to grow. The merger thus can be interpreted as providing the new bank with a new opportunity to earn greater profits with reduced likelihood of government intervention.

In short, the merger can be viewed as another manifestation of the too-big-to-fail doctrine. The merger itself could have had a beneficial effect on the prices of other weak bank stocks among the largest banks because it signaled that big troubled banks would be given more time under the control of existing managers and directors to improve profitability.

Another example involves the closure of the Bank of New England in January 1991. A substantial percentage of Bank of New England's deposits were not explicitly covered by deposit insurance but the depositors were covered nonetheless. The official reason was to avoid possible overall financial instability that could have been caused if uninsured depositors at other large troubled banks withdrew their funds. This act by the deposit insurer indicated concretely that implicit 100 percent deposit-insurance coverage existed for explicitly uninsured depositors at selected large banks. That action involving regulatory forbearance undoubtedly increased the put option value of deposit insurance to the big banks.

Estimating the Put Option Value of Deposit Insurance and Forbearance for Big Banks

We have attempted to take account of this fact by using "option pricing" techniques to estimate both the value of deposit insurance relative to the premium charged (to assess whether a net subsidy has existed) and the "option-adjusted" value of capital from the FDIC's perspective for 63 of the nation's largest banks (or their holding companies). These calculations were based on share prices and other financial statistics as of the second quarter of 1990, the latest date for which we had such information at the time of our report.[18] Insofar as the share prices of any of the banks have deteriorated substantially since June 30, 1990, these estimates may understate any subsidies that exist and overstate the implied market capital when the value of deposit insurance is stripped away.

Nevertheless, the calculations presented in Tables 13 and 14 are illuminating, since in view of deficiencies in existing accounting data, they may provide more useful measures for regulators of true owner-contributed equity capital and of the value of deposit insurance for these banks.

At the least, they may be combined with other information about the banks to better assess their true financial condition.

The results (obtained with the collaboration of Dan Page, a finance professor at Auburn University) show that federal deposit insurance did indeed represent a subsidy to some of the large banks. The columns in the two tables labeled "Put Option/Dep" and "Intrinsic/Assets" are the most important, indicating the implied value of deposit insurance (as a percent of deposits) and the option adjusted equity capital-to-asset ratio, respectively, for three quarters: the first quarter of 1989 and the first two quarters of 1990.

For example, Table 13 indicates that the implied value of deposit insurance to Citicorp in the second quarter of 1990 was 13 basis points, or just under the 15 basis points it paid for the insurance in that quarter. Similarly, Citicorp's option-adjusted equity capital-to-asset ratio in that quarter was 3.98 percent, versus its book-value capital ratio of 5.29 percent.

The differences in the estimates in the two tables reflect differences in assumptions about regulatory forbearance with respect to closing or reorganizing insolvent institutions: Table 14 assumes more forbearance than Table 13. Both tables indicate that the Bank of New England was insolvent as of mid-1990 when the value of the put option resulting from deposit insurance was stripped away (that is, its intrinsic value-to-asset ratio was negative). Table 14 indicates that Southeast Banking Corporation was insolvent by mid-1990 although it and the Bank of New England were not closed until 1991. In general, the results support the view that regulatory forbearance can generate a significant subsidy to weakly capitalized institutions. Furthermore, the results indicate that some institutions with relatively low capital-to-asset ratios received no subsidy, while other banks with significantly higher capital ratios did. It therefore would seem important for the regulatory authorities to investigate thoroughly the robustness of this finding and, correspondingly, the extent to which across-the-board increases in required capital ratios are warranted.

Updating the Put Option Analysis

Events since we conducted our put option analysis have confirmed its usefulness. The Bank of New England, which we estimated was economically insolvent as early as the first quarter of 1990, was seized by regulators in January 1991 and was eventually sold to Fleet/Norstar with

Table 13
Accounting and Market-Value Capitalization of Selected Commercial Banks and Value of Deposit Insurance, 1989 and 1990

Institution (City)	Total Assets ($M)			Equity/Assets (%)		
	1989 1st Qtr	1990 1st Qtr	1990 2nd Qtr	1989 1st Qtr	1990 1st Qtr	1990 2nd Qtr
Citicorp (New York)	172,282	192,714	185,836	5.73	5.00	5.29
BankAmerica (San Francisco)	95,234	98,861	102,950	4.75	5.46	5.35
Chase Manhattan (New York)	93,405	99,782	97,045	5.80	4.85	5.07
J.P. Morgan & Co. (New York)	74,962	70,725	71,964	5.42	4.45	4.49
Bankers Trust N.Y. Corp. (New York)	59,390	55,107	60,959	4.72	2.92	3.16
Security Pacific Corp. (Los Angeles)	57,845	61,124	68,449	4.30	4.97	3.97
Manufacturers Hanover (New York)	56,350	53,743	56,488	4.64	4.84	4.66
NCNB Corp. (Charlotte)	55,236	64,625	67,609	4.79	4.79	4.64
Chemical Banking Corp. (New York)	55,123	48,859	48,390	4.64	4.38	4.59
Wells Fargo & Co. (San Francisco)	44,448	47,016	48,645	5.34	6.10	5.68
First Chicago Corp. (Chicago)	35,585	37,861	37,685	3.91	4.01	4.40
PNC Financial Corp. (Pittsburgh)	28,931	31,719	32,979	5.15	5.07	4.99
Bank of New England (Boston)	25,109	22,972	21,105	5.14	1.76	1.99
First Union Corp. (Charlotte)	24,590	34,207	33,464	5.69	5.58	5.76
Bank of New York Co. (New York)	23,174	45,678	45,729	5.30	4.70	4.64
Mellon Bank Corp. (Pittsburgh)	22,749	22,472	18,342	2.82	4.36	4.58
First Wachovia (Winston-Salem)	22,041	23,556	23,888	6.63	6.93	7.02
Republic New York (New York)	20,405	22,003	21,898	8.00	7.15	7.38
First Interstate Bancorp (Los Angeles)	19,596	21,110	20,531	4.66	5.37	5.26
NBD Bancorp, Inc. (Detroit)	15,871	17,017	18,657	5.56	5.38	5.27
Southeast Banking Corp. (Miami)	13,996	16,729	15,470	4.18	3.97	4.22
First Bank System, Inc. (Minneapolis)	13,575	12,111	11,817	5.13	4.51	4.96
Sovran Financial Corp. (Norfolk)	12,511	13,983	14,638	6.20	6.21	5.88

Intrinsic/Assets (%)			Put Option/Dep (%)			MktVal/Assets (%)			MktVal/BkVal (%)		
1989 1st Qtr	1990 1st Qtr	1990 2nd Qtr	1989 1st Qtr	1990 1st Qtr	1990 2nd Qtr	1989 1st Qtr	1990 1st Qtr	1990 2nd Qtr	1989 1st Qtr	1990 1st Qtr	1990 2nd Qtr
5.48	3.82	3.95	0.08	0.19	0.13	5.50	3.87	3.98	96.13	77.55	75.30
4.60	5.96	6.04	0.05	0.04	0.03	4.64	5.98	6.05	97.56	109.59	113.19
3.50	3.04	2.96	0.09	0.29	0.30	3.53	3.15	3.07	60.97	64.98	60.53
9.61	9.45	9.13	0.00	0.01	0.00	9.61	9.45	9.13	177.22	212.60	203.07
5.87	5.52	5.60	0.01	0.02	0.04	5.87	5.53	5.61	124.34	189.34	177.42
7.72	7.09	6.18	0.00	0.00	0.17	7.73	7.09	6.29	179.51	142.79	158.25
3.18	4.18	4.26	0.21	0.08	0.04	3.27	4.21	4.27	70.47	87.02	91.74
5.51	6.06	5.58	0.03	0.04	0.08	5.53	6.09	5.63	115.60	127.16	121.55
6.26	5.33	6.51	0.01	0.04	0.01	6.26	5.35	6.51	135.01	122.26	141.91
8.12	7.70	8.40	0.00	0.01	0.00	8.12	7.70	8.40	152.17	126.38	147.82
6.64	5.23	5.06	0.00	0.04	0.03	6.64	5.24	5.07	169.98	130.49	115.11
12.18	11.69	8.50	0.00	0.00	0.05	12.18	11.69	8.53	236.33	230.50	171.01
6.34	(4.17)	(0.28)	0.00	8.96	1.89	6.34	1.40	1.03	123.41	79.50	51.79
9.55	5.63	6.08	0.01	0.08	0.09	9.56	5.68	6.14	167.93	101.86	106.51
11.76	5.10	4.69	0.00	0.03	0.10	11.76	5.11	4.73	222.02	108.78	102.00
(3.97)	4.19	5.18	0.01	0.02	0.03	3.98	4.20	5.20	141.04	96.24	113.60
11.03	11.68	11.81	0.00	0.00	0.00	11.03	11.68	11.81	166.43	168.58	168.24
6.59	6.37	7.69	0.00	0.00	0.00	6.59	6.37	7.69	82.34	89.11	104.13
10.92	9.02	10.97	0.00	0.07	0.15	10.92	9.08	11.09	234.34	169.01	210.69
11.96	12.91	12.31	0.00	0.00	0.00	11.96	12.91	12.31	215.16	239.92	233.49
5.32	2.51	1.21	0.02	0.48	1.10	5.33	2.85	2.04	127.46	71.85	48.39
9.37	6.69	7.61	0.00	0.19	0.05	9.37	6.82	7.64	182.77	151.21	154.10
16.38	14.98	11.83	0.00	0.00	0.01	16.38	14.98	11.84	264.26	241.35	201.49

Table 13 (continued)

Institution (City)	Total Assets ($M)			Equity/Assets (%)		
	1989 1st Qtr	1990 1st Qtr	1990 2nd Qtr	1989 1st Qtr	1990 1st Qtr	1990 2nd Qtr
Corestates Financial (Philadelphia)	10,428	9,771	10,474	5.64	6.77	6.53
Valley National Corp. (Phoenix)	10,141	9,190	9,387	5.92	4.76	4.68
Suntrust Banks, Inc. (Atlanta)	10,065	10,075	10,256	7.22	8.14	8.22
MNC Financial (Baltimore)	8,936	10,827	15,630	5.63	4.59	4.25
Comerica, Inc. (Detroit)	8,730	9,627	9,763	5.15	4.68	4.68
Manufacturers National (Detroit)	8,683	8,506	9,042	5.21	6.13	5.90
Northern Trust Corp. (Chicago)	8,415	9,384	9,372	4.52	4.87	5.06
Huntington Bancshares (Columbus)	8,161	8,768	8,825	5.88	6.26	6.35
Ameritrust Corporation (Cleveland)	8,102	8,347	8,527	6.27	5.86	6.02
Meridan Bancorp, Inc. (Reading)	8,060	9,941	10,011	6.40	5.12	5.15
Fleet/Norstar Fin. Grp (Providence)	8,013	11,201	10,875	6.43	4.90	5.19
State Street Boston Corp. (Boston)	7,964	10,480	10,391	7.00	6.13	6.37
Norwest Corp. (Minneapolis)	7,778	8,670	8,416	5.37	4.62	4.83
AmSouth Bancorp. (Birmingham)	7,292	7,516	7,492	7.07	7.05	7.16
First City Bancorp. of Tex. (Houston)	6,305	7,662	7,666	5.04	4.83	4.98
Bancorp Hawaii, Inc. (Honolulu)	6,281	8,251	8,662	6.14	5.60	5.53
Riggs National Corp. (Washington)	6,154	6,492	6,409	4.36	4.22	4.26
Hibernia Corp. (New Orleans)	6,025	6,796	6,851	5.12	4.47	4.68
Society Corp. (Cleveland)	5,978	7,832	7,678	6.00	5.93	6.31
First Tennessee Nat'l. (Memphis)	5,960	6,321	6,178	5.93	5.47	5.74
Midlantic Corp. (Edison, N.J.)	19,146	24,987	30,042	4.91	4.73	4.22
Barnett Banks, Inc. (Jacksonville)	5,624	6,039	6,501	5.60	4.96	4.93
Fifth Third Bancorp. (Cincinnati)	3,614	3,875	4,081	7.24	7.92	8.03

Source: Authors' calculations from *Bank Source,* W.C. Ferguson and Co. and market stock prices from DRI, Inc.

Intrinsic/Assets (%)			Put Option/Dep (%)			MktVal/Assets (%)			MktVal/BkVal (%)		
1989 1st Qtr	1990 1st Qtr	1990 2nd Qtr	1989 1st Qtr	1990 1st Qtr	1990 2nd Qtr	1989 1st Qtr	1990 1st Qtr	1990 2nd Qtr	1989 1st Qtr	1990 1st Qtr	1990 2nd Qtr
16.39	21.80	20.90	0.00	0.00	0.00	16.39	21.80	20.90	290.54	321.83	320.00
5.13	2.55	1.44	0.04	0.45	0.82	5.16	2.96	2.18	87.18	62.17	46.57
28.05	27.03	25.06	0.00	0.00	0.00	28.05	27.03	25.07	388.62	331.98	304.82
15.59	14.42	6.83	0.00	0.01	0.09	15.59	14.42	6.90	276.87	314.16	162.20
8.45	7.72	7.88	0.00	0.00	0.00	8.45	7.72	7.88	163.86	164.85	168.34
7.80	8.59	7.28	0.00	0.00	0.00	7.80	8.59	7.28	149.61	140.17	123.50
9.66	49.48	10.84	0.00	0.00	0.00	9.66	49.48	10.84	213.65	1016.17	214.35
8.55	9.88	9.10	0.00	0.00	0.00	8.55	9.88	9.10	145.21	157.82	143.42
11.33	8.53	7.90	0.00	0.01	0.04	11.33	8.54	7.93	180.76	145.73	131.84
9.31	6.85	6.40	0.00	0.01	0.01	9.31	6.86	6.42	145.49	133.95	124.57
32.68	21.25	19.39	0.00	0.00	0.00	32.68	21.25	19.39	508.44	434.13	373.57
12.34	12.92	14.09	0.00	0.00	0.00	12.34	12.92	14.09	176.15	210.82	220.96
20.99	21.30	23.47	0.00	0.00	0.00	20.99	21.30	23.47	390.58	460.64	486.33
8.25	7.31	6.93	0.00	0.01	0.01	8.25	7.32	6.93	116.75	103.87	96.90
6.15	8.10	6.20	0.00	0.00	0.02	6.15	8.10	6.21	121.84	167.85	124.81
9.34	8.75	9.72	0.00	0.00	0.00	9.34	8.75	9.72	152.05	156.23	175.69
5.59	3.48	3.09	0.01	0.34	0.36	5.60	3.66	3.28	128.31	86.70	77.03
8.08	6.57	2.30	0.03	0.10	0.72	8.11	6.64	2.88	158.48	148.58	61.63
12.91	13.91	14.24	0.00	0.00	0.00	12.91	13.91	14.24	211.81	234.53	225.61
7.06	6.05	5.55	0.00	0.01	0.01	7.06	6.05	5.61	119.19	110.64	97.81
25.96	6.29	5.10	0.00	0.18	0.44	7.69	2.52	1.84	156.72	53.14	43.60
38.94	33.96	31.54	0.00	0.00	0.00	38.94	33.96	31.54	695.14	632.17	639.94
30.19	29.19	30.45	0.00	0.00	0.00	30.19	29.19	30.45	406.80	368.57	379.07

Table 14
Accounting and Market-Value Capitalization of Selected Commercial Banks and Value of Deposit Insurance, 1989 and 1990
(Greater Forbearance)

		Total Assets ($ in Millions)			Equity/Assets (Percent)		
		1989	1990	1990	1989	1990	1990
Citicorp	New York	172,282	192,714	185,836	5.73	5.00	5.29
BankAmerican Corp.	San Francisco	95,234	98,861	102,950	4.75	5.46	5.35
Chase Manhattan Corp.	New York	93,405	99,782	97,045	5.80	4.85	5.07
J. P. Morgan & Co.	New York	74,962	70,725	71,964	5.42	4.45	4.49
Bankers Trust N.Y. Corp.	New York	59,390	55,107	60,959	4.72	2.92	3.16
Security Pacific Corp.	Los Angeles	57,845	61,124	68,449	4.30	4.97	3.97
Manufacturers Hanover Corp.	New York	56,350	53,743	56,488	4.64	4.84	4.66
NCNB Corp.	Charlotte	55,236	64,625	67,609	4.79	4.79	4.64
Chemical Banking Corp.	New York	55,123	48,859	48,390	4.64	4.38	4.59
Wells Fargo & Co.	San Francisco	44,448	47,016	48,645	5.34	6.10	5.68
First Chicago Corp.	Chicago	35,585	37,861	37,685	3.91	4.01	4.40
PNC Financial Corp.	Pittsburgh	28,931	31,719	32,979	5.15	5.07	4.99
Bank of New England Corp.	Boston	25,109	22,972	21,105	5.14	1.76	1.99
First Union Corp.	Charlotte	24,590	34,207	33,464	5.69	5.58	5.76
Bank of New York Co.	New York	23,174	45,678	45,729	5.30	4.70	4.64
Mellon Bank Corp.	Pittsburgh	22,749	22,472	18,342	2.82	4.36	4.58
First Wachovia Corp.	Winston-Salem	22,041	23,556	23,888	6.63	6.93	7.02
Republic New York Corp.	New York	20,405	22,003	21,898	8.00	7.15	7.38
First Interstate Bancorp	Los Angeles	19,596	21,110	20,531	4.66	5.37	5.26
NBD Bancorp, Inc.	Detroit	15,871	17,017	18,657	5.56	5.38	5.27
Southeast Banking Corp.	Miami	13,996	16,729	15,470	4.18	3.97	4.22
First Bank System, Inc.	Minneapolis	13,575	12,111	11,817	5.13	4.51	4.96
Sovran Financial Corp.	Norfolk	12,511	13,983	14,638	6.20	6.21	5.88

Intrinsic/Assets (Percent)			Put Option/Dep (Percent)			MktVal/Assets (Percent)			MktVal/Bk Val (Percent)		
1989	1990	1990	1989	1990	1990	1989	1990	1990	1989	1990	1990
5.34	3.53	3.69	0.57	1.18	1.06	5.50	3.87	3.98	96.13	77.55	75.30
4.27	5.80	5.88	0.59	0.29	0.27	4.64	5.98	6.05	97.56	109.59	113.19
3.03	2.49	2.37	1.42	1.85	1.87	3.53	3.15	3.07	60.97	64.98	60.53
9.61	9.44	9.13	0.01	0.08	0.01	9.61	9.45	9.13	177.22	212.60	203.07
5.83	5.46	5.54	0.22	0.32	0.42	5.87	5.53	5.61	124.34	189.34	177.42
7.72	7.04	5.73	0.01	0.08	0.91	7.73	7.08	6.29	179.51	142.79	158.25
2.61	3.91	4.02	1.61	0.68	0.59	3.27	4.21	4.27	70.47	87.02	91.74
5.25	5.86	5.29	0.41	0.34	0.52	5.53	6.07	5.63	115.60	127.16	121.55
6.19	5.13	6.45	0.15	0.42	0.12	6.26	5.35	6.51	135.01	122.26	141.91
8.12	7.65	8.36	0.00	0.07	0.05	8.12	7.65	8.40	152.17	126.38	147.82
6.62	5.11	4.94	0.05	0.37	0.38	6.64	5.24	5.07	169.98	130.49	115.11
12.18	11.69	8.40	0.00	0.00	0.21	12.18	11.69	8.53	236.33	230.50	171.01
6.29	(5.22)	(1.67)	0.09	10.64	3.89	6.34	1.40	1.03	123.41	79.50	51.79
9.53	5.32	5.81	0.05	0.55	0.49	9.56	5.60	6.14	167.93	101.86	106.51
11.76	4.91	4.42	0.00	0.48	0.76	11.76	5.11	4.73	222.02	108.78	102.00
3.60	3.91	5.01	0.75	0.60	0.33	3.98	4.20	5.20	141.04	96.24	113.60
11.03	11.68	11.81	0.00	0.00	0.00	11.03	11.67	11.81	166.43	168.58	168.24
6.59	6.37	7.68	0.00	0.02	0.00	6.59	6.37	7.69	82.34	89.11	104.13
10.92	8.89	10.79	0.00	0.24	0.38	10.92	9.07	11.09	234.34	169.01	210.69
11.96	12.91	12.31	0.00	0.01	0.00	11.96	12.90	12.31	215.16	239.92	233.49
5.09	1.45	(0.11)	0.34	1.98	2.86	5.33	2.84	2.04	127.46	71.85	48.39
9.37	6.44	7.48	0.00	0.55	0.23	9.37	6.82	7.64	182.77	151.21	154.10
16.38	14.98	11.81	0.00	0.00	0.03	16.38	14.98	11.84	264.26	241.35	201.49

Table 14 (continued)

		Total Assets			Equity/Assets		
		1989	1990	1990	1989	1990	1990
Corestates Financial Corp.	Philadelphia	10,428	9,771	10,474	5.64	6.77	6.53
Valley National Corp.	Phoenix	10,141	9,190	9,387	5.92	4.76	4.68
Suntrust Banks, Inc.	Atlanta	10,065	10,075	10,256	7.22	8.14	8.22
MNC Financial	Baltimore	8,936	10,827	15,630	5.63	4.59	4.25
Comerica, Inc.	Detroit	8,730	9,627	9,763	5.15	4.68	4.68
Manufacturers National Corp.	Detroit	8,683	8,506	9,042	5.21	6.13	5.90
Northern Trust Corporation	Chicago	8,415	9,384	9,372	4.52	4.87	5.06
Huntington Bancshares	Columbus	8,161	8,768	8,825	5.88	6.26	6.35
Ameritrust Corp.	Cleveland	8,102	8,347	8,527	6.27	5.86	6.02
Meridian Bancorp, Inc.	Reading	8,060	9,941	10,011	6.40	5.12	5.15
Fleet/Norstar Financial Group	Providence	8,013	11,201	10,875	6.43	4.90	5.19
State Street Boston Corp.	Boston	7,964	10,480	10,391	7.00	6.13	6.37
Norwest Corp.	Minneapolis	7,778	8,670	8,416	5.37	4.62	4.83
AmSouth Bancorp.	Birmingham	7,292	7,516	7,492	7.07	7.05	7.16
First City Bancorp of Texas	Houston	6,305	7,662	7,666	5.04	4.83	4.98
Bancorp Hawaii, Inc.	Honolulu	6,281	8,251	8,662	6.14	5.60	5.53
Riggs National Corp.	Washington	6,154	6,492	6,409	4.36	4.22	4.26
Hibernia Corp.	New Orleans	6,025	6,796	6,851	5.12	4.47	4.68
Society Corp.	Cleveland	5,978	7,832	7,678	6.10	5.93	6.31
First Tennessee National Corp.	Memphis	5,960	6,321	6,178	5.93	5.47	5.74
Midlantic Corp.	Edison	5,670	9,765	10,101	6.68	6.66	5.51
Barnett Banks, Inc.	Jacksonville	5,624	6,039	6,501	5.60	4.96	4.93
Fifth Third Bancorp	Cincinnati	3,614	3,875	4,081	7.42	7.92	8.03

Source: Authors' calculations from *Bank Source*, W.C. Ferguson and market stock prices from DRI, Inc.

Intrinsic/Assets			Put Option/Dep			MktVal/Assets			MktVal/Bk Val		
1989	1990	1990	1989	1990	1990	1989	1990	1990	1989	1990	1990
16.39	21.80	20.90	0.00	0.00	0.00	16.39	21.79	20.90	290.54	321.83	320.00
4.78	1.28	(0.21)	0.45	1.86	2.65	5.16	2.96	2.18	87.18	62.17	46.57
28.05	27.03	25.06	0.00	0.00	0.01	28.05	27.03	25.07	388.62	331.98	304.82
15.59	14.40	6.64	0.00	0.03	0.37	15.59	14.42	6.90	276.87	314.16	162.20
8.45	7.70	7.83	0.00	0.03	0.06	8.45	7.70	7.88	163.86	164.85	168.34
7.80	8.59	7.24	0.00	0.00	0.07	7.80	8.58	7.28	149.61	140.17	123.50
9.66	49.48	10.84	0.00	0.00	0.01	9.66	49.48	10.84	213.65	1016.1	214.35
8.54	9.87	9.09	0.01	0.01	0.01	8.55	9.88	9.10	145.21	157.82	143.42
11.33	8.47	7.78	0.00	0.09	0.20	11.33	8.49	7.93	180.76	145.73	131.84
9.31	6.75	6.26	0.00	0.13	0.19	9.31	6.84	6.42	145.49	133.95	124.57
32.68	21.25	19.39	0.00	0.00	0.00	32.68	21.25	19.39	508.44	434.13	373.57
12.34	12.92	14.09	0.00	0.00	0.00	12.34	12.92	14.09	176.15	210.82	220.96
20.99	21.30	23.47	0.00	0.00	0.00	20.99	21.30	23.47	390.58	460.64	486.33
8.25	7.19	6.82	0.00	0.17	0.14	8.25	7.29	6.93	116.75	103.87	96.90
6.10	8.10	6.11	0.08	0.00	0.21	6.15	8.10	6.21	121.84	167.85	124.81
9.34	8.74	9.71	0.00	0.02	0.02	9.34	8.75	9.72	152.05	156.23	175.69
5.44	2.78	2.44	0.30	1.66	1.59	5.60	3.66	3.28	128.31	86.70	77.03
7.98	6.30	0.97	0.17	0.43	2.38	8.11	6.62	2.88	158.43	148.58	61.63
12.91	13.91	14.24	0.00	0.00	0.00	12.91	13.90	14.24	211.81	234.53	225.61
7.05	5.92	5.22	0.02	0.16	0.49	7.06	6.05	5.61	119.19	110.64	97.81
25.96	5.98	4.59	0.00	0.55	1.06	25.96	6.44	5.47	388.48	96.73	99.28
38.94	33.96	31.54	0.00	0.00	0.00	38.94	31.35	31.54	695.14	632.17	639.94
30.19	29.19	30.45	0.00	0.00	0.00	30.19	29.19	30.45	406.80	368.57	379.07

substantial government assistance. Southeast Bank in Miami, another large institution which we reported to be insolvent in mid-1990 once the put option value of deposit insurance was stripped away, has also been seized and resolved in a government-assisted merger.

At the same time, of course, the stock prices of many large banks have increased significantly since our report, as we have indicated. In part, this may reflect the imputed value of regulatory forbearance. But the stock market could also be taking account of the impending benefits of interstate banking, which should accrue to large banks, as well as to correcting some possible overreaction in late 1990 and early 1991 about the severity of lending problems in certain banks.

Nevertheless, more recent informed analyses have essentially confirmed a key finding of our put option analysis that a number of large banks were quite weakly capitalized when valued by more realistic measures than book-value accounting. For example, in one recent study, SNL Securities of Charlottesville, Virginia, attempted to mark to market the balance sheets of major U.S. banks. The findings indicated, as of early September 1991, both Citicorp and Chase Manhattan were barely solvent. In addition, the economic or intrinsic value of both Wells Fargo and Fleet/Norstar was below 50 percent of book value.[19]

Citicorp Case Study: "Technically Insolvent?"

The case of Citicorp is especially noteworthy because on July 31, 1991, a widely publicized statement by Congressman John Dingell, Chairman of the House Committee on Energy and Commerce, provoked a debate that dramatically highlights many of the issues we have just discussed: the proliferation of accounting techniques; the use of accounting to tell different stories; the confusion that can result; and the uncertainty of the appropriate policy response.

Mr. Dingell said that Citicorp, the nation's largest bank, was "technically insolvent" and "struggling to survive," as reported in the *New York Times*.[20] The article quoted the Chairman of the FDIC saying that he did not believe Citicorp was "insolvent under any standard." The article further quoted James M. Rosenberg, the money center bank equity analyst for Shearson Lehman Brothers, saying that "Even adjusted for credit risk, Citicorp still shows substantial net worth." The *Wall Street Journal* article reporting Mr. Dingell's comments began by saying that he "made a better Congressman than a bank analyst."[21]

Based upon data as of March 1991, the most recent reporting period before Mr. Dingell's comments, Citicorp reported total equity capital of $8 billion, based on historical cost or book-value accounting under Generally Accepted Accounting Principles (GAAP). Citicorp's reported capital represented 3.7 percent of its total assets of approximately $216 billion.

In other words, a drop in the value of Citicorp's assets of 3.7 percent would have wiped out its total reported equity capital—and the reported buffer protecting the Bank Insurance Fund against losses. Stated still another way, if the reported book value of the assets exceeded true market value by approximately 3.7 percent, there may in fact have been no capital. With the reported capital it had at the time Mr. Dingell spoke, Citicorp would have failed the 1980 minimum net worth requirement for savings and loans.

Almost all experts agree that tangible equity capital, which excludes intangible assets, is a better calculation of reported capital, especially when total equity capital falls as low as 3.7 percent. By this measure at the time Mr. Dingell spoke, Citicorp's capital was $6.6 billion or only 3.1 percent of its total assets. Again, in 1980 by this measure the average savings and loan had double Citicorp's capital.

In June 1991, Mr. Rosenberg—the bank equity analyst—in an equity report entitled "The Big Bank Barbershop: Credit-Risk Haircuts to Book Value" estimated that Citicorp's real capital was only about $4 billion.[22] He adjusted Citicorp's tangible capital for the apparent deterioration in assets, primarily commercial real estate, LDC debt, and loans for highly-leveraged transactions, which he concluded were not accurately valued by the accounting techniques used by Citicorp. This was alluded to in the *New York Times* article without pointing out that the $4 billion represented only 1.84 percent of Citicorp's total assets.

If Mr. Rosenberg was accurate, a fall in the value of Citicorp's assets of 1.84 percent, or a book-value versus market-value error of about that magnitude, would have wiped out the bank's capital. Mr. Rosenberg's report, in fact, indicated that the problem of seriously undercapitalized large banks extended far beyond Citicorp. He reported the overall tangible equity capital of the nation's largest fifteen banks to be 4.2 percent. The average fell to 3.6 percent by Mr. Rosenberg's calculations when allowance for asset deterioration was made. These relatively few banks held over $1 trillion in assets, which represents about a third of the banking industry's assets.

Despite the capital levels discussed above, Citicorp defended itself in the *Wall Street Journal* article reportedly referring to "its capital—a measure of solvency—as being 8 percent of assets." The bank appeared to be referring to its risk-based capital calculated according to the Basel agreement in which different percentages of capital are required for given regulatory estimates of risk associated with specified asset categories. Although the stated goal of the risk-based capital guidelines was to make capital requirements more rigorous, they may instead provide convenient public relation tools for selected banks because of inadequacies in defining risk and the inclusion of loan loss reserves.

Weakly capitalized depositories sometimes argue that a true mark-to-market would be beneficial to them because the estimate of such intangibles as franchise value (a depository's value as a going concern) would be greater than the deterioration of other tangible assets. This has typically not been the case in government-assisted mergers of savings and loans or banks. Bank of New England is a good example: it was seized, closed, and its assets and liabilities—including its franchise value—sold to an acquirer at a loss of $2.5 billion. The value of intangible assets like franchise value is most often (probably always) less than the overstated book value of tangible assets.

As we have indicated above, we long ago reached the point where the deterioration among banks posed a threat to taxpayers. Yet, as with the savings and loan debacle, until the threat is officially acknowledged, it will be generally ignored and it will be impossible to galvanize support for meaningful reform of federal deposit insurance and insured depositories to prevent recurrence. That is why it is important to emphasize the counterfeit nature of reported capital and ferret out the real condition of the banks.

Notes

1. Lewis J. Spellman, *The Depository Firm and Industry: Theory, History, and Regulation*, Academic Press, New York, 1982.

2. George J. Benston, R. Dan Brumbaugh, Jr., Jack M. Guttentag, Richard J. Herring, George G. Kaufman, Robert E. Litan, and Kenneth Scott, "Blueprint for Restructuring America's Financial Institutions: Report of a Task Force," The Brookings Institution, Washington, D.C., 1989. For the importance of capital in establishing appropriate incentives, see Joseph E. Stiglitz, "S&L Bail-Out," in *The Reform of Federal Deposit*

Insurance: Disciplining the Government and Protecting Taxpayers, HarperBusiness, New York, 1992.

3. Throughout most of the book, the data presented for the banking industry refer only to commercial banks. However, in a number of places we note where our aggregate banking industry data also include savings banks. Significantly, as we explain later, our failure cost projections based on the call report data compiled by W.C. Ferguson in Bank Source include both commercial and savings banks.

4. *Quarterly Banking Profile,* Federal Deposit Insurance Corporation, first quarter, 1991.

5. *Ibid.*

6. As we understand the current system, federal regulators are now requiring banks with examination ratings below 1 (the highest ranking) to maintain equity-to-capital ratios of at least 4 percent.

7. See Appendix B in "Banks in Turmoil."

8. Allen N. Berger, Kathlenn A. Kuester, and James M. O'Brien, "The Limitations of Market Value Accounting and a More Realistic Alternative," Federal Reserve Board, September 1990.

9. Robert C. Clarke, Testimony before the Senate Committee on Banking, Housing and Urban Affairs, October 25, 1989.

10. This is reflected in the table in lower ratios of loan loss reserves to equity capital than the ratios of nonaccrual loans to equity capital.

11. John Meehan and Catherine Yang, "The Banks Are Running Out of Running Room," *Business Week,* October 29, 1990, p. 88.

12. Tom Leander, "New England's Banks Are Hurting," *American Banker,* November 15, 1990, p. 2.

13. Ron Suskind, "Some Banks Use Accounting Techniques That Conceal Loan Woes, Regulators Say," *Wall Street Journal,* November 29, 1990, p. 4.

14. Phil Roosevelt, "Home Loans Fall As Bulwarks for Bank Portfolios," *American Banker,* November 13, 1990, p. 1.

15. The adjustment to total capital reflects an addition for loan loss reserves minus an allowance of 1.0 percent of performing loans (to take account of potential additional problems outside the high-risk loan category).

16. Additional financial data on large banks is provided in Appendix D in "Banks in Turmoil." It has been recently reported that many large banks reduced their HLT exposure in the third quarter of 1990, bringing the average ratio of HLTs-to-assets for the 25 largest HLT lenders down

from 4.8 percent in the second quarter to 4.5 percent in the third. (See Steven Lipin, "Big Banks Slash HLT Exposure By Billions," *American Banker*, December 5, 1990, p. 1.) Nevertheless, it is reasonable to assume that the banks sold their best HLT loans, leaving behind those on which they have the highest probability of suffering a loss. Therefore, we do not believe that these banks have significantly lowered their loss exposure from HLT loans.

17. The major bank rating agencies, too, have downgraded the bonds issued by large numbers of banking organizations. For example, through August 1990, Moody's had downgraded the debt of 32 of the 52 largest U.S. bank holding companies; Standard and Poor's, 21; and IBCA, 19. (See IBCA, Ltd., Report on U.S. Banking Industry.)

18. Our option-price adjustment technique is based upon Ehud Ronn and Avinash K. Verma "Pricing Risk-Adjusted Deposit Insurance: An Option-Based Model," *Journal of Finance*, September 1986. Since analysts can differ about the appropriate assumptions to make when calculating option-adjusted estimates of capital, the results shown in Tables 13 and 14 should be interpreted as providing rough orders of magnitude of the value of deposit insurance and the corresponding adjustments to book capital required on account of such insurance. For an application of this technique to savings and loans, see James R. Barth, Daniel E. Page, and R. Dan Brumbaugh, Jr., "Pitfalls in Using Market Prices to Assess the Financial Condition of Depository Institutions," *The Journal of Real Estate Finance and Economics*, June 1992.

19. Reported in Rhonda Brammer, "Good Banks, Bad Banks," *Barron's*, September 9, 1991.

20. *New York Times*, August 1, 1991, p. C17.

21. *Wall Street Journal*, August 1, 1991, p. A14.

22. James M. Rosenberg, "The Big Bank Barbershop: Credit-Risk Haircuts to Book Value," Shearson Lehman Brothers, June 10, 1991.

THREE

Banking In A Long Downward Spiral

Most of the discussion thus far has focused on the current condition of the banking industry and the federal fund that insures its deposits. We now turn to the *future* health of all federally insured depositories and their federal deposit-insurance funds. After the cataclysm of the savings and loan debacle of the 1980s and the deterioration of the banks that began in the 1980s, a crucial issue is whether the health of federally insured depositories and that of the FDIC, now administering both the BIF and the Savings Association Insurance Fund (SAIF), will return to normal. To the contrary, it appears to us that deeper structural problems threaten the existence of federally insured depositories and raise the specter of ongoing deposit-insurance crises.

Competition: Boon to Consumers, Bane of Depositories

The commercial banking industry and the other federally insured depositories have been gradually losing their *raison d'etre*: to provide liquidity by being a safe haven for depositors' funds that are payable on demand and to provide loanable funds to individual and business borrowers. The reasons are simple. Banks and other depositories have been facing increasingly stiff competition from a long and still growing list of nondepositories such as mutual funds, money market mutual funds,

Figure 2. Return on Assets for Banks 1950-1990.

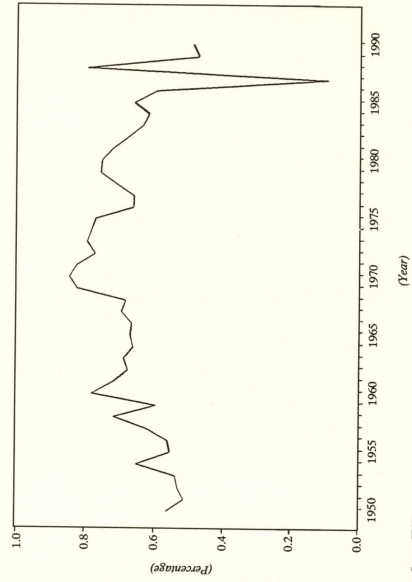

(Percentage)

(Year)

Source: FDIC

insurance companies, pension funds, finance companies, and government sponsored enterprises.

These competitors have been gradually replacing depositories as individuals have been putting a relatively smaller proportion of their savings into depositories and as business borrowers have obtained a relatively smaller proportion of their funds from depositories. We document these trends below and then discuss their powerful implications for the U.S. financial marketplace, federal depository regulation, and deposit insurance. In a nutshell, these trends will continue to provide profound benefits to consumers of financial services but will confront most federally insured depositories and the deposit-insurance system with the almost certain prospect of continued decline in market share.

Inflation Forces Deregulation of Interest Rates: Depository Costs Rise, Competitors Proliferate

When inflation was low, banking was a much easier business. All but the wealthiest customers put their money in banks at low, regulated interest rates, and most individuals and companies had nowhere else to turn for funds except to their bankers. In that world, banks found it simple to earn a spread between the interest rates they paid depositors (though none to checking account customers) and the rates they charged their borrowers. Indeed, as shown in Figure 2, from 1950 through 1970 the industry's return on assets rose steadily. In addition, there were relatively few competitors vying for depositor dollars.

Two major developments in the last twenty years—inflation and technological innovation—produced a sea change in the environment in which banks compete. These two developments are largely responsible for the increased competition for both liabilities and assets that led to the erosion and volatility in return on assets depicted in Chart 2 in the mid-1970s and the dramatic difficulties described throughout Chapter 1.

The explosive jump in inflation in 1973–1974 and 1979–1981 induced depositors to lend their funds to alternative firms that promised returns well above the regulated interest rates banks were limited to paying. Ultimately, the double-digit interest rates available on Treasury securities and money market mutual funds in the late 1970s and early 1980s caused significant deposit withdrawals, or disintermediation. Money market mutual funds that were minuscule in 1978 equaled the dollar volume of demand deposits at banks by 1982, more than $200 billion.[1] These pressures forced Congress to allow banks, savings and loans, and credit unions total freedom in the interest rates they could pay their depositors. The unregulated money market deposit account (MMDA) authorized in 1982 grew to nearly $600 billion by 1986. Over approximately the same period, other checkable deposits authorized for nonbank depositories grew to equal demand deposits. With deposit rates deregulated, banks have had to pay higher, competitive rates for funds which have increased bank costs and reduced bank income.

Technology Spurs Securitization of Depository Assets, and Reduces Depository Revenues

Simultaneously, powerful advances in computer technology significantly improved information processing and helped develop new kinds of financial assets that began to erode the role of banks in lending. Technology also facilitated an increasingly international market for financial assets. Probably most important, technological advances helped launch the securitization of finance, that is, the packaging of individual loans or other assets into bundles sold in the market in various forms of securities.

Fixed rate residential mortgages were the first loans to be securitized, primarily because both the mortgages and the underwriting process for originating them were relatively easily standardized, and because the value of the securities was enhanced by the guarantees of federal or quasi-governmental agencies, such as the Government National Mortgage Association (Ginnie Mae), the Federal National Mortgage Association (Fannie Mae), and the Federal Home Loan Mortgage Corporation (Freddie Mac). Between 1975 and 1988, the volume of mortgage securities outstanding grew by more than a factor of 40, from less than $18 billion to almost $770 billion. By the end of 1988, over 35 percent of all residential mortgages in the United States had been securitized. In essence, the mortgage-backed security enabled many other financial firms than savings and loans to hold fixed-rate mortgages in their portfolios.

Securitization has since spread to other loans, principally variable-rate mortgages, automobile and credit-card loans, although banks have been increasingly selling their business loans as well. From mid-1983 to 1988, the volume of outstanding loan sales by commercial banks jumped from $27 billion to $236 billion.[2] In addition, commercial banks lost business to the corporate paper market as technological advances allowed smaller nonfinancial firms to borrow from corporate debt markets instead of taking out commercial bank loans.

In some ways the development of deeper secondary markets made possible by securitization has been helpful to banks. Unlike the banks of old, the banks of today no longer have to be stuck with loans until they mature. If banks need liquidity or need to sell assets in order to shrink to comply with capital standards, they can in general sell securities more easily than individual loans in their portfolio. Moreover, now that banks have the authority to securitize the loans they make, they can earn fees from origination, sale, and servicing of loans comprising the securities.

How Securitization Squeezes Depository Revenue

Although securitization has provided some benefits, it has had an offsetting, much more powerful, and much less appreciated, negative effect on banks, savings and loans, and credit unions. Simply put, securitization has been one way in which technological development has been eliminating the need, or demand, for depositories.

There are several interesting and provocative ways to describe this revolution. Depositories, for example, are also called intermediaries because they intermediate between lenders (mainly depositors) and borrowers. In this role, depositories have traditionally gathered, evaluated, and monitored information primarily on borrowers that was too costly for lenders themselves to process.

The revolutionary advances in processing information through computers, however, has dramatically improved the ability of lenders and borrowers to gain information about each other directly and has, thus, reduced the demand for depository services. When a nonthrift financial firm or individual purchases a mortgage-backed security, for example, they are holding in their portfolio of mortgage-backed securities a mortgage that in the past almost exclusively would have been held by a savings and loan as a single mortgage.

Another way of describing how securitization reduces the demand for depository services is to point out that depositories transform liquid deposits into illiquid loans. Indeed, it was by taking the risk of holding illiquid loans in portfolio that banks and savings and loans traditionally earned an acceptable return on the capital shareholders provided to them. By turning formerly illiquid depository assets into liquid securities that can be held by many firms and individuals, securitization has been undermining the traditional depository function and therefore its return on capital. The increasingly deep market for individual loan sales is doing the same.

Depositories must charge relatively lower interest rates than they once did on illiquid loans they originated and held in portfolio because they are no longer the sole holders of the loans. Securitization has increased the number of holders of formerly illiquid loans held almost solely by depositories to include pension funds, insurance companies, mutual funds, and individuals themselves. By allowing these other financial service firms to fund assets by purchasing them in the secondary markets, securitization has reduced the interest rates on the assets serving as collateral for the asset-backed securities.

It has been estimated, for example, that the securitization of residential mortgages has effectively lowered mortgage interest rates (below what they would otherwise be) by as much as 50 to 100 basis points.[3] The drop in mortgage rates has been so large that it has substantially exacerbated the plight of most savings and loan institutions. Since 1989 savings and loans have been required by law to invest most of their funds in residential mortgages. But with the exception of two brief periods, savings and loans on average in the 1980s were unable to hold fixed-rate mortgages profitably unless they gambled on the movement of interest rates.[4] This was the strategy that produced the initial savings and loan crisis of the late 1970s and early 1980s.

Proliferating Indices of Bank Decline

Although the big banks are in the most trouble, almost all banks are in a tense struggle for survival under increasing competitive pressure. Securitization, for example, is just one threat that has led to falling spread income for all sizes of banks. Other threats include the ability of a wider range of commercial businesses to find nonbank financing in U.S. and international capital markets, and increasing competition for liabilities. The deterioration in loan quality has also led to industrywide increases in loan charge-offs and other indices of loan problems. As with the big banks these indications of trouble and a decade slide in profitability would have been worse under more appropriate and less tolerant regulatory treatment.

Under these conditions, particularly sustained falling income and increasing competition, it is not surprising to find increasing risk in the banking industry's aggregate balance sheet. Throughout the 1980s banks shifted toward higher-yielding, higher-risk assets and funded them with higher-cost deposits. The current prognosis for the banking industry is a continuing struggle with an ongoing decline in capital that started nearly thirty years ago.

Spread Income and Loan Quality Fall

As nonmortgage loans held by banks are increasingly used to back newly issued securities, the commercial banking industry will be plagued with similar problems. While the pace may be slower, it appears inevitable. As shown in Figure 3, banks of all sizes have already suffered an erosion of their spread, or net interest margin, as a percent of interest-earning assets.[5] The erosion appears to have been greatest at the big banks, although as Figure 3 demonstrates, it has occurred among banks of all sizes.

Increasing competition and the decline of spread income as a percentage of interest-earning assets for small banks are indications that small bank income and capital levels are vulnerable to some of the same threats as the big banks. At this time loans by small banks to small businesses, for example, are relatively more difficult to securitize because it is difficult to standardize underwriting of the relatively large number of small loans with idiosyncratic characteristics. With time securitization will nonetheless become possible for more of these types of loans. As this occurs, small banks, too, will suffer.

Unfortunately for the banks, even Figure 3 understates the problems the industry has been facing. What were once the safest borrowers—blue-chip corporations—essentially have deserted banks as sources of funds, finding it cheaper instead to borrow directly by issuing commercial paper. By 1989, the ratio of nonbank commercial paper outstanding to commercial and industrial (C&I) loans held by banks was over 75 percent, up from less than 10 percent thirty years ago. Increasingly, because of the wider access of information, firms below the blue-chip level have been gaining access to the corporate paper market as well.

With their best customers gone and margins under increasing pressure, banks have chased riskier loans in an effort to maintain their former returns to shareholders. The result is graphically illustrated in Figure 4, which shows that loan charge-offs net of recoveries (loans and leases removed from the balance sheet due to uncollectability less recoveries from past charge-offs) have been rising as a share of total industrywide

Figure 3. Adjusted Net Interest Margin as a Percentage of Interest-Earning Assets 1985-1990.

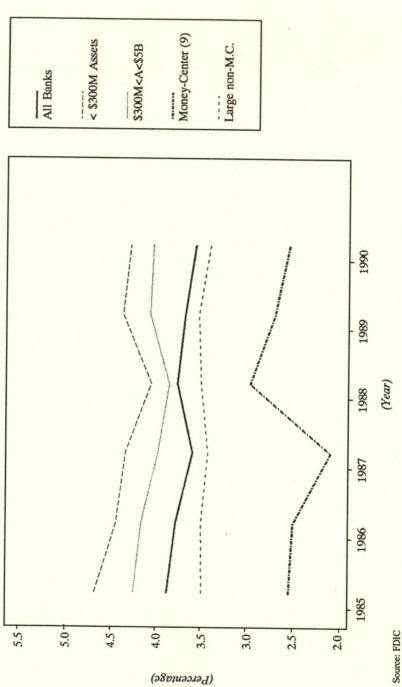

Source: FDIC

Figure 4. Net Loan Charge-Offs to Average Total Loans for Banks 1960-1990.

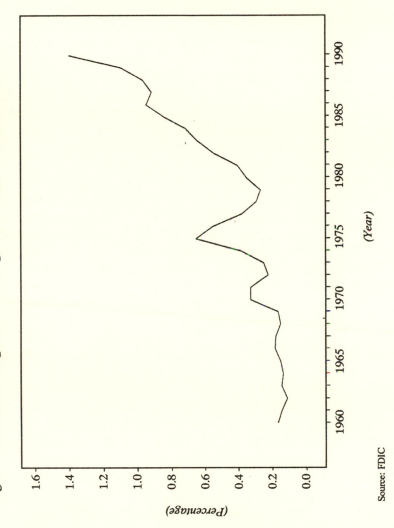

(Percentage)

(Year)

Source: FDIC

loans. The increase has occurred not just during the past several years, but for the past three *decades*.

As Figure 4 shows, however, net charge-offs skyrocketed in the 1980s. Indeed, the drop in banks' net income shown in Figure 2 and the increase in net loan charge-offs shown in Figure 4 would have been even greater and noticed earlier if regulators had not permitted banks to camouflage the deterioration of certain loans, beginning with LDC debt in 1982, with misleading accounting. In addition, reported earnings have been made more volatile by the collective decisions of banks and their regulators not to make more appropriate provisions for loan losses at the time when those assets actually declined in value. Instead, by waiting to adjust accounting values, the problems built up, were generally accompanied by unrealistic denials, and later required significant adjustments of reported income and capital.

Large banks, in particular, have suffered the most. After all, the blue-chip customers that used to borrow from banks used the largest banks, so one would expect to see those institutions experiencing the greatest difficulties with problem loans. The data provided in Appendix Table A-5 bear this out. As discussed earlier, they show that at mid-year 1990, nonaccrual loans held by the largest banks (those with assets above $10 billion) represented almost 2.5 percent of their total loans; in contrast, the same ratio at the smallest banks (those with assets less than $100 million) was only about 0.7 percent.

From the Banks' Income Statement: Falling Aggregate Net Income

The cumulative effects of competition ultimately affect the banking industry's income statement despite accounting conventions that reluctantly acknowledge deterioration. The banking industry's net income, shown in Table 15, fell from 75 basis points in 1980 to 67 basis points in 1990.

The average net income for the 1980s was 61 basis points, significantly below the 81-basis-point average of the 1970s. There were significant fluctuations in net income as well, with a decade low of 12 basis points in 1987 followed by a decade high of 80 basis points in 1988.

The volatility in earnings reflected asset deterioration and inconsistent commercial bank and regulatory policy toward provisioning for loan losses, reductions in income essentially designed to offset expected declines in the value of assets. As Table 15 shows, provisions for loan losses rose throughout the decade. Following the rise from 24 basis points in 1980 to 75 basis points in 1986, the jump in provisions in 1987 to 123 basis points caused the sharp decline in net income for that year. Provisions for loan losses in previous years were below those suggested by the default characteristics of the commercial banks' LDC debt and by the performance of such debt in the secondary market.

Overall net income would have fallen further and the drop would have been more noticeable earlier were it not for bank and regulatory decisions which, beginning in 1982 with LDC debt problems, had permitted banks to camouflage the deterioration of certain loans.

The regulatory decisions also influenced loan loss provisions for domestic real estate and accounted for the large increase in provisions for loan losses from 55 basis points in 1988 to 94 basis points in 1989, as shown in Table 15. The increase in loan loss provisions and the effect they have had on net income reflect the increasing deterioration in assets in the 1980s. The exact timing of the volatility reflects commercial bank and regulatory decisions not to take provisions at a more appropriate time consistent with a reasonable market assessment of deterioration in asset values, decisions that papered over the deterioration for some period of time.

As Table 15 shows, total loan charge-offs quadrupled from 26 basis points in 1980 to 103 basis points in the 1990, consistent with increasing asset deterioration and provisions for loan losses. Charge-offs rose 27 percent in one year between 1989 and 1990.

In addition to provisions for loan losses and total loan charge-offs, the increase in noninterest expense also contributed significantly to the decline in commercial bank income. Noninterest expense increased throughout the decade rising from 251 basis points in 1980 to 328 basis points in 1989, an increase of 77 basis points or nearly 31 percent. Next to provisions for loan losses, the increase in noninterest expense contributed most to the decline in commercial-bank income.

As we briefly mentioned earlier, aggregate net income for commercial banks is artificially higher than it would be otherwise due to removal of closed banks' income from aggregate income accounts. When the BIF closes a bank its income and other performance characteristics are removed from the aggregate database for the entire year in which the closure occurs. This not only affects income but also removes the closed banks negative capital, thus inflating aggregate commercial bank capital levels.

Table 15
Income and Expense of Federally Insured Commercial Banks, 1980 - 1990
(Percent of Total Assets)

	1980	1981	1982	1983	1984	1985	1986	1987	1988	1989	1990
Total Interest and Fee Income	9.51	11.40	10.86	9.28	9.98	9.09	8.09	8.16	8.70	9.62	9.67
Domestic Office Loans	5.45	6.34	6.21	5.48	5.88	5.54	5.07	5.16	5.46	6.12	6.11
Foreign Office Loans	1.39	1.72	1.42	1.01	1.34	1.09	0.82	0.76	0.86	0.97	0.93
Lease Financing Receivables	0.07	0.09	0.09	0.08	0.09	0.09	0.08	0.10	0.11	0.12	0.13
Balances Due From Depository Institutions	0.88	1.20	1.11	0.73	0.67	0.51	0.39	0.40	0.44	0.46	0.38
Interest and Dividend Income on Securities	1.24	1.45	1.53	1.58	1.58	1.50	1.42	1.44	1.50	1.55	1.71
Interest Income on Federal Funds Sold and Repurchase Agreements	0.47	0.60	0.52	0.40	0.42	0.35	0.31	0.30	0.33	0.39	0.38
Total Interest Expense	6.47	8.37	7.72	6.14	6.74	5.76	4.86	4.83	5.27	6.22	6.18
Interest on Domestic Office Deposits	3.42	4.57	4.56	3.90	4.17	3.69	3.16	2.99	3.23	3.76	3.85
Interest on Foreign Office Deposits	1.88	2.30	1.90	1.24	1.43	1.10	0.83	0.87	0.91	1.02	1.03
Expense of Federal Funds Purchased and Reverse Repurchase Agreements	0.90	1.18	0.95	0.70	0.78	0.61	0.54	0.53	0.60	0.76	0.69
Interest on Demand Notes Issued to the U.S. Treasury and Other Borrowed Money	0.24	0.29	0.28	0.27	0.32	0.31	0.26	0.39	0.48	0.63	0.56
Interest on Subordinated Notes and Debentures	0.03	0.03	0.03	0.03	0.03	0.04	0.04	0.05	0.05	0.05	0.04
Interest on Mortgage Indebtedness and Obligations under Capitalized Leases	0.00	0.00	0.00	0.00	0.01	0.01	0.01	0.01	0.01	0.01	0.01
Net Interest Income	3.03	3.03	3.14	3.13	3.24	3.33	3.23	3.33	3.43	3.40	3.49
Provisions for Loan and Lease Losses and Allocated Transfer Risk	0.24	0.25	0.39	0.46	0.55	0.65	0.75	1.23	0.55	0.94	0.96

Table 15 (continued)

Total Noninterest Income	0.77	0.86	0.92	0.99	1.06	1.14	1.22	0.38	1.44	1.55	1.67
Service Charges on Deposit Accoutns	0.17	0.19	0.21	0.23	0.26	0.27	0.27	0.29	0.30	0.31	0.35
Other Noninterest Income	0.60	0.67	0.71	0.76	0.80	0.87	0.95	1.09	1.13	1.24	1.32
Gains on Securities Not Held in Trading Accts.	(0.05)	(0.08)	(0.06)	(0.00)	(0.01)	0.06	0.13	0.05	0.01	0.02	0.01
Total Noninterest Expense	2.51	2.65	2.81	2.86	2.94	3.01	3.07	3.23	3.24	3.28	3.49
Salaries and Employee Benefits	1.33	1.38	1.43	1.45	1.47	1.46	1.46	1.51	1.49	1.49	1.56
Expense of Premises and Fixed Assets, Net of Rental Income	0.40	0.42	0.46	0.48	0.47	0.49	0.49	0.51	0.50	0.50	0.53
Other Noninterest Expense	0.79	.84	0.92	0.93	1.00	1.06	1.12	1.22	1.24	1.28	1.40
Pre-tax Net Operating Income	1.00	0.91	0.81	0.81	0.80	0.86	0.77	0.29	1.09	0.76	0.72
Applicable Income Taxes	0.25	0.19	0.14	0.17	0.19	0.21	0.18	0.18	0.32	0.29	0.24
Income before Extraordinary Items	0.75	0.72	0.67	0.63	0.61	0.65	0.59	0.11	0.77	0.47	0.48
Extraordinary Items, Net of Tax	0.00	0.00	0.00	0.00	0.01	0.01	0.01	0.01	0.03	0.01	0.02
Net Income	0.75	0.73	0.68	0.64	0.62	0.66	0.60	0.12	0.80	0.47	0.50
Total Loan Charge-Offs	0.26	0.26	0.37	0.45	0.52	0.58	0.67	0.67	0.72	0.81	0.98
Total Recoveries	0.07	0.08	0.07	0.09	0.09	0.10	0.10	0.12	0.13	0.12	0.12
Net Additions to Capital Stock	0.00	0.00	0.00	0.12	0.15	0.09	0.11	0.09	0.10	0.05	0.06
Cash Dividends Declared on Preferred Stock	0.00	0.00	0.00	0.00	0.00	0.00	0.00	0.00	0.00	0.00	N/A
Cash Dividends Declared on Common Stock	0.27	0.29	0.30	0.13	0.30	0.31	0.31	0.35	0.42	0.42	0.41
Net Income ($ Millions)	14,009	14,720	14,843	14,923	15,506	18,057	17,514	3,616	24,939	15,659	16,607
Number of Employees	1,485,813	1,497,434	1,498,184	1,509,260	1,526,392	1,561,698	1,563,145	1,544,994	1,527,071	1,531,130	N/A
Number of Banks	14,434	14,408	14,446	14,460	14,477	14,404	14,200	13,699	13,139	12,705	12,342

Source: FDIC; and Ferguson and Co.

The income statement presented in Table 15 offers two apparent bright spots—increases in both net interest and noninterest income—which tend to dim with analysis. Net interest income rose from 303 basis points in 1980 to 340 basis points in 1989, a gain of 37 basis points, or 12 percent. As Figure 4 shows, the overall level averages the higher and more stable net interest income of smaller banks with the lower and more volatile net interest income of larger banks. As Chart 4 also shows, when adjusted for asset growth, all net interest income declined for banks of all sizes.

Noninterest income played a significantly increasing role for commercial banks in the 1980s, more than doubling from 77 basis points in 1980 to 155 basis points in 1989. The increase in noninterest income is consistent with the effects of competition. As profits from traditional loans have fallen, banks have sought revenue from nontraditional sources such as fee income from origination, sale, and servicing of loans and off-balance-sheet activities such as standby letters of credit, foreign exchange contracts, and interest-rate swaps. Some of the most profitable banks in the country earn most of their income from nontraditional activities and their stated strategic plans include growth only in nontraditional activities. Thus, even firms that continue to call themselves banks and benefit from deposit insurance are not really traditional banks anymore, but instead are tending more and more to adapt when possible to the changing and competitive financial marketplace in search of profits.

From the Banks' Balance Sheet: More Risk

The increasingly intense competitive environment helps explain why banks have been taking on more risk. The rising loan losses in the industry, already discussed, make this point self-evident. Table 16, which provides the banking industry's aggregate balance sheet since 1980, illustrates the enhanced risk-taking in the banking industry in more detail.

Banks became less liquid in the 1980s, reducing the share of their assets in cash and investment securities from roughly 36 percent at the beginning of the decade to just 27 percent by the end. An increase in loans took up the slack, rising from 54 percent of total assets to 61 percent. Meanwhile, the composition of bank loan portfolios shifted markedly. C&I loans, the largest component of loans in 1980 at 21 percent, finished the decade at 19 percent. In contrast, real estate loans grew from 15 percent to 23 percent over the same period, replacing C&I loans as the most important lending category.

Table 16
Assets and Liabilities of Federally Insured Commercial Banks, 1980 - 1990
(Percentage of Total Assets)

	1980	1981	1982	1983	1984	1985	1986	1987	1988	1989	1990
Number of Banks	14,434	14,415	14,462	14,468	14,477	14,404	14,200	13,699	13,139	12,705	12,342
Total Assets ($ Billions)	1,856	2,029	2,194	2,342	2,508	2,730	2,941	3,001	3,131	3,299	3,388
Cash and Due from Depository Institutions	17.89	16.14	15.24	14.59	12.90	12.48	12.89	11.94	11.36	10.63	9.38
Securities	18.02	17.37	17.60	18.84	15.37	16.09	16.49	17.35	17.12	16.95	17.84
Federal Funds Sold and Securities Purchased Under Agreements to Resell	3.79	4.49	4.73	3.99	4.41	4.87	4.74	4.35	4.08	4.45	4.33
Loans and Leases, Net	54.23	55.19	55.20	55.57	59.39	58.87	58.75	59.31	60.23	60.74	60.61
Plus: Allowance for losses	0.54	0.56	0.61	0.66	0.75	0.85	0.98	1.65	1.49	1.63	1.63
Loans and Leases, Total	54.78	55.75	55.81	56.23	60.13	59.72	59.73	60.96	61.72	62.37	62.24
Plus: Unearned Income	1.13	1.04	0.93	0.82	0.76	0.66	0.55	0.51	0.50	0.46	0.41
Loans and Leases, Gross	55.91	56.79	56.74	57.05	60.89	60.38	60.28	61.46	62.23	62.83	62.65
Real Estate Loans, Total	14.50	14.35	14.03	14.38	15.37	16.06	17.52	19.99	21.56	23.09	24.46
Construction and Land Development	1.98	2.22	2.38	2.59	3.04	3.27	3.63	3.99	4.10	4.12	3.72
Secured by Farmland	0.46	0.41	0.38	0.40	0.41	0.42	0.43	0.48	0.50	0.51	0.51
Secured by 1-4 Family Residential Properties	7.95	7.64	7.22	7.14	7.24	7.28	7.57	8.76	9.64	10.64	11.81
Secured by Multifamily Residential Properties	0.35	0.35	0.35	0.40	0.43	0.46	0.54	0.60	0.58	0.60	0.62
Secured by Nonfarm Nonresidential Properties	3.45	3.31	3.29	3.48	3.83	4.15	4.77	5.57	6.04	6.53	7.02
Real Estate Loans Booked in Foreign Offices	0.32	0.43	0.41	0.37	0.43	0.49	0.59	0.58	0.71	0.69	0.78
Commercial and Industrial Loans	21.07	22.40	22.98	22.41	22.53	21.16	20.43	19.65	19.18	18.76	18.16
Agricultural Production Loans	1.74	1.66	1.69	1.70	1.61	1.32	1.07	0.98	0.97	0.94	0.98
Loans to Financial Institutions	4.37	4.68	4.88	4.67	2.88	2.49	2.39	2.14	1.88	1.75	1.51

Table 16 (continued)

	1980	1981	1982	1983	1984	1985	1986	1987	1988	1989	1990
Loans to Individuals, Total	10.10	9.51	9.08	9.59	10.64	11.31	11.41	11.70	12.07	12.14	11.91
Credit Cards and Related Plans	1.61	1.63	1.68	1.93	2.44	2.87	3.12	3.43	3.74	3.97	3.94
All Other Loans to Individuals	8.49	7.88	7.40	7.66	8.20	8.44	8.29	8.28	8.33	8.18	7.97
All Other Loans	3.37	3.41	3.33	3.57	7.05	7.15	6.51	5.96	5.48	3.81	4.50
Lease Financing Receivables	0.75	0.78	0.76	0.73	0.81	0.89	0.94	1.03	1.10	1.13	1.13
Bank Premises and Fixed Assets (Including Capitalized Leases)	1.44	1.50	1.55	1.56	1.53	1.49	1.45	1.50	1.46	1.46	1.52
Other Real Estate Owned	0.12	0.13	0.20	0.22	0.23	0.26	0.31	0.37	0.36	0.42	0.63
Intangible Assets	0.00	0.00	0.00	0.07	0.09	0.10	0.15	0.16	0.16	0.18	0.27
All Other Asset	4.51	5.19	5.47	5.15	6.07	5.83	5.23	5.02	5.23	5.17	5.42
Total Liabilities, Limited-Life Preferred Stock and Equity Capital ($ Billions)	1,856	2,029	2,194	2,342	2,508	2,730	2,941	3,001	3,131	3,299	3,388
Total Deposits	79.82	78.30	77.77	78.67	78.24	77.56	77.64	77.81	77.67	77.25	78.18
Individuals, Partnerships, Corporations	54.31	54.42	55.36	57.80	58.46	58.35	59.63	59.89	67.31	67.53	64.05
U.S. Government	0.18	0.16	0.14	0.15	0.16	0.19	0.18	0.19	0.18	0.18	0.17
States and Political Subdivisions in the U.S.	4.36	4.04	3.96	3.56	3.70	3.75	3.57	3.53	3.47	3.30	3.11
Deposits in Foreign Offices	15.84	15.70	13.98	13.17	12.66	11.79	10.67	11.38	10.06	9.45	8.66
All Other Deposits	5.13	3.98	4.33	4.00	3.26	3.49	3.59	2.81	6.60	6.14	2.09
Domestic Office Deposits, Total	64.25	62.61	63.79	65.50	65.58	65.77	66.97	66.42	67.60	67.80	69.52
Demand Deposits	23.25	18.93	16.91	16.63	16.51	16.51	17.37	15.18	14.65	13.96	13.68
Savings Deposits	10.82	11.02	13.89	19.75	20.15	21.57	24.22	24.03	23.68	22.70	23.43
Time Deposits	29.89	32.65	32.99	29.12	29.00	27.69	25.38	27.21	29.27	31.14	32.30
Transaction Accounts	0.00	22.15	20.68	20.89	20.98	21.35	23.32	21.48	21.14	20.26	20.19

Table 16 (continued)

	1980	1981	1982	1983	1984	1985	1986	1987	1988	1989	1990
Nontransaction Accounts	0.00	40.46	43.10	44.61	44.60	44.42	43.65	44.95	46.47	47.54	49.34
Federal Funds Purchased and Securities Sold under Agreements to Repurchase	7.18	8.07	8.20	7.62	7.53	8.13	8.45	7.91	7.50	8.37	7.23
Demand Notes Issued to the U.S. Treasury and Other Liabilities for Borrowed Money	2.27	2.24	2.51	2.35	2.77	3.49	3.66	4.04	4.57	4.26	4.05
Mortgage Indebtedness	0.12	0.13	0.13	0.12	0.12	0.11	0.10	0.09	0.09	0.07	0.06
Liability on Acceptances Outstanding	0.00	0.00	0.00	0.00	2.47	1.86	1.38	1.26	1.06	0.83	0.65
Subordinated Notes and Debentures	0.35	0.32	0.33	0.30	0.41	0.54	0.58	0.59	0.55	0.60	0.71
All Other Liabilities	4.45	5.11	5.19	4.94	2.32	2.11	2.01	2.26	2.27	2.42	2.65
Total Liabilities	94.20	94.17	94.13	94.00	93.85	93.80	93.80	93.95	93.72	93.79	93.54
Limited-Life Preferred Stock	0.00	0.00	0.00	0.00	0.00	0.00	0.00	0.00	0.00	0.00	0.00
Total Equity Capital	5.80	5.83	5.87	6.00	6.14	6.20	6.20	6.04	6.28	6.21	6.46
Perpetual Preferred Stock	0.01	0.01	0.01	0.03	0.03	0.04	0.05	0.05	0.06	0.05	0.05
Common Stock	1.17	1.16	1.13	1.10	1.12	1.07	1.01	1.01	0.96	0.93	0.91
Surplus	2.04	1.99	1.97	2.05	2.11	2.15	2.17	2.35	2.40	2.49	2.71
Undivided Profits	2.59	2.67	2.75	2.83	2.89	2.96	2.98	2.64	2.87	2.77	2.81
Foreign Currency Translation Adjustment	0.00	0.00	0.00	0.00	(0.02)	(0.01)	(0.01)	(0.01)	(0.01)	(0.01)	(0.02)
Loans and Leases 30-89 Days Past-Due	0.00	0.00	1.17	1.18	1.19	1.14	1.11	1.07	1.05	1.18	N/A
Loans and Leases 90 Days or More Past-Due	0.00	0.00	0.54	0.49	0.37	0.34	0.33	0.29	0.28	0.29	0.33
Loans and Leases in Nonaccrual Status	0.00	0.00	1.11	1.26	1.37	1.26	1.31	1.82	1.52	1.59	1.98
Income Earned, Not Collected on Loans	0.94	1.09	0.97	0.87	0.87	0.71	0.56	0.59	0.66	0.70	N/A
Total Brokered Deposits	0.00	0.00	0.00	0.94	0.98	0.93	1.05	1.24	1.72	1.96	2.14

Source: FDIC and Ferguson and Co.

Moreover, within the real estate loan category, banks shifted toward the riskiest borrowers. The share of construction and development loans doubled, from 2 percent to 4 percent of total assets. In addition, loans secured by nonfarm, nonresidential real estate, or commercial mortgages, also nearly doubled, from 3.5 percent to 6.5 percent. Though these percentages may seem small, each percentage point given the size of the commercial banking industry, represents over $20 billion.

At the same time that banks were rushing into commercial real estate lending, savings and loans had already invested heavily in such lending. In combination, the two types of depositories gave rise to the enormous overhang of excess supply that is now depressing commercial real estate prices in many major metropolitan markets today and will likely continue to depress them for some time. We believe that the excess lending for commercial real estate, in many cases by open but insolvent savings and loans and banks gambling for resurrection, played an important role in precipitating the 1990 recession. In combination with federal tax law changes that in 1981 stimulated demand for commercial real estate but then in 1986 reduced that same demand, the explosive lending by depositories was particularly damaging.

The other noteworthy increase, also shown in Table 16, occurred in credit card loans which rose from approximately 1.6 percent of total assets in 1980 to 4 percent in 1989. With annual percentage rates that equal or exceed rates paid on junk bonds, many of these loans must also be considered risky. The growth of these loans occurred during an overall U.S. economic expansion and their performance in the recession, including their possible expansion as consumers use unused balances, is an important issue. Also at issue is the performance of home equity loans encouraged by tax law changes in 1986 and carried on the banks' books as consumer loans. Homeowners with falling incomes can borrow from existing home equity loans while the house collateralizing the loan could be falling in value.

⅄ Ironically, in the search for more risk banks have been chasing their own tails. As they have lost their best customers, banks have turned to increasingly risky lending. As those loans have turned sour, banks have intensified their securitization of assets and their loan sales, in an effort to shrink, if necessary, in order to meet the new and higher capital requirements recently imposed. But, as noted above, while securitization adds liquidity, it also lowers spreads. With lower margins, banks are encouraged to seek out even riskier borrowers who promise compensating, higher returns. But riskier borrowers—the kryptonite of the banking industry—eventually mean even more loan losses. And so the vicious cycle continues. The spiral is downward.

Table 17 shows dramatically that all the risks are not on the banks' balance sheets. Overall, the off-balance-sheet items in the banking industry as a whole are approximately 4 times the volume of balance-sheet items and increasing.[6] The largest categories by far are foreign exchange contracts and interest rate swaps. In some cases, the total volume of loan commitments and standby and commercial letters of credit is large.

The ultimate problem posed by off-balance-sheet items was revealed by the closure of the Bank of New England in 1991. As we discussed above, the bank was almost certainly insolvent long before closure even though it was reporting a positive capital-to-asset ratio of approximately one percent. Within days of closure, the FDIC reported that estimated losses were $2.5 billion or about 10 percent of the bank's assets. What was not reported at the time was that the off-balance-sheet items of the bank exceeded the on-balance-sheet assets and involved primarily complicated foreign exchange transactions and interest-rate swaps. According to various newspaper reports following the closure, closure was postponed in order to allow the bank to unwind these transactions. The worry was that closure before the transactions were unwound could precipitate defaults by the Bank of New England that would impose losses on other banks. As a result, according to the reports, the bank may have been left open for approximately a year during which great risks were taken, especially involving speculation in interest rates.

Liabilities Also Reveal Risk-Taking

As Table 16 also shows, total deposits decreased slightly as a percentage of total liabilities from 1980 through 1989 reflecting primarily the decline in foreign office deposits. Domestic deposits increased and by 1989 represented almost 68 percent of total assets. As with assets, there were significant shifts within liabilities in the 1980s. Demand deposits decreased by slightly more than 9 percentage points to approximately 14 percent in 1989. At the same time savings deposits more than doubled to approximately 23 percent and time deposits grew slightly. Interest-bearing transaction accounts, which did not exist nationwide in 1980, accounted for approximately 20 percent of liabilities in 1989.

Table 17
Off-Balance-Sheet Items of Selected Large Bank Holding Companies, December 31, 1989 ($ Millions)

Bank Holding Co.	Assets	Loan Commitments	Standby Letters of Credit	Commercial Letters of Credit	Foreign Exchange Contracts	Interest Rate Swaps
Bankers Trust (NY)	55,658	13,952	6,992	728	218,831	155,615
Citicorp (NY)	230,643	51,751	26,031	4,582	588,393	187,463
Chase Manhattan (NY)	107,369	30,895	12,377	2,149	268,940	134,757
Manufacturers Hanover (NY)	60,479	19,888	7,025	1,622	141,625	103,848
Bank of N.Y. (NY)	48,857	18,169	4,113	1,999	33,031	20,018
J.P. Morgan (NY)	88,964	32,371	9,959	119	248,489	118,081
Marine Midland (NY)	27,067	4,924	3,540	268	89	4,929
Chemical (NY)	71,513	26,414	5,268	875	165,316	252,096
First Chicago (IL)	47,907	29,864	5,965	1,113	170,869	38,531
Bank of America (CA)	98,764	40,549	9,642	2,100	133,009	32,434
Mellon Bank (PA)	31,467	16,286	3,152	353	14,480	7,229
PNC Financial (PA)	45,661	8,537	4,010	313	246	1,247
BancOne (OH only)	26,514	4,498	1,314	226	69	4,965
National City (OH)	22,972	4,379	1,053	130	352	2,149

Source: Federal Reserve Y-9 Reports and published financial statements; Walker F. Todd and James B. Thomson, "An Insider's View of the Political Economy of the Too Big to Let Fail Doctrine," 65th Annual Western Economic Association International Conference, San Diego, California, Session 146, July 2, 1990 (Revision of August 15, 1990).

Overall there was an important shift away from noninterest-bearing demand deposits in commercial banks to deposits that paid interest, and as part of this shift, time and savings deposits increased. As a result of the higher deposit costs, either the income of banks had to fall or greater risk-taking was needed to maintain income.

The combined effects of the shift in assets toward real estate and the shift in deposits toward interest-bearing time and savings accounts suggest increased risk. The shift in assets and liabilities also reduced the distinctions that had separated the functions of commercial banks from savings and loans. Distinctions were further reduced by the simultaneous shift, due to changes in regulation, in the assets of savings and loans toward commercial real estate and commercial loans and toward checkable deposits.

Figure 5 graphically portrays the net effect on capital within the banking industry. Although the aggregate capital of the industry as reflected in Table 16 appears stable, we have shown that within it the decline of the big banks poses severe problems.

Figure 5 shows that the problem of declining capital has been apparent in relatively modern times since 1960. Overall capital was substantially higher in the 1960s and 1970s than in the 1980s and today. This should be kept in mind whenever one hears a banker or regulator talk about a given bank's capital relative to its peers.

Finally, the dramatic decline in capital relative to assets after the implementation of deposit insurance is a reminder that deposit insurance has substituted for capital as a buffer against losses by depositors. It should surprise no one that taxpayers are increasingly at risk when both capital and deposit insurance reserves are declining as they have been in recent years.

A Shrinking Share of U.S. Financial Assets in Depositories

Table 16 shows that overall the number of banks declined by approximately 2,092 in the 1980s from 14,434 in 1980 to 12,342 in 1990 while their total assets grew approximately 73 percent from about $1.9 trillion in 1980 to $3.4 trillion in 1990. Yet, as Table 18 shows, the total assets of domestic financial service firms more than doubled from $4 trillion to $10.5 trillion over the same period. Thus, the assets of banks grew but grew less than the overall growth of U. S. financial assets held by financial service firms.

Figure 5. Bank Equity Capital to Total Assets 1934-1990.

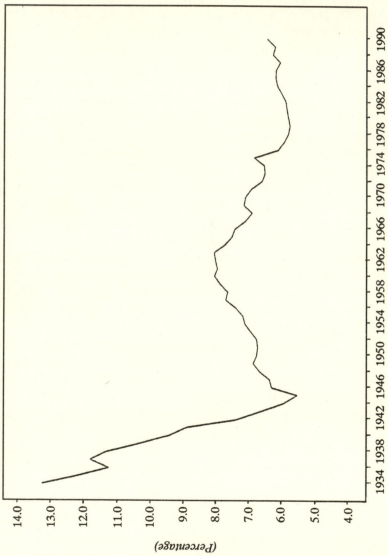

(Percentage)

(Year)

Source: FDIC

In addition, Table A-10 in the Appendix shows a substantial increase in foreign ownership of U.S. banks. Since 1980 the number of banks owned by foreign individuals has nearly tripled to approximately 29 percent and the percentage of domestic banking assets held by foreign-controlled banks has doubled to approximately 21 percent. This indicates that the share of domestic financial assets in banks controlled by domestic firms has shrunk substantially more than Table 18 alone would indicate. Given the often more liberal banks' ownership and bank activities limitations imposed by foreign countries, Table A-10 suggests that purely domestic banks may be at a competitive disadvantage relative to both foreign banks and foreign-owned domestic banks.

The combination of stiffer competition for deposit funds and the gradual replacement of bank intermediation with direct intermediation performed by the securities markets helps explain why the banking industry has dramatically shrunk relative to other types of financial intermediaries. Table 18 illustrates the dramatic shift in the share of financial assets held by banks during the past four decades, from over 50 percent in 1950 to just barely more than 30 percent in 1989. Most of the slack has been taken up by mutual funds and pension funds. As both banks and savings and loans react to deteriorating asset quality and the recently implemented new and higher capital requirements, the share of financial assets held by depositories should continue to shrink.

It is important to view this long-run development with favor, not alarm. The economic forces that created and drive the expansion of nondepository financial institutions benefit the U.S. economy. The proliferating number of financial competitors and the expanding array of financial products they offer are largely due to greatly improved technologies and result in products and services provided more efficiently.

These benefits tend to be obscured by the deterioration, first, of the savings and loans and then more recently, of commercial banks. Some tend to equate the troubles among these institutions with a reduction in financial services offered. Yet, as Table 18 illustrates, nondepository institutions clearly seem to be taking the place formerly occupied by banks and savings and loans in the U.S. financial sector.

Similarly, it is tempting to tie the welfare of the largest banks, which have been under severe pressure, with the welfare of the entire banking industry. While clearly large banks are important, Table 19 highlights the fact that large banks—as measured by concentration ratios—have been becoming progressively less important in the overall banking system.

Table 18

Percentage Distribution of U.S. Financial Assets Held by All Financial Service Firms, 1950 - 1989

	1950	1960	1970	1980	1981	1982	1983	1984	1985	1986	1987	1988	1989
Depository Institutions[1]													
Commercial Banks	51.2	38.2	38.6	36.8	36.3	35.2	34.2	34.0	33.1	31.9	31.2	30.8	30.7
U.S.-Chartered	50.5	37.5	36.6	31.4	30.6	29.9	29.1	28.9	27.9	25.5	26.5	24.9	24.1
Foreign Offices in U.S.	0.4	0.6	0.7	2.5	2.8	2.3	2.0	2.0	2.1	2.6	2.3	2.8	3.5
Domestic Affiliates	0.0	0.0	1.1	2.6	2.6	2.7	2.8	3.0	3.1	3.0	3.0	2.9	2.9
Banks in U.S. Possessions	0.3	0.1	0.3	0.3	0.3	0.3	0.2	0.1	0.1	0.1	0.1	0.2	0.2
Savings and Loans	5.8	11.8	12.8	15.2	14.6	14.2	14.9	15.7	14.8	13.9	14.1	14.2	11.7
Mutual Savings Banks	7.6	6.9	5.9	4.3	3.9	3.5	3.5	3.3	3.1	2.9	3.0	3.0	2.7
Credit Unions	0.3	1.1	1.3	1.7	1.6	1.7	1.8	1.8	1.9	2.0	2.1	2.0	1.9
Contractual Intermediaries													
Life Insurance Companies	21.3	19.4	15.0	11.5	11.4	11.5	11.5	11.1	11.1	11.0	11.3	11.7	12.0
Other Insurance Companies	4.0	4.4	3.7	4.3	4.2	4.1	4.1	3.9	4.0	4.2	4.4	4.5	4.7
Private Pension Funds[2]	2.4	6.4	8.4	11.6	10.9	11.7	12.4	11.5	11.9	11.5	11.4	10.9	11.0
State and Local Government Retirement Loans	1.7	3.3	4.5	4.9	5.0	5.3	5.7	5.7	5.7	5.7	5.8	6.3	6.9

Table 18 (continued)

Others	1950	1960	1970	1980	1981	1982	1983	1984	1985	1986	1987	1988	1989
Finance Companies	3.2	4.6	4.8	5.0	5.1	4.8	4.8	4.8	4.9	5.0	5.1	5.1	4.9
Mutual Funds	1.1	2.9	3.5	1.5	1.3	1.6	2.0	2.2	3.4	5.1	5.2	5.0	5.3
Security Brokers and Dealers	1.4	1.1	1.2	1.1	1.4	1.7	1.7	1.9	2.2	2.3	1.6	1.4	2.2
Money Market Mutual Funds	0.0	0.0	0.0	1.9	4.2	4.5	3.3	3.7	3.4	3.6	3.6	3.5	4.1
REITS[3]	0.0	0.0	0.3	0.1	0.1	0.1	0.1	0.1	0.1	0.1	0.1	0.1	0.1
SCO Issuers[4]	0.0	0.0	0.0	0.0	0.0	0.0	0.1	0.2	0.4	0.8	1.2	1.4	1.8
Total Assets ($ Billions)	294	597	1,340	4,032	4,455	4,916	5,503	6,232	7,141	8,185	8,840	9,667	10,534

Source: Flow of Funds Accounts, Board of Governors of the Federal Reserve System.

[1]   Commercial banks consists of U.S. chartered commercial banks, domestic affiliates, Edge Act corporations, agencies and branches of foreign banks, and banks in U.S. possession. Foreign banking offices in U.S. includes Edge Act corporations and offices of foreign banks.   IBFs are excluded from domestic banking and treated like branches in foreign countries. Savings and loan associations include all savings and loan associations and federal savings banks insured by FSLIC.   Mutual savings banks includes all federal and mutual savings banks insured by FDIC.

[2]   Private pension funds includes Federal Employees' Retirement Thrift Savings Fund.

[3]   REITS are real estate investment trusts.

[4]   SCO issuers are securitized credit obligations.

Table 19
Concentration Ratios for Federally Insured Commercial Banks, 1980 - 1990

Year	TOP 5 (%) Number	Assets	TOP 10 (%) Number	Assets	TOP 25 (%) Number	Assets	TOP 50 (%) Number	Assets	TOP 100 (%) Number	Assets	Total Number	Total Assets ($ Bil)
1980	0.03	20.97	0.07	30.02	0.17	40.26	0.35	47.05	0.69	54.30	14,435	1,856
1981	0.03	20.14	0.07	29.32	0.17	39.71	0.35	46.48	0.69	53.88	14,415	2,029
1982	0.03	19.39	0.07	28.33	0.17	38.75	0.35	45.56	0.69	53.20	14,453	2,194
1983	0.03	17.80	0.07	26.42	0.17	36.46	0.35	43.57	0.69	51.63	14,468	2,342
1984	0.03	17.16	0.07	25.16	0.17	34.86	0.34	42.38	0.69	51.11	14,531	2,508
1985	0.03	16.60	0.07	24.47	0.17	33.93	0.35	41.68	0.69	50.74	14,406	2,731
1986	0.04	15.57	0.07	23.54	0.18	33.04	0.35	40.91	0.70	50.56	14,205	2,941
1987	0.04	14.82	0.07	22.65	0.18	32.41	0.36	40.76	0.73	50.56	13,719	2,999
1988	0.04	13.97	0.08	21.41	0.19	31.23	0.38	40.06	0.76	50.52	13,136	3,131
1989	0.04	13.70	0.08	21.06	0.20	31.19	0.39	39.73	0.79	50.82	12,711	3,299
June 1990	0.04	14.05	0.08	21.79	0.20	31.85	0.40	40.54	0.80	51.41	12,513	3,361

Source: FDIC.

This no doubt reflects the inability of these institutions to grow, given the squeeze rising loan losses have put on their capital positions.

Developing a Policy Perspective As Depositories' Uniqueness Erodes

It is now unmistakable that the changing financial marketplace is eroding the special characteristics of depositories, including banks.[7] The appropriate government policy response, however, should *not* be to protect depositories from competition. Although this approach in the short run could result in the appearance of stability it would in reality retard, but not halt, the development of new financial products and services.

Depositories have been unique in the past because they alone provided savers with deposits that could be redeemed at face value at any time. Other intermediaries and securities firms did not traditionally provide liquidity. At the same time depositories funded primarily illiquid loans. Other intermediaries and security firms tended to invest in more liquid securities of business firms. The unique characteristic of funding illiquid assets with liquid liabilities created the particular danger against which deposit insurance provided protection.

Depositors of a solvent depository could perceive it to be insolvent and run to get their deposits. The depository would then have to sell illiquid assets or demand immediate repayment of loans in order to return cash to the depositors. The forced asset sales could produce losses at otherwise healthy institutions and calling in loans could have an adverse effect on real economic activity. Deposit insurance eliminated the prospect of runs and the associated adverse consequences.

Now, however, there is a proliferation of firms providing liquid liabilities. There is also a proliferation of ways to turn illiquid assets into liquid assets. In essence, the market has found ways to provide assets and liabilities in depositories and other financial service firms that have the effect of reducing the need for deposit insurance. These developments represent significant benefits to consumers as well. Ironically, the same developments have spelled disaster for savings and loans and the prospect of disaster for banks as competition has eaten away at profitability and hence capital.

Certain aspects of deposit insurance tend to compound the problem. Unless the deposit-insurance system contains incentives to take excessive risk through examination and supervision, and takes prompt corrective action against inadequately capitalized and insured depositories, losses can escalate through unsuccessful risk-taking. The losses can take the form of excessive investment in unproductive projects. When the risk-taking fails, if the losses are large enough, they can be imposed on taxpayers.

Notes

1. Robert E. Litan, "Remedy for S&L's: Operation 'Clean Sweep,'" *Challenge*, November–December 1990 (reprinting of Testimony before the Senate Judiciary Committee, August 14, 1990), Figure 3.

2. Gary Gorton and George Pennacchi, "Financial Innovation and the Provision of Liquidity Services," in *The Reform of Federal Deposit Insurance: Disciplining the Government and Protecting Taxpayers*, James R. Barth and R. Dan Brumbaugh, Jr., eds., HarperBusiness, New York, 1992. Gorton and Pennacchi emphasize how technological innovation in the production and transmission of information is leading to a separation of nonmarketable assets and demandable liabilities and, in the process, reducing the role of banks in the financial system and reducing the need for deposit insurance and regulation.

3. James A. Rosenthal and Juan M. Ocampo, *Securitization of Credit: Inside the New Technology of Finance*, John Wiley & Sons, 1988.

4. Andrew S. Carron and R. Dan Brumbaugh, Jr., "The Viability of the Thrift Industry," *Housing Policy Debate*, Volume 2, Issue 1.

5. Table 15 presents detailed income and expense data for the banking industry in the 1980s. On the surface, it shows, among other things, a rising trend in reported net interest income as a percent of assets. However, this figure is not adjusted for the tax-free status of municipal securities as shown in Chart 3.

6. Eileen Maloney and George Gregorash, "Banking 1989: Not Quite a Twice Told Tale," *Economic Perspectives*, Federal Reserve Bank of Chicago, July–August 1990.

7. For a description of these issues in the context of the credit union industry, see James R. Barth and R. Dan Brumbaugh, Jr., "The Credit Union Industry: Financial Condition and Policy Issues," California Credit Union League, February 1991.

FOUR

Déjà Vu All Over Again? The Condition of the Bank Insurance Fund

One need cite nothing more than the hundreds of billions of taxpayer dollars that are now needed to honor the deposit-insurance guarantee for failed savings and loans to indicate the importance of a timely and accurate estimate of how much banking failures may cost the federal government. Although the budgetary cost per se is important, as is the distribution of the cost between the banking industry and taxpayers, there are other more subtle reasons why a timely and accurate estimate of the cost to close or reorganize banks is important.

A Framework for Understanding Deposit-Insurance Cost Estimates

As the savings and loan debacle taught us, when the Federal Home Loan Bank Board as head of the FSLIC realized that the FSLIC's reserves were inadequate to close all insolvent savings and loans—long before the FSLIC's financial statements indicated insolvency—forbearance began. Among other things, fewer insolvent savings and loans were closed so as to maintain the appearance of solvency for the FSLIC. Lower capital levels and broader measures of capital were adopted that allowed savings and loans insolvent by previous guidelines to appear solvent by the new guidelines. The deteriorated but open savings and loans took great risks, which for the most part, did not succeed. As a result, the total cost to resolve failed savings and loans skyrocketed.

We believe that an earlier, more accurate official acknowledgment of the cost to close all insolvent savings and loans could have led to less forbearance and hence lower ultimate resolution costs. Denial and understatement long ago crept into official accounts of the bank problems, and so has regulatory forbearance. Thus, accurately estimating the costs that the BIF faces may help reduce the tendency toward forbearance and lead to the adoption of more cost-effective closure or reorganization policies.

An Almost Certain Understatement of Actual Losses with Most Estimates

We begin by presenting our best baseline estimates of the government's deposit-insurance liabilities over the three years mid-1990 through mid-1993, based upon bank call report data through mid-1990. Four significant qualifications, however, suggest that these estimates, and all of the official estimates made during the same time by the GAO and CBO, are likely to understate actual losses. First, the baseline estimates assume no further change in the health of banks throughout the next three years. If economic conditions worsen relative to those that prevailed in mid-1990, as they certainly did as a result of the recession that began in July, the baseline loss estimates will prove to be too low. For this reason, we later simulate the potential effects of a recession on the government's liabilities for bank failures.

Second, the baseline estimates assume that insolvent banks are closed on the same timetable that the FDIC has operated on in the past. This assumption will prove inaccurate if because of falling cash reserves the FDIC engages in more forbearance than previously for weak and troubled banks. We present data made public for the first time in our congressional report showing that the overall bank closure rate has been slowing even though bank distress has been escalating.

In addition, the historical failure costs per dollar of assets for large banks have been below those of small banks. Yet, the big banks are those in the most distress at the moment and may be the biggest beneficiaries of regulatory forbearance. As we show below, the BIF's costs will rise substantially above the baseline estimates if future big bank failures begin to cost as much per dollar of assets as small bank failures do today.

It is possible that a policy of forbearance coupled with intensive examination and supervision of the insolvent banks could be cheaper than liquidating them or providing cash assistance in mergers. Some agricultural banks that were granted forbearance in the mid-to-late 1980s, for example, appear to have come back to life. Whether their resurrection reflected random luck or risk-taking guided by adequate supervision is uncertain. More certain is the conclusion that the forbearance practiced in the 1980s for savings and loans—whereby hundreds of institutions actually reporting themselves to be insolvent were permitted to gamble for resurrection without meaningful supervision and regulation—had disastrous results.[1]

Third, our baseline loss estimates may be understated because we were unable to review nonpublic information about individual banks in the possession of the federal bank regulators. For this reason, we had no choice but to rely heavily on bank call reports in constructing our baseline estimates. As we have already discussed, these reports tend to paint rosier pictures of the health of banks—especially weak banks—than is objectively warranted. The GAO reports, for example, that in its study of past bank failures, the most recent call reports prior to failure significantly understated the deterioration that had already occurred in bank loan portfolios .[2] Two of us have previously found the same to be true with banks that failed in early 1990.[3] None of this should be surprising. Leo Crowley, the first Chairman of the FDIC, noted in 1935 that "a great many of your bank statements in the past did not really show the true conditions of the banks."[4]

Fourth, we were able to obtain new data, unpublished before our congressional report, on the size of problem banks, the rate at which they have been failing, and new overall closure rate data. As our analysis of these data shows, our baseline estimates may significantly understate the costs that the BIF will encounter. Despite these qualifications, we believe the baseline loss estimates shown below remain useful as at least a conservative lower bound for the government's deposit-insurance liabilities as of mid-1990. Their primary usefulness lies in the fact that they indicate that the BIF had woefully inadequate funding as of mid-1990 even if given almost every benefit of doubt and rosy scenario that can be devised.

Methodological Overview for Baseline and Recession Scenarios

Our analysis covers both commercial and savings banks insured by the BIF, although we do not break out separately the results for these different types of depositories. Our methodology for estimating likely liabilities for future bank insolvencies is very similar to that recently used by the CBO.[5] Based on historical data we describe below, we calculate the probability that banks with different capital-to-asset ratios will fail during the next three years. We apply those probabilities to the distribution of banks across capital-to-asset categories as of June 30, 1990 to arrive at a projection of future bank failures and the corresponding bank assets those failures will involve. We then multiply various historical loss ratios (FDIC losses as a percent of banks assets reported prior to failure) by the projected assets of failed banks to estimate the government's three year bank failure costs.

Like CBO, we include in our projections banks with a wide range of failure probabilities. In contrast, GAO previously projected the costs of only 35 institutions it estimated were "highly likely" to fail.[6] Although we, too, identify those banks that are either virtually certain or highly likely to fail in the months ahead, we believe a more expansive estimate of potential failed banks is more prudent. As we discuss below, even some supposedly well-capitalized banks failed in the 1987–1989 period. The same was true for most of the major failed Texas banks earlier in the 1980s, as William Seidman (when FDIC chairman) has noted.[7] Failure to take account of such probable failures in the future will lead to understatements of the government's likely failure costs.

Baseline Estimates of the Condition of the BIF

To estimate the condition of the BIF we begin by estimating the probability of future bank failures based on characteristics of recent failures. Although few large banks have failed in the past, we expect this pattern to change and have made appropriate adjustments in our estimates. We then present the costs or losses associated with recent failures and project three-year baseline failure costs based on failure probabilities and loss ratios. By comparing the projected baseline failure costs to BIF reserves a picture of the baseline conditions of the BIF emerges.

Estimating the Probability of Bank Failures

We calculated our failure probabilities by sorting all 631 banks that the FDIC liquidated or assisted during the 1987–1989 period into four different capital-to-asset categories. Since these 631 institutions represented more than 60 percent of all banks that failed during the 1980s, and an even greater percentage of losses, we believe their experience provides a sufficient database from which to project the likelihood of future bank failures. In addition, since the resolutions in the sample have occurred in the not-too-distant past, they should provide a reliable basis for extrapolating from current financial data.

We chose the capital-to-asset ratio as our sorting device, despite the well-known flaws in accounting data based on historical values, because previous analysis has found this ratio to be a reasonable and readily available indicator of likely bank failure.[8] The reason its use is reasonable is straightforward. Banks with low reported capital ratios are more likely to conceal their true financial condition with accounting devices that artificially inflate capital ratios (such as understating loan loss reserves or booking capital gains on selected assets). In addition, weakly capitalized banks obviously are more susceptible to economic downturns that cause borrowers to default and asset values to decline. Finally, and perhaps most important, since insolvency is defined by regulators as the absence of reported capital, it is appropriate to gauge the probability of resolution by an institution's capital position.

We recognize that it is possible, and perhaps even desirable, to employ a more complicated, multivariate model of bank failure prediction. However, we rejected such an approach for several reasons. First, we wanted to use a technique that is easy to replicate, well-documented in the literature, and not dependent on forecasts of explanatory variables. The capital-to-asset ratio meets these tests. In addition, the estimated coefficients from multivariate models tend to be highly sensitive to the time periods for which the analysis is performed. Of course, this criticism can be advanced against our use of the capital-to-asset ratio as well. Nevertheless, as we note below, the resolution probabilities calculated from the capital-to-asset ratios for each of the years ending 1986–1988 are quite stable, which provides us with some comfort in making projections based on those probabilities.[9] Most important, however, there is no evidence that a more complicated procedure would significantly affect our results. Tables 20 and 21 report the results of our bank resolution analysis for banks in two size categories, those with assets below and above $500 million, "small" and "large" banks, respectively.[10]

Table 20 provides the more useful information since all but fifteen of the bank resolutions during the 1987–1989 period involved banks with assets less than $500 million. As expected, the table illustrates that the banks with the higher capital-to-asset ratios were far less likely to be resolved than those with weak capital positions. As shown in the tables in Appendix Table A-6, it is noteworthy that on average in every year of the 1980s, banks with capital-to-asset ratios below 3 percent lost money. In addition, for banks in all capital categories, resolution became more likely with the passage of time.

Table 20
Bank Resolution Probabilities by Capital-To-Asset Categories
Banks with $0-500 Million in Assets
All Failures 1987-1989 Based on Year-End 1986-1988 Data

| Capital-to-Asset Category | Year | Number of Banks | Number of Failures and Cummulative Failure Probability ( ) | | |
			One Year Later	Two Years Later	Three Years Later
Greater Than 6 Percent	1986	12,191	28 (0.2)	122 (1.0)	243 (2.0)
	1987	12,051	27 (0.2)	81 (0.7)	
	1988	11,649	10 (0.1)		
Greater Than 3 Percent But No Higher Than 6 Percent	1986	1,130	46 (4.1)	126 (11.2)	186 (16.5)
	1987	1,034	53 (5.1)	144 (13.9)	
	1988	860	27 (3.1)		
Greater Than 1.5 Percent But No Higher Than 3 Percent	1986	109	24 (22.0)	33 (30.3)	41 (37.6)
	1987	161	19 (11.8)	48 (29.8)	
	1988	149	35 (23.5)		
Between 0 and 1.5 Percent	1986	92	39 (42.3)	54 (58.7)	56 (60.9)
	1987	94	36 (38.3)	53 (56.4)	
	1988	91	45 (49.5)		

Source: W. C. Ferguson and Co., *Bank Source*; and Authors' Calculations.

For example, Table 20 indicates that of the 12,191 banks reporting capital-to-asset ratios above 6 percent at year-end 1986, only 0.2 percent (28) were resolved during the next year; a cumulative total of 1.0 percent (122) had been resolved within two years (by the end of 1988); and 2.0 percent (243) had been resolved within three years (by the end of 1989). At the other extreme, of the 92 banks at year-end 1986 reporting positive capital ratios below 1.5 percent, over 58 percent (56) had been resolved by the end of 1989. Similar findings are reported in the table for banks reporting similar financial condition at year-ends 1987 and 1988. As just suggested, the failure probabilities for each of the years are rather similar, suggesting a relatively stable relationship has existed between reported capital positions and the likelihood of future resolution.

Table 21
Bank Resolution Probabilities by Capital-To-Asset Categories
Banks With Assets Above $500 Million
All Failures 1987-1989 Based on Year-End 1986-1988 Data

Capital-to-Asset Category	Year	Number of Banks	Number of Failures and Cummulative Failure Probability ( )		
			One Year Later	Two Years Later	Three Years Later
Greater Than 6 Percent	1986	415	0 (0)	3 (0.7)	3 (0.7)
	1987	475	5 (1.5)	7 (1.5)	
	1988	518	0 (0)		
Greater Than 3 Percent But No Higher Than 6 Percent	1986	135	0 (0)	5 (3.7)	12 (8.9)
	1987	165	1 (0.6)	9 (5.5)	
	1988	153	1 (0.7)		
Greater Than 1.5 Percent But No Higher Than Per- cent	1986	3	0 (0)	0 (0)	0 (0)
	1987	11	0 (0)	0 (0)	
	1988	4	0 (0)		
Between 0 and 1.5 Percent	1986	2	0 (0)	0 (0)	0 (0)
	1987	1	0 (0)	0 (0)	
	1988	5	2 (40.0)		

Source: W.C. Ferguson and Co., *Bank Source*; and Authors' Calculations.

Factoring Big-Bank Problems into Consideration

Since few large banks were resolved by the FDIC during the 1987–1989 period, the resolution probabilities reported for these banks in Table 21 are much less reliable. Nevertheless, the results shown in Table 21 are strikingly different from those in Table 20 in one major respect. In all of the capital categories, the large banks were less likely to be resolved than small banks during the 1987–1989 period. Thus, for example, Table 20 shows that about 30 percent of small banks reporting capital-to-asset ratios of between 1.5 percent and 3.0 percent in 1986 and 1987 were resolved by the FDIC within two years. In contrast, none of the large banks with identical capital-to-asset ratios were resolved. Again, a similar picture emerges for banks in each of the other capital categories.[11] This difference in resolution probabilities for small and large banks illustrates an important distinction between resolution or failure and insolvency. Unlike a private insurer that has no control over when claims will arrive and in what amounts, the FDIC, in conjunction with federal and state bank regulators, determines when to close a bank and thus when to file a claim on the BIF. The fact that the FDIC resolved large banks with identical capital-to-asset ratios less frequently than small banks during the 1987–1989 period may reflect the relatively small sample size for large banks or reflect regulatory forbearance for troubled larger banks.[12]

Both explanations are probably correct. But, we believe it is important in projecting future bank failure costs to account for the possibility, if not the likelihood, that from now on the failure probability of larger banks may be much closer, and indeed equal, to that of smaller banks. Allowing for this outcome is especially important given the concentration of current banking problems in the largest banks.

Resolution Costs per Dollar of Failed-Bank Assets

Table 22 reports data on the FDIC's resolution cost experience for each year since 1985 for banks in various categories compiled from data supplied by the FDIC.

The costs reflect the FDIC's loss estimates for all these failed banks as of June 30, 1990.[13] The first three sections of Table 22 illustrate the differences between resolutions of state and national banks. From 1985 to 1987, state-chartered banks accounted for most of the assets in banks resolved by the FDIC, whereas in 1988 and 1989 national banks accounted

Table 22
Bank Losses by Type of Bank Charter and Size of Bank, 1985 - 1989 ($ Millions)

		1985	1986	1987	1988	1989	Average 1985-1989
NATIONAL BANKS	Number of Resolutions	30	49	76	94	111	72
	Total Losses for Year	273	713	717	4411	4291	2081
	Total Assets of Resolved Banks	1,254	2,863	3,044	45,487	22,499	15,029
	Largest Estimated Loss	53	173	88	1,667	1,167	630
	Smallest Estimated Loss	1.0	0.4	0.0	0.6	0.7	0.5
	Average Estimated Loss	9	15	9	47	39	24
	Average Assets of Failed Banks	42	58	40	479	203	164
	Average Loss/Assets (Percent)	21.8	24.9	23.5	9.8	19.1	19.8
STATE BANKS	Number of Resolutions	90	96	127	126	96	107
	Total Losses for Year	577	1,018	1,301	1,120	1,706	1,144
	Total Assets of Resolved Banks	7,083	3,967	6,155	7,136	7,039	6,276
	Largest Estimated Loss	173	93	118	72	271	145
	Smallest Estimated Loss	0.1	0.0	0.0	0.1	0.3	0.1
	Average Estimated Loss	6	11	10	9	18	11
	Average Assets of Failed Banks	79	41	48	57	73	60
	Average Loss/Assets (Percent)	8.1	25.7	21.1	15.7	24.2	19.0

Table 22 (continued)

		1985	1986	1987	1988	1989	Average 1985-1989
COMBINED STATE AND NATIONAL BANKS	Number of Resolutions	120	145	203	221	207	179
	Total Losses for Year	850	1,732	2,017	5,530	5,598	3,145
	Total Assets of Resolved Banks	8,337	6,830	9,198	52,623	29,538	21,305
	Largest Estimated Loss	173	173	118	1,667	1,167	660
	Smallest Estimated Loss	0.1	0.0	0.0	0.1	0.3	0.1
	Average Estimated Loss	7	12	10	25	29	17
	Average Assets of Failed Banks	70	47	45	238	143	109
	Average Loss/Assets (Percent)	10.2	25.4	21.9	10.6	20.3	17.7
ASSETS < $500 MILLION	Number of Resolutions	119	143	202	207	198	174
	Total Losses for Year	676	1,466	2,001	2,003	2,932	1,816
	Total Assets of Resolved Banks	3,058	5,535	7,998	10,972	11,818	7,876
	Largest Estimated Loss	53	89	118	127	172	112
	Smallest Estimated Loss	0.1	0.0	0.0	0.1	0.3	0.1
	Average Estimated Loss	6	10	10	10	15	10
	Average Assets of Failed Banks	26	39	40	53	60	44
	Average Loss/Assets (Percent)	22.1	26.5	25.0	18.3	24.8	23.3

Table 22 (continued)

ASSETS > $500 MILLION		1985	1986	1987	1988	1989	Average 1985-1989
	Number of Resolutions	1	2	1	13	9	5
	Total Losses for Year	173	266	16	3,527	3,065	1,409
	Total Assets of Resolved Banks	5,279	1,295	1,200	41,651	17,720	13,429
	Largest Estimated Loss	173	173	16	1,667	1,167	639
	Smallest Estimated Loss	173.4	93.0	16.0	0.9	98.7	76.4
	Average Estimated Loss	173	133	16	271	341	187
	Average Assets of Failed Banks	5,279	648	1,200	2,975	1,969	2,414
	Average Loss/Assets (Percent)	3.3	20.5	1.3	9.1	17.3	10.3

Source: Authors' calculations based on data supplied by the FDIC.

for most of those assets. Notably, however, over the entire 1985–1989 period state banks have not been significantly more expensive to resolve than failed national banks. This contrasts with the savings and loan experience, where failed state-chartered institutions have cost the FSLIC (and now the RTC) substantially more than federally chartered institutions.[14]

The last sections of Table 22 confirm the finding of previous analysts that small bank failures have higher resolution cost ratios than large bank failures.[15] Thus, during the 1985-1989 period the FDIC lost an average of 23 cents on the dollar of assets for small failed banks but only 10 cents on the dollar for large failed banks. This differential was considerably narrower, however, in 1989: 25 percent for small banks and 17 percent for large banks.

The averages reported in Table 22 conceal enormous differences in resolution costs across different states.[16] As one might expect, the resolution cost ratios have been quite large, often in excess of 30 percent in most years, for failed banks in the "oil patch" states of Louisiana, Oklahoma, and Texas. But they have also been quite high elsewhere throughout the country, notably in Arkansas, Colorado, Kansas, Minnesota, Missouri, Utah, and Wyoming.

Finally, Table 23 lists the largest bank failures, by absolute size of loss, between 1985 and 1989.

Most important, the table illustrates how high these ratios are for these failures: most are above 30 cents on the dollar, many are above 50 cents on the dollar, and most are even above the average resolution cost ratios for the most recent year, 1989. Table 23 serves as a strong reminder of how expensive bank failures can be and the likelihood that the loan loss reserves for troubled institutions are probably significantly understated.

Projected Three-Year Baseline Failure Costs

Given the uncertainties inherent in projecting the future on the basis of historical experience, we estimated the government's baseline three-year failure cost liability under various combinations of assumptions concerning failure probabilities and loss ratios. We chose three years because that is the longest time period for which our data permitted us to calculate resolution or failure probabilities.

Table 24 presents the three pairs of three-year failure probabilities that we used to make our projections: (1) those CBO calculated for all FDIC

Table 23
Largest Bank Failures By Estimated Loss, 1985 - 1989

Institution (State)	Type	Inception Date	Charter	Assets ($ Mil)	Estimated Loss ($ Mil)	Loss/ Assets (%)
Mbank-Aggregate (TX)	AT	03/29/89	N	15,736	2,581	16.40
First Republic Bank, Agg (TX)	PA	07/29/88	N	18,124	1,667	9.20
TAB/Aggregate (TX)	AT	07/20/89	N	4,753	933	19.62
First City Bancorp. (TX)	AT	04/20/88	N	11,200	926	8.27
First American Bank (FL)	TA	12/15/89	S	1,880	271	14.41
First Service Bank (MA)	DT	03/31/89	S	888	230	25.92
Alliance Bank (AK)	PA	04/21/89	S	849	200	23.56
Bowery Savings Bank (NV)	AT	10/01/85	S	5,279	173	3.28
The First National Bank (OK)	PA	07/11/86	N	693	173	24.92
Guardian Bank N.A. (NY)	PO	06/21/89	N	420	172	41.05
First National Bank (LA)	DP	11/18/88	N	272	127	46.75
First Interstate Bank (AK)	PA	12/11/87	S	368	118	32.06
The First State Bank (TX)	DP	02/17/89	S	262	113	43.19
United Bank-Houston (TX)	DP	04/30/87	S	217	109	50.20
Western Bank-Westheimer (TX)	DP	10/01/87	S	292	98	33.60
Park BSNK (FL)	PA	02/14/86	S	602	93	15.44
Bossier Bank And Trust (LA)	PA	06/12/86	S	222	89	40.08
The Security National (OK)	PA	01/08/87	N	203	88	43.40
United Bank Of TX (TX)	DP	06/04/87	S	191	85	44.47
Louisiana Bank And Trust (LA)	PA	02/16/89	S	258	84	32.64
The County Bank (FL)	PA	02/13/87	S	146	73	49.70
Bank Of Dallas (TX)	TA	02/05/88	S	187	72	38.53
Yankee Bank For Finance (MA)	DA	10/15/87	N	464	70	15.14
Utica National Bank (OK)	PA	07/20/89	N	163	70	42.88
American Bank and Trust (LA)	PA	09/26/86	S	183	69	37.70
Banc Oklahoma Corp. (OK)	AK	11/24/86	N	468	65	13.88
Citizens National Bank (OK)	DP	08/14/86	N	166	62	37.27
Central National Bank (NY)	PO	09/10/87	N	165	60	36.09
The Jefferson Guaranty (LA)	AT	01/13/88	S	287	58	20.01
Sunshine State Bank (FL)	PO	05/23/86	S	104	57	54.25
Bank Of Commerce (OK)	PA	05/08/86	S	166	56	33.88

Table 23 (continued)					
Institution (State)	Type	Inception Date	Charter	Assets ($ Mil)	Estimat- ed Loss ($ Mil)	Loss/ Assets (%)
Capital Bank & Trust (LA)	PA	10/30/87	S	387	56	14.49
United Oklahoma Bank (OK)	PA	03/17/87	S	147	53	36.01
Moncor Bank, N.A. (NM)	PA	8/30/85	N	238	53	22.17
American Exchange Bank (OK)	PA	08/20/87	S	92	45	48.33
Rose Capital Bank (TX)	PA	09/21/89	S	56	43	76.12
Stockmens Bank (WY)	DP	09/20/87	S	118	41	34.69
Caribank (FL)	TA	12/08/88	S	533	40	7.43
Northwest Bank & Trust (TX)	TA	06/23/88	S	97	39	40.00
First Bank And Trust Co. (TX)	DP	12/18/86	S	95	38	40.66
Alaska National Bank (AK)	DP	10/22/87	N	187	38	20.45
Union Bank And Trust (OK)	PA	07/21/88	S	115	38	33.38
Guaranty Bank (TX)	TA	06/02/88	S	82	38	46.31
Cordell National Bank (OK)	DP	12/05/86	N	77	37	47.94
La Salle State Bank (LA)	TA	09/07/89	S	38	37	97.65
The Farmers National (OK)	PA	12/03/87	N	64	35	55.58
Harris County Bank, N.A. (TX)	DP	02/25/88	N	74	34	45.33
New Mexico National (NM)	PA	07/17/86	N	152	33	21.63
Century Bank (AZ)	PA	10/19/89	S	119	33	27.34
The First National Bank (MO)	PA	10/11/85	N	180	33	18.09
First City Bank, N.A. (OK)	PA	06/21/85	N	66	32	49.04
Forestwood National (TX)	DP	07/27/89	N	55	32	57.62
Banker Trust (LA)	DT	03/10/89	N	86	31	36.14
The National Bank (LA)	PA	01/12/89	N	78	30	39.22
The First National Bank (OK)	DP	05/26/86	N	67	30	45.46
The Citizens Bank (UT)	PA	10/18/85	S	46	30	66.87
Liberty National Bank (TX)	PA	05/25/89	N	63	30	48.19
The Bank Of Commerce (LA)	PA	06/12/86	S	66	30	45.60
First National Bank (TX)	PA	06/19/86	N	77	30	38.45
United Mercantile Bank (LA)	PA	01/21/88	S	74	30	40.16
Metropolitan Bank (LA)	PA	11/07/86	S	66	29	43.53
First Bank (TX)	TA	02/09/89	S	143	29	20.10
Texas National Bank (TX)	DP	02/16/89	N	49	28	58.23

Table 23 (continued)						
Institution (State)	Type	Inception Date	Charter	Assets ($ Mil)	Estimated Loss ($ Mil)	Loss/ Assets (%)
Western Bank (TX)	PA	09/04/86	S	63	28	43.94
The First National Bank (OK)	PO	11/06/86	N	89	27	30.73
First Bankers Trust (LA)	TA	09/14/89	S	26	27	104.04
First State Bank and Trust (TX)	PA	05/24/86	S	140	27	19.23
Northwest Bank (TX)	DP	01/21/88	S	54	26	47.52
Citizens Bank, Houston (TX)	TA	02/09/89	S	100	25	24.77
Alaska Mutual (AK)	AT	01/01/88	S	823	25	3.02
Heritage National Bank (TX)	PA	12/10/87	N	48	24	49.58
Alaska Continental Bank (AK)	PA	08/03/88	S	39	24	61.35
Republic Bank (OK)	PA	11/19/87	S	55	24	42.67
The First National Bank (OK)	DP	03/10/88	N	62	23	37.64
First Capitol Bank (TX)	DP	07/28/88	S	45	23	51.72
Commerce Bank-Plano (TX)	DP	01/07/88	S	37	23	63.01
Security National Bank (PA)	PA	10/23/86	N	38	22	58.28
Round Rock National Bank (TX)	DP	10/27/88	N	34	22	65.88
Livingston Bank (LA)	PA	03/16/89	S	102	22	21.61
Parkway Bank and Trust (TX)	PA	06/09/88	S	39	22	55.25
Merchants State Bank (TX)	TA	01/19/89	S	139	21	15.37
First National Bank (TX)	PO	02/19/87	N	66	21	32.05
Waxahachie Bank (TX)	PA	09/10/87	S	65	21	32.77
Tracy Collins Bank (UT)	AT	12/30/88	S	206	21	10.19

Source: FDIC.

bank resolutions between 1987 and the first half of 1990 based only on bank call reports at year-end 1986;[17] (2) average failure rates calculated from bank call reports at year-ends 1987 and 1988; and (3) those we calculated for 1989 failures alone based on year-end 1988 data.[18]

For bank data reported at year-ends 1987 and 1988, we estimated three-year failure likelihoods by extrapolating from the relationship between the third and earlier year failure probabilities calculated from the 1986 data.[19] We believe it is important to supplement the CBO failure probabilities, which were based on only one snapshot of the banking system at year-end 1986, with the more recent snapshots taken at year-ends 1987 and 1988. This enables us to assess the sensitivity of future cost projections to the use of more recent call report information.

Those probabilities are presented in pairs in Table 24. For each set, the first column reports the actual or extrapolated three-year resolution rates

Table 24
Alternative Three-Year Bank Resolution Probabilities

Banks		CBO[1]		1988-1989			
Equity Capital-to-Asset Ratio	Size	Actual	No Differ-ential	Average	Average/ No Dif-ferential	1989	1989 / No Differential
> 6 %	Small[2]	1.5	1.5	1.2	1.2	1.0	1.0
> 6 %	Large[3]	1.3	1.5	1.1	1.2	0.7	1.0
3 to 6 %	Small	10.1	10.1	16.5	16.5	12.4	12.4
3 to 6 %	Large	3.1	10.1	5.0	16.5	4.8	12.4
1.5 to 3 %	Small	46.1	46.1	38.6	38.6	40.2	40.2
1.5 to 3 %	Large	0.0	46.1	0.0	38.6	0.0	40.2
0 to 1.5 %	Small	49.0	49.0	63.4	63.4	68.2	68.2
0 to 1.5 %	Large	18.7	49.0	20.0	63.4	40.0	68.2
< 0 %	Small	100.0	100.0	100.0	100.0	100.0	100.0
< 0 %	Large	100.0	100.0	100.0	100.0	100.0	100.0

Source: Authors' calculations based on data in Reischhauer, 1990 and *Bank Source*, W. C. Ferguson & Co.

[1] CBO probabilities were calculated for a 3 1/2 year time frame, based on assets in failed banks as a percentage of total assets of all banks in the relevant capital category. The CBO probabilities shown here are adjusted for a 3 year percentage of all banks in the relevant capital category.

[2] Small banks: Less than or equal to $500 million in assets.

[3] Large banks: Greater than $500 million in assets.

Table 25
Failed Bank Resolution Costs as a Percentage of Assets

Bank Equity Capital-to-Asset Ratio	Size	CBO	1985-1989 Average	1989 Average
> 6 %	Small[1]	.21	.23	.25
> 6 %	Large[2]	.07	.10	.17
3 to 6 %	Small	.13	.23	.25
3 to 6 %	Large	.11	.10	.17
1.5 to 3 %	Small	.12	.23	.25
1.5 to 3 %	Large	.00	.10	.17
0 to 1.5 %	Small	.27	.23	.25
0 to 1.5 %	Large	.24	.10	.17
< 0 %	Small	.10	.23	.25
< 0 %	Large	.10	.10	.17

Source: Reischauer Testimony and authors' calculations from FDIC data.

[1] Small banks: Less than or equal to $500 million in assets.
[2] Large banks: Greater than $500 million in assets.

for small and large banks separately. However, as we have just noted, the significant differences in actual resolution probabilities for small and large banks in the past suggest that the FDIC and other regulators have engaged in forbearance. To remove any downward bias this introduces in the loss estimates, we include a second set of failure probabilities (the column labeled "No Differential") for each sample period that assigns the resolution likelihoods for small banks to large banks as well.

Table 25 reports the three alternative resolution cost ratios that we used to make our cost projections: those reported by CBO for bank failures since 1986; and those we calculated from FDIC data for two different time periods, 1985 through 1989 and for just 1989.[20]

Again, we believe it is useful to supplement the CBO resolution cost ratios with the additional information. The resolution cost ratios for 1989 should be especially relevant for projecting future resolution costs since they reflect the FDIC's most recent experience. For computational simplicity, however, our three resolution cost scenarios do not assign different loss ratios for banks in different capital categories prior to failure (as is the case with the CBO projections), although we do distinguish between costs experienced for small and large banks. Finally, Table 26 sets forth the distribution of banks by capital-to-asset categories as of June 30, 1990 to which our failure probabilities and resolution cost ratios are applied. As already discussed, we used the database compiled by W.C. Ferguson, which includes both commercial and savings banks insured by the FDIC, whereas the FDIC data refer only to commercial banks. This difference in coverage, we are certain, accounts for most (but not all) of the differences between the Ferguson and FDIC data series reported in the table for the numbers of banks and assets in the various capital categories.[21]

Table 26 Banks and Assets Two Different Capital-To-Asset Categories, June 30, 1990				
	Ferguson (Commercial and Savings Banks)		FDIC	
Capital Ratio	Banks	Assets ($ Billions)	Commercial Banks	Assets ($ Billions)
> 6 %	11,699	1,913.9	11,180	1,663.0
3 to 6 %	1,065	1,632.4	1,138	1,667.8
1.5 to 3 %	3101	12.0	92	9.7
0 to 1.5 %	61	31.4	56	18.9
< 0 %	37	3.8	35	1.5
Total	12,963	3,543.5	12,501	3,360.9

Source: *Bank Source*, W. C. Ferguson & Co. and FDIC.

Table 27 reports our estimates, based on varying combinations of the assumptions displayed in Tables 25 and 26, of the federal government's projected three-year liabilities for future bank failures. The estimates vary considerably. Most of the differences arise between the baseline scenarios that rely on the historical resolution probabilities observed for large and small banks and the scenarios in which large banks are assumed to fail with the same probability as small banks.

For example, within all of the base-case scenarios, the projected three-year costs range between $12 and $24 billion. The estimated cost range for the high scenarios is a little more than twice as high, $25 to $57 billion. Given the uncertainty about which of the various failure-probability and resolution-cost assumptions will prove to be the most accurate indicator of future BIF experience, we average the projections over all assumption combinations. Thus, the bottom of Table 27 illustrates our average baseline three-year projection of $17 billion and our average high cost projection of $36 billion. Our estimates compare to the recent three-year cost estimates advanced by the GAO of $7.5 to $14.2 billion for 1991–1993, CBO of approximately $15 billion, and OMB of approximately $16 billion.[22]

Table 27 Estimated Three-Year Bank Failure Costs Under Alternative Assumptions Concerning Failure Probability and Resolution Costs ($ Billions)				
	Resolution Cost Assumptions			
Failure Probability Assumptions	CBO	1985-1989 Average	1989 Average	Average Over All Resolution Cost Scenarios
CBO	Base	12.2	13.0	18.5	14.6
	High	26.4	25.2	39.2	30.3
1988-89 1987-89 1989	Base	15.8	16.5	23.9	18.7
	High	38.3	35.9	56.8	43.7
	Base	15.8	15.2	22.4	17.8
	High	30.8	28.4	44.7	34.6
Average Probability Over All Scenarios	Base	14.6	14.9	21.6	17.0
	High	31.8	29.8	46.9	36.2

Source: Authors' calculations based on data in *Bank Source*, W. C. Ferguson & Co.

As we have also argued, the baseline estimate may prove to be far too low. It assumes continued differentials in resolution probabilities between troubled small and large banks. To the extent this differential reflects a regulatory policy of forbearance, the government is exposed to potentially far higher losses. If the past is a guide, gambling for resurrection will occur that even intensive supervision may not be able to detect, let alone thwart, in time. The baseline estimate also assumes no increased difficulties due to the recession that began in July 1990. Furthermore, to the extent that publicly available accounting data have obscured deterioration the baseline estimate will understate the cost.

To illustrate some of the details behind these aggregate cost projections, we provide in Table 28 a list of open banks as of June 30, 1990 that were reporting themselves to be insolvent and thus were certain to be resolved by the FDIC. Table 29 supplements this list with very weakly capitalized banks at that date—with capital-to-asset ratios below 1.5 percent—that are highly likely to be resolved by the FDIC at some point in the future.

Table 28
Selected Characteristics of Reporting Insolvent Banks, June 30, 1990
($ Thousands)

Name of Institution	State	Assets	Net Income	Equity Capital-to-Asset Ratio (%)
City National Bank	TX	35,577	(3,561)	(10.23)
Cherry Creek National Bank	CO	85,818	(10,519)	(9.67)
Fort Worth State Bank	TX	20,689	(2,503)	(7.15)
First Comanche Bank	TX	33,116	(3,675)	(5.40)
United Bank of Waco	TX	250,030	(2,486)	(5.36)
Security National Bank	TX	15,067	(172)	(5.17)
City National Bank of Irving	TX	32,126	(1,415)	(5.14)
Bay City Bank & Trust Co.	TX	79,609	(11,844)	(4.88)
Western National Bank of Texas	TX	34,013	(1,605)	(4.07)
Citizens National Bank	TX	51,326	(3,547)	(3.95)
The First National Bank of Levelland	TX	62,249	(1,355)	(3.84)
First Bank of Plano	TX	9,248	(49)	(3.83)
The Pawnee National Bank	OK	14,206	(180)	(3.65)
New Hampshire Savings Bank	NH	816,193	(11,818)	(2.94)

Table 28 (continued)				
Name of Institution	State	Assets	Net Income	Equity Capi-tal-to-Asset Ratio (%)
Citizens National Bank	TX	12,791	(545)	(2.48)
Trinity National Bank	TX	25,849	(1,081)	(2.07)
First National Bank of Corpus Cristie	TX	117,002	800	(2.00)
Chishom National Bank	TX	20,886	(478)	(1.91)
The First State Bank	TX	20,075	(94)	(1.84)
First National Bank of Kennedale	TX	27,485	(1973)	(1.71)
Metropolitan National Bank	TX	19,851	(531)	(1.59)
Boundary Waters State Bank	MN	12,662	(8)	(1.40)
Citizens Bank	TX	15,876	(73)	(1.27)
The Bank of Wilson	OK	12,982	(8)	(1.24)
Maine Savings Bank	ME	1,496,905	(14,348)	(0.98)
United Peoples Bank	TX	32,673	(1,106)	(0.98)
Woodway Bank & Trust	TX	35,375	(1,230)	(0.98)
Amercian Bank of Commerce	TX	17,389	(1,002)	(0.85)
First National Bank of Cedar Hills	TX	11,478	(152)	(0.78)
Washington County State Bank	TX	84,690	(3,034)	(0.65)
Peoples State Bank	TX	36,728	(2,145)	(0.54)
Freedom National Bank of New York	NY	99,777	(602)	(0.33)
American Bank of Commerce	OK	14,366	(24)	(0.24)
Southwestern Bank & Trust Co.	OK	76,027	113	(0.23)
Western Bank	TX	42,148	(187)	(0.13)
Great Western National Bank	TX	13,377	(152)	(0.11)
First National Bank of Crosby	ND	12,433	(138)	(0.09)
Totals		3,798,092	(82,727)	(2.36)

Source: *Bank Source*, W. C. Ferguson & Co.

Table 29
Weakly Capitalized Banks, June 30, 1990
(Capital-to-Asset Ratio Less Than 1.5 Percent) ($ Thousands)

Institution (State)	Assets	Net Income	Equity Capital-to-Asset Ratio (%)
Gleneagles National Bank (TX)	19,787	4	0.07
Northside Bank (TX)	54,654	(344)	0.07
The Brooklyn Savings Bank (CT)	130,931	1	0.16
First State Bank (OK)	7,695	(63)	0.17
United Mercantile (CA)	47,663	(293)	0.21
Georgetown National Bank (TX)	26,953	(104)	0.24
First American Bank for Savings (MA)	526,176	(4,226)	0.29
MBank Waco, National Assoc. (TX)	323,476	(16)	0.29
ProBank (TX)	31,750	85	0.31
Ingram State Bank (TX)	23,452	(340)	0.32
Stone Oak National Bank (TX)	17,664	(528)	0.33
The Chireno State Bank (TX)	14,290	(332)	0.44
Coffeyville State Bank (KS)	14,228	(121)	0.46
The Peoples Bank & Trust Co. (LA)	117,050	(333)	0.46
The Community Bank of Nebraska (NE)	9,799	(445)	0.54
The Farmers & Merchants Bank (ND)	3,049	(14)	0.58
First National Bank of Sachse (TX)	15,837	9	0.58
Western American National Bank (TX)	32,988	(318)	0.59
United Valley Bank (CA)	22,651	(378)	0.60
Farmers State Bank of Madisonville (TX)	38,022	5	0.68
American Bank & Trust Co. (LA)	351,544	298	0.72
The First National Bank of Carthage (TX)	38,727	(800)	0.72
Citizens National Bank (CO)	11,788	(678)	0.76
The First National Bank of Wortham (TX)	8,078	5	0.77
Tascosa National Bank of Amarillo (TX)	92,735	13	0.81
Village Green National Bank (TX)	34,907	19	0.83
Union Security Bank & Trust Co. (LA)	26,967	(4)	0.85
Goldome Savings Bank (NY)	10,254,871	(35,328)	0.86
First National Bank of Rowlett (TX)	23,234	14	0.87
The Capital National Bank in Austin (TX)	41,138	54	0.89
Community Guardian Bank (NJ)	63,840	(520)	0.89

Table 29 (continued)			
Institution (State)	Assets	Net Income	Equity Capital-to-Asset Ratio (%)
The State Bank of Omaha (TX)	22,267	(113)	0.96
First American Bank and Trust Co. (OK)	56,401	(91)	0.98
City Bank and Trust (NH)	125,552	(1,459)	1.00
Bank of Healdton (OK)	27,179	(327)	1.01
The Permanent Savings Bank (NY)	329,994	(47)	1.02
Merchants Trust & Savings Bank (LA)	43,925	(206)	1.03
The Merchants Bank & Trust Co. (CT)	305,523	(6,054)	1.08
Bank of Shawsville (VA)	46,653	256	1.09
Chickasha Bank & Trust Co. (OK)	44,185	16	1.11
Southwest National Bank (NM)	46,353	339	1.15
United Bank of Aurora (CO)	72,941	(3,557)	1.16
Dripping Springs National Bank (TX)	21,831	(767)	1.19
Bank of the Hills (TX)	325,998	(8,114)	1.20
Lone Star Bank, National Assoc. (TX)	20,172	(26)	1.22
NBC Bank- Eagle Press (TX)	134,675	(1,045)	1.22
The Hondo National Bank (TX)	20,098	(18)	1.23
Bank of New England (MA)	13,265,155	22,419	1.24
Peoples Bank (TX)	21,951	15	1.24
Americn State Bank of Erskine (MN)	11,674	11	1.28
Connecticut Savings Bank (CT)	1,200,088	(69,582)	1.32
Lone Star National Bank (TX)	43,110	(519)	1.37
American Bank & Trust Co. (LA)	57,897	(19)	1.38
Pontchartrain State Bank (LA)	163,698	(1,126)	1.38
The First National Bank of Arvada (CO)	26,812	(1,178)	1.39
Merchants National Bank (MA)	180,373	(5,976)	1.42
Bank of Arlington (TX)	65,249	(715)	1.43
Capitol Bank and Trust Co. (MA)	498,420	(21,992)	1.43
The National Bank of Washington (DC)	1,650,969	(61,043)	1.43
Altantic Trust Co. (NH)	20,784	(382)	1.46
First National Bank of Huntsville (TX)	103,724	241	1.47
Totals	31,379,595	(205,737)	1.08

Source: *Bank Source*, W. C. Ferguson & Co.

For reasons discussed above, of course, many more banks than those shown in Table 29 will fail during the next three years. However, it is noteworthy that just those banks shown in the table now control over $35 billion in assets and at an average resolution cost ratio of 15 percent (a highly conservative figure) are likely to cost the BIF at least $5 billion.[23]

Implications of the Growing Problem Bank List

The FDIC provided us with limited information about problem banks that permit a different method of estimating likely future resolution costs. A problem bank is one that receives one of the two worst ratings (either a 4 or a 5 on a 1 to 5 scale) under the "CAMEL" system used by federal bank examiners to rate the health of the banks they supervise.[24] For all problem banks since 1984, Table 30 depicts the percentage that later failed through 1989. This table, included in our congressional report, was the first public description of the deposit size of problem banks. Beginning in 1986 the data distinguish between problem banks below and above $300 million in deposits (delineating small and large banks, respectively).

Higher Failure Rates

Table 30 illustrates that the probability of subsequent failure among problem banks has risen over time. For example, among small problem banks, the first year failure probability rose from just over 10 percent for banks so designated in 1986 to over 15 percent for banks so designated in 1988. Similarly, for large banks, the first year failure probabilities rose from almost 6 percent based on 1986 data to over 20 percent using 1988 data. This contrasts with our Tables 20 and 21, which generally show that failure probabilities among banks in different capital-to-asset categories have been roughly stable during the 1986–1988 time frame.

Initially, the rising failure rate among problem banks seems to contradict the notion that the FDIC has practiced forbearance. So, too, does the fact that, with few exceptions, the failure rates for small and large banks shown in Table 30 are roughly the same. In fact, however, the FDIC's experience with problem banks suggests that forbearance has been very much in evidence. As mentioned earlier, not only are the failure-cost ratios quite high, but Table 31 and Figure 6 illustrate that both the mean and median length of time that failed banks were desig-nated problem banks prior to failure generally increased throughout the 1980s, markedly so since 1985. The same trends are evident for the maximum and 75th percentile periods of problem-bank designation before failure.

Table 30 Cumulative Failure Probabilities of Problem Banks, 1985 - 1989								
Problem Banks as of Year-End:								
Year	1984	1985	1986		1987		1988	
Size Category[1]	Total	Total	< 300	+300	< 300	+300	< 300	+300
Number	938	1322	1484	69	1368	57	1177	69
Deposits ($ Billions)	165.9	274.8	58.4	176.3	55.5	155.2	50.6	134.5
Percent Failed Cumulative Year-End:								
By 1985 Banks	9.5							
By 1985 Deposits	1.5							
By 1986 Banks	16.4	8.5						
By 1986 Deposits	4.3	2.3						
By 1987 Banks	20.8	15.5	10.4	5.8				
By 1987 Deposits	5.7	4.1	8.7	0.9				
By 1988 Banks	23.2	19.4	17.2	8.7	10.9	7.0		
By 1988 Deposits	7.0	5.9	15.8	1.6	9.2	8.5		
By 1989 Banks	24.4	22.2	22.7	21.7	21.3	29.8	15.4	20.3
By 1989 Deposits	10.1	8.5	22.8	9.8	21.5	19.4	18.9	10.8

Source: Authors' calculations based on FDIC data.

[1] Size categories are above (+) and below (<) $300 million in deposits.

Evidence of Forbearance in Problem-Bank and Closure Data

It is possible, of course, that as the decade wore on, it objectively took problem banks longer to fall over the edge of insolvency. We are skeptical. We do not believe it is a coincidence that during the first half of the decade—when annual bank failures were running at 100 or less—the typical failed bank was resolved in about 15 months since first appearing on the problem list, and toward the end of the decade—when the annual failure rate was above 200—the typical failed bank was not resolved for anywhere from 21 to 28 months (1987 through 1989) after

Figure 6. Number of Months Failed Banks Received the Lowest Regulatory Examination Rating Before Closure 1980-1989.

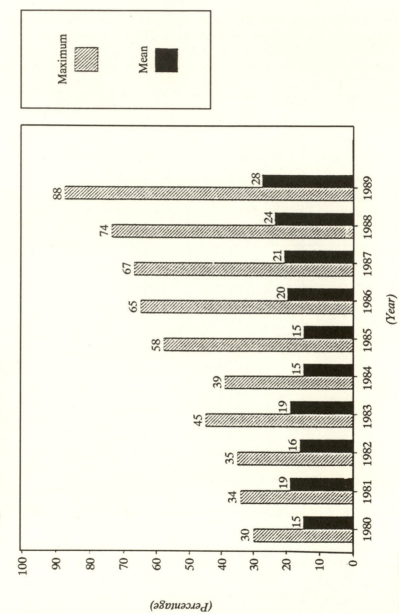

Source: FDIC

first being designated a problem bank. In the late 1980s when the FDIC was handling approximately 200 bank resolutions per year, its personnel and financial resources were stretched and thus the agency was not in a position to move on problem institutions as fast as it did during more quiescent times.[25] This is a far more likely reason for the significant lengthening in the period failed banks were on the problem list before being closed.[26]

Table 31								
Number of Consecutive Months Failed Banks Received								
Examination Ratings of 4 or 5 Before Closure, 1980 - 1989								
			Months Rated 4 or 5					
Year of Failure	Failed Banks	Banks Included	Mean	Maximum	75th Per-centile	Median	25th Per-centile	Minimum
1980	10	7	15	30	24	13	10	0
1981	7	6	19	34	28	19	10	7
1982	32	26	16	35	28	12	8	1
1983	45	39	19	45	27	15	10	3
1984	78	76	15	39	21	13	7	0
1985	116	113	15	58	20	13	8	0
1986	138	135	20	65	28	19	10	0
1987	184	182	21	67	27	19	11	0
1988	200	166	24	74	32	21	13	0
1989	206	202	28	88	38	27	18	0
1980 - 1989	1,016	952	21	88	29	19	11	0

Source: FDIC.

Note: Ratings used are average CAMEL ratings from bank regulatory examinations. The examination data are from all examination records available on FDIC on-line and archived databases.

Higher Estimated Costs Based on Problem-Bank Failures

In any event, it is possible to use the failure probabilities calculated from the problem bank database to provide an alternative illustrative estimate of the FDIC's likely future losses. Using the most recent failure rate data in Table 30, we believe it can be conservatively projected that during the next three years (mid-1990 through mid-1993) banks currently on the problem list will fail in sufficient numbers to account for 25 percent and 20 percent of the deposits held by small and large problem banks, respectively. Indeed, the table shows that for banks on the problem list at year-end 1987, small banks accounting for 21.5 percent of all small problem bank-deposits had failed by the end of 1989 (two years later). The corresponding figure for large banks was 19.4 percent.

Applying the 25- and 20-percent failure rates to the aggregate deposits held by small and large problem banks as of September 30, 1990 ($46.6 billion for the 958 small banks on the list and $198.8 billion for the large banks) yields deposits subject to probable failure in the next three years of $12 billion (small) and $40 billion (large) for the two bank groups.[27]

Each of these two figures must in turn be multiplied by an appropriate resolution cost ratio. The ratios shown in Table 25 earlier reflect FDIC losses as a share of failed bank *assets*; the loss ratios should be somewhat lower when calculated as a share of deposits (since the typical failed bank should have more deposits than assets). To be conservative, therefore, we assume cost ratios for the small and large problem banks, respectively, of 20 percent and 15 percent (ratios below those for 1989, as shown in Table 25). Applying these loss ratios to the deposits subject to failure yields estimated BIF losses during the next three years of $8.3 billion.

This estimate, however, understates likely future losses because it fails to account for the many banks that may fail in the next three years that are not currently on the problem list. As it is, Table 30 illustrates that 52 banks that failed during the 1980s never appeared on the problem list, an average of about 5 per year, or 0.045 percent of the roughly 11,500 commercial banks not now on the problem list. If this were the only group of banks that the problem list missed, then any upward revision to the $8.3 billion loss estimate would be relatively minor.

A closer look at Table 31, however, reveals that a more substantial upward adjustment is in order. The table reveals that at the 25th percentile, failed banks were on the problem list for an average of only 11 months. Put another way, one-fourth of the banks that fail each year have been on the list less than a year. Based on the failure rates shown in Table 30, it is likely that at least 30 percent of the 958 banks (not the deposits) will fail in the next three years, a total of almost 290 or about 95 per year. If in the first year, these 95 banks represent three-fourths of the total failures, then another 32 banks will fail in that year. By similar reasoning, 64 banks will fail in the second year that are not currently on the problem list, and another 96 banks will fail in the third year that are not on the list. In total, the failure of another 192 banks during the next three years must be accounted for, or 1.7 percent of the roughly 11,500 banks not now on the list.

Since as shown in Tables 20 and 21 most failed banks have assets under $500 million—or the bank size grouping in which resolution probabilities based both on numbers and assets of failed banks are quite similar—we believe it is appropriate to assume that 1.7 percent of the $3.1 trillion in assets of nonproblem banks, or approximately $53 billion, are likely to be held by banks in this group that will fail during the next three years. Applying a conservative resolution cost ratio of 15 percent yields an additional $7.9 billion in resolution costs. When added to the $8.3 billion in likely costs from failures now on the problem list, the total potential three-year resolution cost to the BIF is an estimated $16.2 billion, a figure well within the range of cost estimates under our base case assumptions shown in Table 27.

In sum, a narrow focus on likely failures within the problem bank category, or on any other single grouping of likely potential bank failures, can result in a substantial understatement of likely bank resolution costs. This is because no single test or screen for bank failures is perfect: some future failures will be missed, more so as the prediction period lengthens.

Yet, even the $16.2 billion cost estimate probably understates the BIF's future resolution costs. This is because the calculations just presented assume relatively identical resolution probabilities for banks under and above $300 million in deposits. As noted above, this size distinction conceals the likelihood that the resolution probabilities for much larger banks on the problem list historically have been well below those for smaller banks. If the future failure rates for problem banks in the two size groupings are equal, then the BIF's projected losses based on an analysis of problem bank experience would probably be much higher.

Since we did not have access to the identities of the banks on the problem list we could not determine how many, if any at all, large banks were included. Yet from our foregoing discussion, we believe that the largest banks, as a group, pose the greatest risks to the FDIC. We include Table 32 to show the interbank dependence among selected large banks. The table highlights the dangers that difficulties among one or more large banks can transmit to the others.

Table 32
Correspondent Balances and Interbank Deposits of Selected Large Banks, June 30, 1989 ($ Millions)

Name of Institution	Demand Deposits Due To All Banks	Time and Savings Deposits Due To All Banks	Demand Deposits Due Foreign Banks	Time And Savings Deposits Due Foreign Banks	Interbank Deposits as Percent of Total Deposits
Bankers Trust (NY)	2,230	574	1,151	0	8.9
Citibank, (NY)	2,256	49	1,603	18	2.2
Chase Manhattan (NY)	1,924	178	1,144	29	3.4
Manufacturers Hanover (NY)	1,689	314	679	58	4.6
Bank of N.Y. (NY and DE)[1]	1,371	82	1,063	4	5.0 (est.)
Morgan Guaranty (NY)	1,043	494	523	51	3.1
Marine Midlan (NY)	366	493	210	22	5.1
Chemical (NY and TX)	866	120	57	74	2.5 (est.)
First Chicago (IL)	631	412	201	28	3.6
Bank of America (CA)	1,410	87	411	59	2.1
Mellon Banks (PA)	533	139	88	0	3.3 (est.)
Pittsburgh National (PA and KY)[1]	393	471	NA	NA	4.8 (est.)
Bank One (OH,IN, TX and WI)[1]	439	792	NA	NA	7.6 (est.)
National City (OH)	82	4	NA	NA	1.5

Source: *American Banker, Top Numbers 1990*; and Walker F. Todd and James B. Thomson, "An Insider's View of the Political Economy of the Too Big to Let Fail Doctrine", 65th Annual Western Economic Association International Conference, San Diego, California, Session 146, July 2, 1990 (Revision of August 15, 1990).

[1] Multistate bank holding companies' totals might be overstated due to double-counting of intra-company claims.

The BIF's Net Cash Reserves: Increasing Insurance Premiums Struggling to Keep Pace with Losses

At year end 1990, the FDIC reported its reserves, or the equivalent of its net worth, at $8.5 billion, or just 0.43 percent of total insured deposits held in U.S. commercial banks, as shown in Table 33. Both the table and Figure 7 illustrate that, at this ratio, the fund was in the poorest condition in its history and well below the 1.25 percent target for the BIF set in the Financial Institutions Reform, Recovery, and Enforcement Act of 1989 (FIRREA).

To help stanch the flow of red ink the FDIC announced in 1990 that it would raise bank insurance premiums beginning in 1991 from 15 to 19.5 basis points. As part of the budget agreement reached in October 1990, the Administration projected that the FDIC would raise bank insurance premiums still further, to 23 basis points, the same level as for savings and loan deposits, which was done in July 1991.

GAO and CBO Income and Reserve Projections

Table 34 provides the net income and reserve level projections for the BIF made by GAO and CBO in 1990, adjusted for the FDIC's earlier projection of a $3 billion loss for 1990 and for two different levels of sustained bank deposit insurance premiums, 19.5 and 23 basis points, respectively.

We have listed two of the three projection scenarios made by GAO, which differ primarily in the degree of future losses expected (the projections for its scenario 2 differed little from those for scenario 1).

Table 34 indicates that even as adjusted by the higher BIF loss projections for 1990 made by the FDIC, both GAO and CBO project that the BIF would have sufficient reserves to cover future expected failure costs in their base cases. Those projections assume that the economy would weaken no further from its position in September 1990 when the agencies issued their loss projections.

Specifically, the table shows that at the current 19.5 basis point premium level, GAO projects the BIF fund balance to remain above $10 billion throughout the 1991–1995 period and to hit $21.5 to $30 billion by 1995 (calendar year). CBO is more pessimistic, projecting the fund balance to fall below $7 billion (in fiscal year 1992) and not even to recover to $10 billion by 1995.

Table 33
Insured Bank Deposits and the Bank Insurance Fund, 1934 - 1990
($ Millions)

Year (12/31)	Insurance Coverage ($)	Deposits in Insured Banks[1]		% Insured Deposits	Bank Insurance Fund Reserves	Ratio of Bank Insurance Fund Reserves to:	
		Total	Insured			Total Deposits	Insured Deposits
1990	100,000	2,608,362	1,976,744	75.0	8,500.0	.33	.43
1989	100,000	2,464,725	1,872,953	76.0	13,210.0	.54	.70
1988	100,000	2,330,768	1,750,259	75.1	14,061.1	.60	.80
1987	100,000	2,201,549	1,658,802	76.9	18,301.3	.83	1.10
1986	100,000	2,167,596	1,634,302	75.4	18,253.3	.84	1.12
1985	100,000	1,974,512	1,503,393	76.1	17,956.9	.91	1.19
1984	100,000	1,806,520	1,389,874	76.9	16,529.4	.92	1.19
1983	100,000	1,690,576	1,268,332	75.0	15,429.1	.91	1.22
1982	100,000	1,644,697	1,134,221	73.4	13,770.9	.89	1.21
1981	100,000	1,409,322	988,898	70.2	12,246.1	.87	1.24
1980	100,000	1,324,463	948,717	71.6	11,019.5	.83	1.16
1979	40,000	1,226,943	808,555	65.9	9,792.7	.80	1.21
1978	40,000[6]	1,145,835	760,706	66.4	8,796.0	.77	1.16
1977	40,000[5]	1,050,435	692,533	65.9	7,992.3	.76	1.15
1976	40,000	941,923	628,263	66.7	7,268.8	.77	1.16
1975	40,000	875,985	569,101	65.0	6,716.0	.77	1.18
1974	40,000	833,277	520,309	62.5	6,124.2	.73	1.18
1973	20,000	766,509	465,600	60.7	5,615.3	.73	1.21
1972	20,000	697,480	419,756	60.2	5,158.7	.74	1.23
1971	20,000	610,685	374,568	61.3	4,739.9	.78	1.27
1970	20,000	545,198	349,581	64.1	4,379.6	.80	1.25
1969	20,000	495,858	313,085	63.1	4,051.1	.82	1.29
1968	15,000	491,513	296,701	60.2	3,749.2	.76	1.26
1967	15,000	448,709	261,149	58.2	3,485.5	.78	1.33
1966	15,000	401,096	234,150	58.4	3,252.0	.81	1.39
1965	10,000	377,400	209,690	55.6	3,036.3	.80	1.45
1964	10,000	348,981	191,787	55.0	2,844.7	.82	1.48
1963	10,000	313,304[2]	177,381	56.6	2,667.9	.85	1.50
1962	10,000	297,548[3]	170,210	57.2	2,502.0	.84	1.47
1961	10,000	281,304	160,309	57.0	2,353.8	.84	1.47

Table 33 (Continued)

Year (12/31)	Insurance Coverage ($)	Deposits in Insured Banks[1]		% Insured Deposits	Bank Insurance Fund Reserves	Ratio of Bank Insurance Fund Reserves to:	
		Total	Insured			Total Deposits	Insured Deposits
1960	10,000	260,495	149,684	57.5	2,222.2	.85	1.48
1959	10,000	247,589	142,131	57.4	2,089.8	.84	1.47
1958	10,000	242,445	137,698	56.8	1,965.4	.81	1.43
1957	10,000	225,507	127,055	56.3	1,850.5	.82	1.46
1956	10,000	219,393	121,008	55.2	1,742.1	.79	1.44
1955	10,000	212,226	116,380	54.8	1,639.6	.77	1.41
1954	10,000	203,195	110,973	54.6	1,542.7	.76	1.39
1953	10,000	193,466	105,610	54.6	1,450.7	.75	1.37
1952	10,000	188,142	101,841	54.1	1,363.5	.72	1.34
1951	10,000	178,540	96,713	54.2	1,292.2	.72	1.33
1950	10,000	167,818	91,359	54.4	1,243.9	.74	1.36
1949	5,000	156,786	76,589	48.8	1,203.9	.77	1.57
1948	5,000	153,454	75,320	49.1	1,065.9	.69	1.42
1947	5,000	154,096	76,254	49.5	1,006.1	.65	1.32
1946	5,000	148,458	73,759	49.7	1,058.5	.71	1.44
1945	5,000	157,174	67,021	42.4	929.2	.59	1.39
1944	5,000	134,662	56,398	41.9	804.3	.60	1.43
1943	5,000	111,650	48,440	43.4	703.1	.63	1.45
1942	5,000	89,869	32,837	36.5	616.9	.69	1.88
1941	5,000	71,209	28,249	39.7	553.5	.78	1.96
1940	5,000	65,288	26,638	40.8	496.0	.76	1.86
1939	5,000	57,485	24,650	42.9	452.7	.79	1.84
1938	5,000	50,791	23,121	45.5	420.5	.83	1.82
1937	5,000	48,228	22,557	46.8	383.1	.79	1.70
1936	5,000	50,281	22,330	44.4	343.4	.68	1.54
1935	5,000	45,125	20,158	44.7	306.0	.68	1.52
1934	5,000[4]	40,060	18,075	45.1	291.7	.73	1.61

Source: FDIC.

[1] Deposits in foreign branches are omitted from totals because they are not insured. Insured deposits are estimated by applying to deposits at the regular Call dates the percentages as determined from the June Call Report submitted by insured banks. [2] December 20, 1963. [3] December 23, 1962. [4] Initial coverage was $2,500 from January 1 to June 30, 1934. [5] $100,000 for some savings deposits of in-state units governmental units provided in 1974. [6] $100,000 for individual retirement accounts and Keogh accounts provided in 1978.

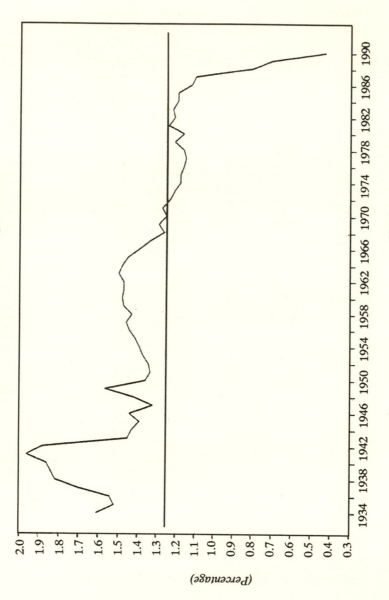

Figure 7. Bank Insurance Fund Reserves Relative to Insured Deposits 1934-1990.

(Percentage)

(Year)

Source: FDIC

On the assumption that a further increase in the deposit-insurance premium to 23 basis points throughout the period will not add to bank failure costs, Table 34 also shows that the GAO projections imply that the BIF reserve fund will rise to $27 to $35 billion by 1995; for CBO, the reserve fund increases to approximately $15 billion.

Table 34
GAO and CBO Income and Cash Flow Projection for the BIF, 1991 - 1995
(Adjusted for Previous Premium Increases and Assumed $3.0 Billion Loss in 1990)
($ Billions)

			1991	1992	1993	1994	1995
GAO[1]	Assessible Base[2]		$2,585	$2,763	$2,954	$3,158	$3,376
	19.5 Basis Point Premium: 1991-1995	Net Income-Scenario 1	3.8	4.1	4.3	4.6	5.0
		Net Income-Scenario 3[3]	2.0	2.4	2.6	3.0	3.3
		Fund Balance-Scenario 1	12.0	16.1	20.4	25.0	30.0
		Fund Balance-Scenario 3	10.2	12.6	15.2	18.2	21.5
	23.0 Basis Point Premium: 1991-1995	Net Income-Scenario 1	4.7	5.1	5.3	5.7	6.2
		Net Income-Scenario 3	3.1	3.4	3.6	4.1	4.5
		Fund Balance-Scenario 1	12.9	18.0	23.3	29.0	35.2
		Fund Balance-Scenario 3	11.3	14.7	18.3	22.4	26.9
CBO[1]	Assessible Base[4]		$2,527	$2,641	$2,760	$2,894	$3,024
	19.5 Basis Point Premium: 1991-1995	Net Income	(1.2)	(0.2)	0.4	0.8	1.5
		Fund Balance	7.0	6.8	7.2	8.0	9.5
	23.0 Basis Point Premium: 1991-1995	Net Income	0.3	0.7	1.4	1.9	2.7
		Fund Balance	8.5	9.2	10.6	12.5	15.2

Sources: GAO, 1990; Reischauer, 1990; CBO worksheets; authors' calculations.

[1] GAO projections are for calendar years; CBO's for fiscal years. [2] Same as for FDIC projections. [3] Preexisting GAO scenario #3 assumed 19.5 basis point premium in 1991 only. [4] Assumes annual deposit growth of 4.5 percent.

Still, only under the most favorable loss assumptions of GAO's scenario 1 and a 23 basis point insurance premium level throughout the period would GAO's projected 1995 reserve level of $35 billion hit the 1.25 percent target ratio of BIF reserves to insured deposits set by Congress in FIRREA.[28]

A More Appropriate Framework

As noted above, our three-year minimum baseline BIF loss projection of $17 billion is somewhat above even that of the CBO, the more pessimistic of the projections shown in Table 34. What does our baseline loss projection imply for the sufficiency of the BIF's reserves in each of the next three years? We are reluctant to answer this question by making year-by-year income and reserve level projections like those made by GAO and CBO. Our reason is simple. As we have already explained, the FDIC manages its caseload by deciding when to close or assist troubled banks. Accordingly, we believe it is unproductive to predict precisely year-to-year how and when the FDIC will exercise the discretion it has under existing law.

Instead, we believe it is more illuminating to emphasize that on any reasonable set of assumptions, the FDIC is unlikely to have sufficient resources during the next three years to cover likely bank failure costs. To explain why, we begin by noting that based on GAO's projected assessment base between 1991 and 1993 (which, as shown in Table 34, is somewhat higher than that of CBO), the BIF should realize total premium income of approximately $16 billion on a 19.5 basis point premium; on a 23 basis point premium, estimated premium revenue rises to roughly $19 billion. In addition, the FDIC should realize interest income during this period of about $3 billion, bringing its estimated total income during the next three years to $19 to $22 billion, depending on the level of insurance premiums. Assuming the BIF had approximately $9 billion in reserves at year-end 1990, then it will have a total of $28 to $31 billion to handle bank failures during the next three years.

BIF Cash Reserve Shortage at Any Moment Even with Baseline Estimates

At this level of resources, the FDIC should cover our minimum baseline loss estimate of $17 billion, with some room to spare. However, the

BIF's resources are clearly inadequate, even at a 23 basis point premium level, to cover the $36 billion high baseline cost, let alone the additional costs we project under many of the recession scenarios outlined in the next section.

In fact, however, the FDIC has even less margin for comfort than these projections imply. As we have stressed throughout this report, in order to avoid running the dangers of forbearance, the FDIC must be assured of having sufficient cash resources to liquidate or reorganize insolvent institutions promptly. Table 35 shows that as of the end of June 1990, the FDIC had a total of $11 billion in cash and investment securities (down from a 1980s peak of $16.2 billion in 1988).

Given the lags between expenditures and receipts from asset sales, CBO projects that the BIF's cash resources will fall to the neighborhood of only $5 billion in 1992–94.[29]

Moreover, as both the GAO and CBO have highlighted, the FDIC currently has a potential off-balance sheet liability totaling perhaps as much as $8 billion, representing the amount by which it would be obligated to pay past acquirers of insolvent banks who may, at any time, decide to put back to the FDIC certain problem assets they inherited from failed banks they had purchased. In acknowledging this potential liability to the GAO in particular, the FDIC claimed in its comments on the GAO's report that the put options extended only to some "undetermined portion" of those assets, and that even if exercised, those puts would pose "liquidity" issues rather than reserve concerns (since the FDIC might not eventually post a loss on the subsequent sale of those assets).[30] These comments implied that the FDIC's contingent liability was somewhat less than $8 billion.

In fact, however, it has been recently reported that two major acquirers of failed banks—Banc One of Texas and Team Bank of Fort Worth—could exercise options to return up to $20 billion in problem assets to the FDIC, a much more substantial sum.[31] As it is, NCNB Texas has returned almost $2.5 billion in assets to the FDIC this year and last; Banc One and Team Bank together have exercised puts totaling an additional $2.65 billion.

Put more simply, these "liquidity issues" mean that even under the CBO's base-case projections—which, as we have observed, are more optimistic than ours—the BIF's potential cash outlays in the event these puts are exercised could exhaust the BIF's cash reserves. In addition, in our high cost baseline scenario the additional cash drain for meeting the

Table 35
Bank Insurance Fund
Statements of Financial Position, 1980 - 1990
($ Millions)

	As of December 31										June 30
	1980	1981	1982	1983	1984	1985	1986	1987	1988	1989	1990
ASSETS											
Cash and cash equivalents	$ 2	0	1	89	4	1,705	2,092	1,325	2,928	4,814	2,082
Investment in U.S. Treasury obligations, net	10,494	12,005	13,252	13,992	14,436	14,160	14,553	14,792	13,293	8,814	7,985
Accrued Interest receivable on investments and other assets	235	238	349	393	394	499	504	455	652	279	258
Net receivables from bank assistance and failures	881	976	1,422	2,416	6,462	5,662	5,208	5,891	5,814	5,498	7,266
Property and buildings	23	23	34	37	42	47	51	73	77	98	119
Total Assets	$11,635	13,242	15,058	16,927	21,338	22,073	22,408	22,536	22,764	19,614	17,710

Table 35 (continued.)

| | As of December 31 | | | | | | | | | | June 30 |
	1980	1981	1982	1983	1984	1985	1986	1987	1988	1989	1990
LIABILITIES AND THE FUND BALANCE											
Accounts Payable, accrued liabilities and other	$ 35	36	98	80	100	81	118	55	65	50	23
Liabilities for estimated bank assistance	569	129	96	164	0	0	150	1,237	3,877	3,820	2,905
Liabilities incurred from bank assistance & failures	13	831	1,091	1,254	0	4,021	3,881	2,832	4,651	2,412	3,285
Estimated losses from corporation litigation	0	0	3	0	0	14	6	110	122	122	
Total Liabilities	$ 617	996	1,288	1,498	4,808	4,116	4,155	4,234	8,703	6,404	6,335
Fund Balance	11,020	12,246	13,771	15,429	16,529	17,957	18,253	18,302	14,061	13,210	11,375
	$11,637	13,242	15,059	16,927	21,337	22,073	22,408	22,536	22,764	19,614	17,710

Source: FDIC.

put obligations would clearly force the FDIC into a forbearance stance even if it also drew on its current $5 billion line of credit with the Treasury.[32]

In sum, even under the baseline assumptions we have outlined, before taking account of any downside effects of a recession, the BIF can have a cash reserve problem at any time. If the Administration and Congress wish to avoid putting the FDIC in a position where it almost assuredly has to grant forbearance to troubled banks that merit resolution, a way must soon be found to come up with additional cash.

Table 36
Net Outlays for the Bank Insurance Fund of the
Federal Deposit Insurance Corporation,
Fiscal Years 1980-1990 ($ Millions)

Fiscal Year	Actual Outlay	Estimated Outlay and Date			
1990	6,429	3,904 July 1990	1,961 Jan. 1990	1,909 July 1989	(1,324) Jan. 1989
1989	1,929	4,307 July 1989	3,807 Jan. 1989	502 Feb. 1988	(458) Jan. 1987
1988	2,146	2,268 Feb. 1988	1,535 Jan. 1987	(2,150) Feb. 1986	(2,500) Feb. 1985
1987	(1,438)	4,046 Jan. 1987	(1,900) Feb. 1986	(2,000) Feb. 1985	(2,220) Feb. 1984
1986	262	(1,658) Feb. 1986	(1,500) Feb. 1985	(1,987) Feb. 1984	(2,410) Jan. 1983
1985	(1,942)	(1,000) Feb. 1985	(1,696) Feb. 1984	(2,180) Jan. 1983	(2,850) Jan. 1982
1984	(248)	(1,424) Feb. 1984	(2,020) Jan. 1983	(2,050) Feb. 1982	(1,600) Jan. 1981
1983	(613)	(2,300) Jan. 1983	(2,000) Feb. 1982	(1,550) Jan. 1981	(1,600) Jan. 1980
1982	(1,440)	(1,800) Feb. 1982	(1,500) Jan. 1981	(1,550) Jan. 1980	(1,300) Jan. 1979
1981	(1,726)	(1,450) Jan. 1981	(1,500) Jan. 1980	(1,250) Jan. 1979	NA
1980	(922)	(1,450) Jan. 1980	(1,192) Jan. 1979	(1,075) Jan. 1978	NA

Source: Office of Management and Budget.

FDIC's Estimates: Wrong and Optimistic

We conclude our base-case projections of future bank resolution costs by observing that the FDIC itself in the past has erred substantially in making projections of its outlays, even when doing so for short periods into the future. Table 36 presents information on FDIC's actual and estimated outlays during the 1980s.

Table 36 illustrates the significant gaps between even the FDIC's recent outlay estimates and the actual outlay figures. For example, even though the BIF's net outlays by fiscal year-end 1990 reached $6.4 billion, as recently as January 1990, the FDIC estimated that total to be only $2 billion.

Indeed, even three months before the end of the year, the FDIC's net outlay estimate for fiscal year 1990 was nearly 40 percent below the final actual figure. For other years, Table 36 illustrates similar variances between estimated and actual outlays.

The table shows, moreover, that as the FDIC encountered an increasingly large and costly number of bank failures, the BIF contributed to, rather than reduced, the federal budget deficit. Given the importance the FDIC's outlays now have for the federal budget deficit, it is imperative that both the Administration and the Congress be given timely and accurate information about bank failure costs and outlays. We suspect that the principal reason OMB decided to generate its own estimates of the FDIC's outlays is the FDIC's relatively poor past record of doing so. Indeed, it should be a source of concern to the Congress that the GAO, CBO and OMB apparently cannot rely on the FDIC for accurate estimates of the outlays and condition of the BIF.

Effects of Recession on Bank Failure Costs

Our baseline estimates will understate the government's actual liabilities for bank failure costs because the economy entered a recession in July 1990. As a result, banks throughout the country will suffer additional loan losses and many of those with weak capital positions will become insolvent. It is very difficult, however, to estimate the effects of a recession on the BIF with precision primarily because recessions vary in intensity and length. They can also have very different regional effects and later recoveries can also vary greatly.

Table 37
Estimated Three-Year Bank Failure Costs Based Upon
Alternative Assumptions Concerning Recession Scenarios,
Failure Probabilities, and Resolution Costs
($ Billions)

			No Recession	Mild Recession	"New England Style" Recession	"Texas Style" Recession
CBO Failure Probability	CBO Resolution Costs	Base	12.2	13.3	15.4	16.9
		High	26.4	28.9	30.9	33.0
	1985-1989 Resolution Costs	Base	13.0	14.6	17.8	20.9
		High	25.2	31.4	38.0	51.8
	1989 Resolution Costs	Base	18.5	20.4	24.6	28.6
		High	39.2	48.9	59.0	81.0
1988-1989 Failure Probability	CBO Resolution Costs	Base	15.8	17.9	21.6	23.8
		High	38.3	42.7	49.4	49.2
	1985-1989 Resolution Costs	Base	16.5	19.4	24.4	28.6
		High	35.9	43.6	53.2	65.5
	1989 Resolution Costs	Base	23.9	27.4	34.2	39.2
		High	56.8	68.6	83.1	101.9
1989 Failure Probability	CBO Resolution Costs	Base	15.8	17.6	20.5	21.8
		High	30.8	34.1	39.0	38.6
	1985-1989 Resolution Costs	Base	15.2	17.7	21.9	25.2
		High	28.4	35.0	42.7	55.1
	1989 Resolution Costs	Base	22.4	25.5	31.3	35.3
		High	44.7	55.0	66.6	86.0
Average of All Scenarios		Base	17.0	19.3	23.5	26.7
		High	36.2	43.1	51.3	62.5

Source: Authors' calculations based on data in *Bank Source*, W. C. Ferguson and Co.

Three Scenarios Based on Recent Regional Recessions

Accordingly, we have estimated the potential effects on the BIF of three possible recessions differing in severity. We constructed our three recession scenarios by projecting how the distribution of banks across our different capital categories (each with its own probability of resolution) would change if all banks outside the Southwest uniformly experienced the same deterioration in their capital-to-asset ratios as the reductions surviving banks already have experienced in Texas and New England. We assume in each recession scenario that because of rising oil prices banking conditions will not deteriorate any further in three key Southwestern states whose economies are heavily dependent on oil production: Louisiana, Oklahoma, and Texas.

Specifically, in our worst-case scenario we assume that all non-Southwestern banks suffer the same 1.5 percentage point drop in their capital-to-asset ratios as the average surviving bank in Texas suffered between 1986 and 1988.[33] Our New England-style scenario assumes that all non-Southwestern banks suffer a 1.0 percentage point reduction in their capital-to-asset ratios, or about the same degree of equity deterioration as the average surviving banks in Connecticut and Massachusetts experienced between mid-1989 and mid-1990.[34] Finally, our mild-recession scenario assumes a 0.5 percentage point across-the-board deterioration in the capital-to-asset ratios of all non-Southwestern banks.[35]

Baseline Estimates Adjusted to Reflect the Recession's Effects

When combined with the resolution probabilities and cost ratios previously discussed, these various recession shocks produce additional failures and associated costs. Table 37 displays the results from these simulations, together with the earlier projections assuming no recession, for each of the combinations of failure probability and resolution cost assumptions discussed above. The difference in resolution costs attributable to any of these recessions can be easily calculated by subtracting the no-recession cost estimate for each combination of assumptions from the cost estimate for the appropriate recession scenario.

Thus, for example, Table 37 illustrates that the additional three-year resolution costs of a mild recession under the base-case CBO failure probabilities and resolution costs is estimated to be $1.1 billion above the

$12.2 billion of losses already embedded (on a probabilistic basis) in the banking system. Using the same assumptions but equalizing the probabilities of resolution for small and large banks, the additional cost of a mild recession is estimated at $2.5 billion (above the base estimate of $26.4 billion). Similar calculations that are reported in Table 38 reveal the ranges of incremental three-year resolution costs (in billions of dollars) across all of the assumption combinations.

Table 38 Estimated Three-Year Incremental Bank Failure Costs ($ Billions)		
	Base Case Assumptions	High
Mild Recession	1.1 - 3.5	2.5 - 12.2
"New England" Style	3.2 - 10.3	4.5 - 26.3
"Texas" Style	4.7 - 15.3	6.6 - 45.1

Source: Authors' calculations based upon FDIC data.

The bottom rows of Table 37 present the average three-year resolution costs over all assumption combinations for each of the recession scenarios, as well as the baseline, no-recession scenario. Given the significant uncertainties pertaining to which combination of assumptions will prove to be the most accurate indicators of actual future bank failure costs, we believe these averages represent the most useful set of failure cost projections for each of the recession outcomes.

In brief, the averages demonstrate that under so-called base-case assumptions—that is, assuming continued differentials between the probabilities of resolving large and small troubled banks—the average incremental cost of the three recessions are $2.3 billion (mild), $6.5 billion (New England), and $9.7 billion (Texas). If, however, the large and small troubled banks are resolved with the same frequency during the next three years—our high-cost assumption—then the corresponding average incremental three-year failure costs are $6.9 billion (mild), $15.1 billion (New England), and $26.3 billion (Texas).

Put another way, the average cost estimates in Table 37 suggest that under base-case assumptions, the total bank failure costs during the next three years will range between $17 billion and almost $27 billion, but under the high cost assumptions, will range between $36 billion and $62.5 billion.[36] To be sure, the foregoing cost estimates for the various recession scenarios could overstate the actual cost if the current recession truly has temporary effects and no banks engaged in any of the gambling-for-resurrection behavior that so many savings and loans displayed in the 1980s. However, if there is gambling for resurrection, then the delay in closing insolvent banks could produce resolution costs substantially larger than those just shown.

Indeed, there are two reasons why the above estimates are conservative even in the absence of forbearance. First, they assume that the various recessions affect all banks equally and uniformly. In fact, however, the weakest banks may very well suffer the greatest impacts because the same factors that have contributed to the current weakness—such as heavy asset concentrations in commercial real estate and HLT loans—are also likely to be sources of substantial additional deterioration in capital-to-asset ratios in any recession. Second, the reductions in capital-to-asset ratios that define our recession scenarios are drawn from the experiences of the average surviving banks in Texas and New England. This survivorship bias understates the actual degree of deterioration in capital-to-asset ratios in these states since the averages reported earlier do not reflect the substantial erosions of capital in banks in these states that have failed.

Conclusion: Effective Present-Value Insolvency for the BIF

Given the likely downward biases in our cost estimates, our judgment is that the BIF most likely faces bank resolution costs between the middle and high end of our cost ranges through 1993. Assuming, therefore, that the recession amounts to no more than what we labeled a mild recession, bank resolution costs through 1993 should range between $31 billion and $43 billion, a level that clearly exhausts the resources of the BIF given the January 1991 premium rate of 19.5 basis points. This would continue to be the case unless the government imposes a substantial—and, as we have indicated, what may prove to be a counterproductive—increase in the insurance premium.

We have distinguished between "technical" and "effective" insolvency for the BIF. As long as there is a federal guarantee of insured deposits and as long as the federal government can tax or print money, the BIF cannot technically be insolvent. The most important consequence of this fact is that widespread runs will not occur. But the BIF without adequate cash reserves can behave as if it were insolvent because it will not be able to close or reorganize all insolvent banks in a timely and cost effective manner. This effective insolvency creates moral hazard that manifests itself in forbearance.

Notes

1. This phenomena has been noted in numerous academic analyses of the savings and loan crisis (see, for example, Lawrence J. White, *The S&L Debacle: Public Policy Lessons for Bank and Thrift Regulation*, Oxford University Press, 1991; George J. Bentson and George G. Kaufman, "Understanding the Savings and Loan Debacle," *The Public Interest*, Spring 1990; and Edward J. Kane, *The S&L Insurance Mess: How Did It Happen?*, Urban Institute Press, 1988). In addition, each of us has separately made the same point (James R. Barth, *The Great Savings and Loan Debacle*, American Enterprise Institute, 1991; R. Dan Brumbaugh, *Thrifts Under Siege*, Ballinger, 1988; and Robert E. Litan, "Remedy for S&L's: Operation 'Clean Sweep,'" *Challenge*, November-December 1990).

2. General Accounting Office, *Bank Insurance Fund: Additional Reserves and Reforms Needed to Strengthen the Fund*, September 1990, p. 58.

3. R. Dan Brumbaugh, Jr., and Robert E. Litan, "The Banks Are Worse Off Than You Think," *Challenge*, January–February 1990.

4. Leo T. Crowley, Statement in Hearings Before the House Committee on Banking and Currency, *Banking Act of 1935*. A graphic illustration of the gap between call reports for weak banks and reality was provided by the recent failure of the National Bank of Washington. According to NBW's call report for as late as the first quarter of 1990, the bank had an equity capital-to-asset ratio of 5.0 percent. Yet by the time the bank failed and was sold by the FDIC to Riggs National Bank in August 1990, the FDIC was estimating that it would suffer potential losses of over $500 million, or nearly 30 percent of the bank's $1.8 billion in reported assets. (See Joel Glenn Brenner, "GAO: Closing of NBW Came Far Too Late," *Washington Post*, September 20, 1990, p. E1.)

5. One of the authors of this book (Litan) met with CBO's economists during the summer of 1990 to discuss the rough outlines of our estimating methodology, which CBO eventually adopted. The same methodology, as described in the text, is used here.

6. General Accounting Office, *Bank Insurance Fund: Additional Reserves and Reforms Needed to Strengthen the Fund*, September 1990, p. 30.

7. In early November 1990, Seidman commented that the "Texas banks were the best capitalized banks in the country, and that was clearly true about many of the New England banks." This experience, Seidman observed, "has revealed that high capital alone can't be the answer." (See Bill Atkinson, "Texas Bust Tied to Lack of Exams," *American Banker*, November 5, 1990, p. 2.)

8. See, for example, Joseph F. Sinkey, Jr., "Identifying 'Problem' Banks," *Journal of Money, Credit and Banking*, May 1978, pp. 184–193; Joseph F. Sinkey, Jr., *Problem and Failed Institutions in the Commercial Banking Industry*, JAI Press, 1979; and Coleen C. Pantalone and Marjorie B. Platt, "Predicting Bank Failure Since Deregulation," *New England Economic Review*, Federal Reserve Bank of Boston, July–August 1987, pp. 37–47.

9. We are also able to compare our results with those reported by CBO, since its analysis was quite similar.

10. CBO's analysis separated banks into three size categories: banks with less than $100 million in assets; those with assets between $100 million and $500 million; and those with assets above $500 million. Since CBO's findings for banks in the first two categories were very similar, we merged the banks in these categories together, analyzing all banks with under $500 million in assets together.

11. We do not report failure probabilities for banks reporting capital-to-asset ratios below 0 between 1986 and 1988. Although approximately 70 of these banks remained open for parts of these years, virtually all were eventually closed. Accordingly, we assign a 100 percent three-year resolution probability to these banks for purposes of projecting the government's future bank failure liabilities.

12. It is conceivable that large banks have been resolved less frequently (given their capital ratios) because their call reports tend to provide more

reliable indications of their financial health, however. If anything, the converse is more likely to be true. During the 1980s, the largest banks made the heaviest commitment to loans to developing countries and yet for much of the decade did not recognize, as was obvious to virtually everyone else, that those loans were worth far less than the amounts stated on the banks' balance sheets.

13. The lost estimates are shown in Appendix F of "Banks in Turmoil."

14. See James R. Barth, *The Great Savings and Loan Debacle*, American Enterprise Institute, 1991.

15. This result also is implied in John F. Bovenzi and Arthur J. Murton, "Resolution Costs and Bank Failures," *FDIC Banking Review*, Fall 1988.

16. Depicted in Appendix G of "Banks in Turmoil."

17. The failure probabilities calculated by CBO cover a 3.5-year time frame, so we multiplied them by a factor of 6/7 to put them on a 3-year basis. In addition, the CBO failure probabilities shown in Table 24 for banks below $500 million in assets represents a weighted average of CBO's probabilities for banks in its two lowest-size categories.

18. The CBO failure probabilities shown in the table are based on the assets of failed banks as a percentage of total assets for all banks in the relevant capital-to-ratio categories. In contrast, the rest of the probabilities shown in the table refer to the number of failed banks as a percentage of all banks in these categories.

19. Described in Appendix H of "Banks in Turmoil."

20. Again, we report the resolution cost ratios used by CBO for banks under $500 million as the weighted average of the ratios in CBO's two lowest-size categories.

21. One weakly capitalized savings bank, Goldome Savings Bank of New York with over $10 billion in assets, accounts for almost all of the difference in reported assets for the 0–1.5 percent capital-to-asset category. The fact that the FDIC's figures in Table 26 for the 3–6 percent capital-to-asset category are somewhat higher than those for Ferguson is probably due to differences in the ways in which the categories were defined (in particular, whether the category includes banks with capital-to-asset ratios equal to 3 or 6 percent).

22. The three-year figure for CBO's losses is 75 percent of the four-year loss estimate of $20.8 billion provided in Robert Reischauer, Testimony before the House Committee on Banking, Currency, and Housing, September 12, 1990. OMB's implicit estimate for three-year costs which

begin in fiscal year 1991 is $1 billion higher than CBO's, reflecting the higher net operating losses that OMB projects for FDIC during this period. Our $12.2 billion three-year loss projection using CBO failure probabilities and resolution costs is made on the basis of June 30, 1990 data whereas the actual CBO three-year loss projection of approximately $15 billion is based on December 31, 1989 data. As noted in the introduction, both OMB and CBO reported likely future failure costs very close to ours shortly after we presented our congressional report.

23. This calculation assumes that currently insolvent banks will be resolved and that the banks reporting capital-to-asset ratios between 0 and 1.5 percent will be resolved with the probabilities shown in Tables 20 and 21.

24. The CAMEL acronym stands for capital adequacy; asset quality; management; earnings; and liquidity. All banks are rated on a 1 to 5 scale (the best earning a "1" and the worst meriting a "5") based on each of these factors. The average score over all five factors is the bank's composite CAMEL rating.

25. We believe there is a simple reason why the failure probabilities calculated from the problem bank designations for the small and large banks shown in Table 30 are roughly comparable, whereas those based on capital-to-asset ratios are not. The size cutoff for problem banks reported by the FDIC as shown in Table 30 is $300 million in deposits, whereas the size distinction for the banks in our analysis in Tables 20 and 21 is somewhat larger, $500 million in assets. Since relatively few banks over $500 million in assets have failed, the FDIC's "large" problem bank category undoubtedly includes many failed banks between the $300 million deposit and $500 million asset thresholds, banks that we believe have been resolved at roughly the same rate as banks below the $300 million deposit cutoff for problem banks.

26. Additional data provided by the FDIC on problem banks in the 1980s are presented in the Appendix.

27. The problem-bank breakdowns were provided by the FDIC.

28. According to the GAO and the FDIC, total insured bank deposits will hit $2795 billion in 1995. A 1.25 percent ratio of BIF reserves to that level of insured deposits translates into a reserve level of $35 billion.

29. In addition, the FDIC had net receivables at mid-year 1990 of $7.3 billion. This is a book-value figure, however; it is not clear if the FDIC could realize this same amount in the market place. (We suspect not.)

30. General Accounting Office, *Bank Insurance Fund: Additional Reserves and Reforms Needed to Strengthen the Fund*, September 1990, pp. 111–12.

31. Barbara Rehm, "New Pressure on FDIC Fund, Bank Capital," *American Banker*, December 11, 1990, p. 1.

32. As part of the budget agreement package enacted in the fall of 1990, the FDIC was given the authority to borrow up to nine times its reserves from the Treasury for *working capital* purposes only. While this new authority could ease the BIF's cash flow problems in the short run, it does not remove the need for additional *permanent financing* under many of our estimated scenarios, as discussed further below. Indeed, if we are correct that the BIF's reserves will continue to dwindle, then this working capital borrowing authority also will diminish in scope.

33. Actually, according to *Bank Source*, the average capital-to-asset ratio of Texas banks during this period dropped from 6.33 percent to 4.87 percent, or by 1.46 percentage points (which we rounded to 1.5 percent).

34. According to *Bank Source*, the average Connecticut bank experienced a 1.23 percentage point drop in its capital-to-asset ratio during this period; the average Massachusetts bank a reduction of 0.86 percentage points. The simple average reduction for the two states combined was 1.05 percentage points.

35. Of course, as the economy weakens, banks in New England will probably deteriorate even further; indeed it is possible that, measured by the decline in their average capital-to-asset ratios, these banks will suffer as badly as Texas banks did from 1986 through 1988. However, the "New England-style" recession we simulate here reflects only the average deterioration in the capital-to-asset ratios of New England banks that occurred through the second quarter of 1990.

36. David Cates, a well-respected bank analyst, recently has estimated that a severe recession would lead to $40 billion in bank failure costs, using a different methodology from the one described above. Interestingly, as shown in Table 37, the midpoint of our cost range for a Texas-style recession, averaged over all assumption combinations, is $45 billion, a figure quite close to his estimate. (See Brett Duval Fromson, "Will the FDIC Run Out Of Money?" *Fortune*, October 8, 1990, pp. 119–27.)

FIVE

———————

Recapitalizing the Bank Insurance Fund

Charting a Course Between "Type 1" and "Type 2" Errors

In an atmosphere of as much uncertainty as surrounds the BIF's operational solvency, economic policy inevitably charts a course between what statisticians call "type 1" and "type 2" errors. It either reflects a course on which, if errors result, costs are higher than expected or it reflects a course on which, if errors result, costs are lower than expected. Throughout the entire savings and loan debacle, the former course has been chosen at every turn. The denial, understatement, and forbearance amply described in this book about the banking crisis indicate that the same mistakes are being made in the banking crisis. The financing recommendations that we make strongly urge a course that would entail a more rigorous evaluation of deteriorated banks, more realistic estimates of the BIF's obligations, and more rigorous estimates of the banking industry's ability to fund further recapitalization of the BIF than government officials have provided. We believe that is the low-cost approach.

Officials versus Some Experts: Whom to Believe?

Throughout the debate about the recapitalization of the FSLIC and now in the debate about recapitalizing the BIF, official estimates have consistently underestimated the costs of resolving failed institutions and overestimated BIF resources. Again, in a replay of the FSLIC crisis, independent analysts have provided their own higher and thus far more accurate estimates of costs. Notwithstanding important similarities between the official behavior in the savings and loan crisis and the banking crisis, and despite the relative accuracy of independent cost estimates in the savings and loan crisis, significant credibility is still accorded official estimates. The reaction of most taxpayers who have one is probably a sense of ambiguity, unease, and doubt about official estimates.

When we use the term "official" we mean the FDIC, and before it the Federal Home Loan Bank Board (FHLBB), the FSLIC, and the Office of Thrift Supervision (OTS). But we also mean Congress and the Administration. Congress and the Administration have long been well enough informed about the incentive of underfunded deposit-insurance agencies to understate the costs of closing insolvent savings and loans and banks that they should have developed their own far more comprehensive and direct funding plan. Yet, thus far they have not done so.[1] For taxpayers, this inaction combined with the debate among the deposit-insurance agencies and experts has added to the ambiguity.

The combination of mind-numbing technicalities with apparently remote analogies to the savings and loan debacle is another impediment to gaining the appropriate perspective. In 1985 two of us (Barth and Brumbaugh) published for the first time that the FSLIC was insolvent.[2] We multiplied the FSLIC's present-value cost to close insolvent savings and loans as a percentage of total assets times the total assets of open savings and loans reporting insolvency. Our view was that the difference between the FSLIC's reserves at the time, approximately $6 billion, and the $15.8 billion present-value cost of closure that we had estimated was needed immediately to close all reporting insolvent savings and loans, represented FSLIC's insolvency.

The official response that developed emphasized the ability of the FSLIC to add to its reserves primarily through future premium income. In congressional testimony in March of 1986, the FHLBB Chairman said that expenditures in "the $16 billion range" could be needed but that "this does not imply that FSLIC needs $16 billion immediately. Rather, the FSLIC will likely resolve all its known cases over the next three years."[3] The Chairman reassured the Congress that future FSLIC income could cover any needed expenditures.

More recently, the pattern has been repeated for banks. When two of us (Brumbaugh and Litan) in August 1988 applied a variation of the method just described to the banking industry and reported that the BIF was significantly overstating its reserves, FDIC officials denied and criticized our findings. When asked about critics who said the FDIC was overestimating the Bank Insurance Fund, the Chairman of the FDIC said, "I don't find any evidence that supports their view that we are somehow not looking realistically at the situation. (Academics) lean towards finding news. These economists predict in order to make astrologers look good."[4]

The Big Difference Between the Savings and Loan Debacle and the Banks

It is easy to see that the recitation of failure cost numbers can become numbing even to experts let alone taxpayers and that debates harking backward could seem like irrelevant history. Yet, the debate today about the recapitalization of the BIF is almost identical to the debate surrounding the recapitalization of the FSLIC. It centers on the "size of the problem": how many banks are insolvent and what will it cost to close them, and when. That is also the center of the debate out of which radiate issues of regulatory forbearance, excessive risk-taking by banks, the ability of examination and supervision staffs to limit excessive risk-taking, and ultimately whether the present-value cost to close insolvent banks will grow. Thus, the nature of the BIF's recapitalization can significantly affect many other important issues that will influence the future of banking.

There is, however, an important difference between the savings and loan debate and the bank debate that makes the banking debate even more difficult to resolve. In the savings and loan case, there were a large number of savings and loans reporting insolvency for long periods.[5] In the bank case, as shown in Chapter 2, there is a significant number of banks with an extraordinarily large volume of assets that have been reporting low, but not negative, capital for a long time. Among experts it is well known that banks in this condition use accounting techniques to bolster their reported capital over its market value. Yet, in the absence of official reports of insolvency an additional degree of uncertainty exists.

Even with reported insolvency in the savings and loan debacle, the government was reluctant to raise adequate funds promptly to close those savings and loans reporting insolvency. We can be certain that the government will be even more reluctant to act in the absence of reported insolvency. The government has actually made it more difficult to perceive and act on insolvency because it has created a proliferation of sometimes contradictory capital standards.

In the savings and loan crisis, there were until recently essentially three measures of reported capital: RAP capital based on Regulatory Accounting Principles; GAAP capital; and tangible capital based on removing goodwill and other intangibles from GAAP capital. Only tangible capital ever showed any statistically significant relationship to a market value measure of capital.[6]

In the banking crisis, there is reported equity capital based essentially on GAAP, Tier 1 and Tier 2 regulatory adjustments, tangible capital, and (more recently) risk-based capital with phased in minimum standards. As a result, for example, analysts in mid-1991 cited with worry Citicorp's tangible capital of 3 percent and the bank responded that its capital was really closer to 8 percent, apparently calculated by the risk-based standard.

It is clearly in the self-interest of poorly capitalized banks to have a proliferation of these kinds of accounting calculations of capital. It allows the banks to assert that they are adequately capitalized despite strong indications to the contrary. This thwarts the ability or willingness of the government to take prompt corrective action against a bank when reliable indicators of significant trouble emerge. That the government would tolerate this may seem counterintuitive but there is a culprit—the BIF's moral hazard. The economic self-interest of a cash-deficient BIF is, like the FHLBB and the FSLIC before it, to take comfort in capital calculations that obscure deterioration and make the public perception of the problem more ambiguous. This approach buys the fund time and the opportunity to benefit from an unexpected economic bonanza.

It also demonstrates that once moral hazard creeps into the deposit-insurance system, the economic interests of taxpayers and the deposit insurer diverge, and the interest of the deposit insurer moves toward that of deteriorated insured depositories.

How Much Is Needed and From Where Should it Come?

As Chapter 4 suggests, the BIF has insufficient cash to close or reorganize insolvent institutions promptly, and the issue has now become how much more money should the BIF have and from where should the money come. The banking industry itself or taxpayers through general appropriations are essentially the only sources of funds. Economic efficiency would appear to dictate pinning the cost on banks, which after all, have reported book-value capital of over $200 billion at year-end 1990. At some point, higher bank contributions could be self-defeating.

The CBO reportedly has projected that a deposit-insurance premium of 43 basis points would be required to enable the BIF to meet FIRREA's target ratio of 1.25 percent of BIF resources to insured deposits by 1995. In addition, it is reported that the CBO projected that a premium increase of this magnitude could push another forty banks into insolvency although how much added cost these additional insolvencies would impose on the BIF is not known.[7]

Calculating What the Banks May Be Able to Afford

Precise estimates of the added bank failure costs that may be attributable to the various proposals for greater bank contributions—a premium increase, a required capital infusion, or a borrowing to be paid back by the banks—are impossible. We present the following illustrative calculations, however, in an attempt to find some quantitative boundary.

Our analysis assumes that any further increase in bank-insurance premiums would be fully absorbed by most banks rather than passed on to customers. Although such an assumption is extreme for smaller banks with customers who, in practice, have limited options for depositing or borrowing funds, we believe it is quite realistic for larger banks, which rely on depositors and borrowers that are highly rate-sensitive.[8] Further, we assume that the net after-tax effect of any premium increase would be reduced by 35 percent, the marginal corporate tax rate.

A Modest Additional Increase in the Premium or a One Percent Capital Infusion

Based upon these assumptions, consider first the effect of another 10 basis point increase in the insurance premium that would raise the rate from the 19.5 basis point level scheduled for January 1, 1991 to 29.5 basis points. Assuming no increase in bank failure costs, such an increase would raise BIF revenues by approximately $8 billion over a three-year period. On a present-value basis, assuming a 10 percent discount rate and a 5 percent growth rate in deposits, such a premium increase would provide roughly $50 billion in additional revenues to the fund.[9]

Compared to the 15 basis point premium level as of June 30, 1990, the date used for our cost analysis, another 10 basis point increase in the rate would represent a total increase of almost 15 basis points. On an after-tax basis, this would translate into 10 basis points on assessable deposits, and approximately 7.5 basis points on assets (since assessable deposits fund about 75 percent of the banking industry's assets). Sustained in perpetuity and discounted at a 13 percent rate (roughly the average post-tax rate of return in the corporate sector in the 1980s), such a premium increase has the equivalent present-value effect of reducing the average bank capital-to-asset ratio by the equivalent of 58 basis points (7.5/.13).

This reduction in capital is a little more than the average 50 basis point decline in the average bank capital-to-asset ratio that we simulated in our mild recession scenario, which we estimate to cost an additional $2.3 to $6.9 billion in Table 30. On this basis, therefore, a 10 basis point premium increase would impose higher bank failure costs of $2.7 to $8 billion, on roughly a present-value basis, compared to the present-value gains of additional revenue of about $50 billion.

A required capital infusion of 1 percent of bank deposits would have almost the same effect. On an after-tax basis, such a requirement would lower the capital-to-asset ratio by 65 basis points on assessable deposits, or about 50 basis points on assets. Using the figures just presented, this implies an approximate present-value cost of higher failures of $2.3 to $6.9 billion.

A premium increase of 20 basis points—or almost 25 basis points above the 15 basis point rate in mid-1990—would have a larger effect, although it would produce greater revenue gains: approximately $16 billion over three years and $100 billion on a present-value basis. On an after-tax basis, such an increase would translate to almost 16 basis points on assessable deposits, or roughly 12 basis points on assets. Discounted at a 13 percent rate, this would reduce average bank capital-to-asset ratios by almost a full percentage point, or the same reduction we simulate in our New England recession scenario, producing higher bank failure costs of $6.5 to $15.1 billion on roughly a present-value basis.

The results suggest it is doubtful that the added bank failure costs resulting from any of the premium increases simulated, including the 1 percent of deposit capital infusion, would come anywhere close to offsetting the added revenue the BIF would obtain. These calculations, however, do not account for any additional risks that banks generally might take in an effort to compensate for the reduction in their after-tax income induced by a premium increase. Regardless of whether or not banks would take higher risks, they would be placed at a greater ongoing competitive disadvantage as the result of the higher premiums. Thus the possibility of higher failures exists both through greater risk-taking and as the result of higher costs in an increasingly competitive environment.

Meeting Higher Capital Requirements While Paying Higher Premiums

Making the banking industry shoulder the full burden of any higher bank failure costs through higher premiums would make it that much more difficult for banks to meet the new capital standards recently implemented by the regulators, especially in view of the evidence already noted that many banks currently fail to meet the regulatory targets. Under these circumstances, these banks may choose to shrink their assets rather than attempt to raise capital or to cut dividends (discussed in Chapter 6).

But by shrinking their assets, these banks would be further curtailing the availability of credit. The negative macroeconomic effects from credit contraction could outweigh any modest boost to BIF resources that the higher premiums might provide. Even without these macroeconomic feedback effects, to the extent a higher premium rate would induce the banking industry as a whole to shrink, it would reduce any gains the BIF might expect in its total premium income from a higher premium rate.

Indeed, Leo Crowley expressed sentiments over five decades ago that would support this argument. While acknowledging that banks should pay "their fair share" of the FDIC's bank failure costs, Crowley noted that banking is no longer merely a private business proposition. The stability of the banking system affects the economic prosperity of the country. For this reason, Crowley concluded that a "contribution from other sources to help build our [the FDIC's] reserves might be considered."[10]

All this said, there also is a powerful countervailing reason, at least at this point, for assessing the full cost of bank failures on banks themselves. Unlike the savings and loan crisis that has produced costs beyond the abilities of healthy institutions to pay for the necessary cleanup, the banking industry is reporting more than enough capital to absorb substantial additional failure costs in the short run. As we noted in Chapter 4, the average three-year cost for potential bank failures, even in the worst of the recessions we simulated, was $63 billion, an amount far below the $216 billion in book-value capital that had been invested in the banking industry by end of second quarter, 1990. Even assuming a substantially lower amount of aggregate bank capital, measured at market prices for assets and liabilities, the banking industry almost certainly has the wherewithal to deal with at least moderately larger bank failure costs in the years immediately ahead.

To be sure, higher bank insurance premiums will cut into existing bank capital and make it even more difficult for banks to raise even more. But as we discuss in Chapter 6, to the extent banks remain reluctant or are unable to go to the equity markets, they should bolster or preserve capital by cutting, or even eliminating, shareholder dividends. Why should taxpayers pay when shareholders of many banks have yet to be hit fully first? When all is said and done, however, it is hard to be completely sanguine about raising bank premiums further because it is impossible to calculate the effects of increasing competition and future instability of banks to meet the competition due to regulatory restraints.

When Does it Become Counterproductive to Tax Banks?

There is a limit beyond which it would be unproductive to continue taxing the banks. To a rough first approximation, the core earning power of the banking industry assuming no extraordinary loan losses (clearly a major assumption) is about $25 billion annually. At 23 basis points, the premium raises about $6 billion in total revenue. Clearly, a doubling or a tripling of the premium would impose substantial additional costs on the industry in relation to its annual income. Accordingly, if future bank failure costs reach or exceed the upper ranges of some of our failure probability/resolution cost scenarios, it would be unreasonable to make healthy banks bear the whole cost of bank failures in an increasingly competitive financial marketplace.

Timing of Bank Failures and Who Should Pay

The critical problem that both banks and federal policymakers face, however, is the timing and uncertainty of future bank failure costs. As our previous discussion indicates, in a mild recession the BIF may need an additional $10 billion over the next three years, perhaps more beyond then (which our estimates did not take into account). We would feel far more comfortable if the BIF had access to substantially greater resources in order to protect itself against reasonable worst-case outcomes. Moreover, we believe that the BIF needs the funds immediately in order to avoid the typical problems associated with forbearance.

There are basically three options for bolstering BIF resources that rely exclusively on the banking industry to fund the additional costs. The first would continue to raise annual premiums. The second would require the banks to make a large capital contribution to the BIF, such as the 1 percent of insured deposits capital contribution required of credit unions insured by the National Credit Union Share Insurance Fund (and recently suggested for banks by Representative Frank Annunzio, Chairman of the House Subcommittee on Financial Institutions Supervision, Regulation, and Insurance.[11] Given the current $2.5 trillion in assessable deposits in the banking industry, a 1 percent deposit charge would raise approximately $25 billion. The third option would substantially increase the BIF's line of credit with the U.S. Treasury Department, to perhaps something like $70 billion from the current $5 billion. This is in essence the option proposed, subsequent to our Congressional testimony, by the Administration in 1991.

Of these three options, two of us (Barth and Litan) favor (2) and (3) over (1), since the latter option cannot provide the BIF immediately and with certainty sufficient resources to handle any of our high-cost recession scenarios. Yet, that is precisely what the BIF currently needs to enable the FDIC to take prompt corrective action against inadequately capitalized institutions.

We all believe that the line of credit option has an important advantage not shared by the one-time capital infusion. If the BIF's three-year resolution costs balloon upward of $70 billion, even another $25 billion infusion from the banks would not provide the BIF with sufficient resources to handle bank insolvencies on a timely basis. A larger line-of-credit window at the U.S. Treasury Department would cure this problem.

Of course, if the ultimate borrowing were to grow too large, the banking industry cannot be expected to repay all of it. At a $25 billion level, however, Barth and Litan believe that the burden can be borne by banks (without question more easily if the banking laws also were modified, as discussed in Chapter 6). For example, repayment of $25 billion at an 8.5 percent interest rate over ten years would obligate the industry to pay approximately $3.6 billion per year. At current levels of assessable deposits, such an amount could be amortized with a premium increase of approximately 14 basis points (above the planned 19.5), an increase that would decline over time as the assessable deposit base increases.[12]

Brumbaugh believes the costs of additional bank failures will be larger than those we have estimated and discussed above because, in his opinion, substantial market-value insolvency is obscured by book-value accounting. In addition, he fears that any higher premium would have a significantly adverse effect on healthy banks. He also considers it inequitable to tax healthy banks further. Accordingly, Brumbaugh favors an infusion of funds into the BIF from general revenues. But if that option is rejected by Congress, he supports the approach advocated by Barth and Litan, since in his opinion, the dangers of leaving insolvent institutions open is greater than the costs to the banking industry from higher deposit-insurance premiums or other indirect costs.

Notes

1. See Thomas Romer and Barry R. Weingast, "Political Foundations of the Thrift Debacle," in *The Reform of Federal Deposit Insurance: Disciplining the Government and Protecting Taxpayers*, James R. Barth and R. Dan Brumbaugh, Jr., eds., HarperBusiness, New York, New York, 1992.

2. James R. Barth, R. Dan Brumbaugh, Jr., Daniel Sauerhaft, and George H.K. Wang, "Insolvency and Risk-Taking in the Thrift Industry: Implications for the Future," *Contemporary Policy Issues*, Volume III, Number 8, Fall 1985.

3. Statement of Edwin J. Gray, Chairman, Federal Home Loan Bank Board, before the Committee on Banking, Housing and Urban Affairs, United States Senate, March 13, 1986.

4. Paul Starobin, "Will the Banks Be Next?" *National Journal*, December 30, 1989, pp. 3090–3095.

5. James R. Barth, *The Great Savings and Loan Debacle*, American Enterprise Institute, Washington, D.C., 1991. For more detailed information about the costs of resolving failed banks, savings and loans, and credit unions, as well as the delay in closing them, see James R. Barth, Testimony on Deposit Insurance Reform, Before the Senate Committee on Banking, Housing, and Urban Affairs, March 12, 1991.

6. See, for example, James R. Barth, R. Dan Brumbaugh, Jr., and Daniel Sauerhaft, "Failure Costs of Government-Regulated Financial Firms: The Case of Thrift Institutions," Federal Home Loan Bank Board Working Paper 123, October 1986.

7. Debra Cope and Robert M. Garrson, "Study Raises Doubts Fees Can Revive FDIC," *American Banker*, September 26, 1990, p. 1.

8. In particular, most large banks rely heavily on large uninsured deposit accounts for funding, or customers that would be sensitive to placing their funds in foreign banks or in the securities markets (especially money market funds) if the domestic banks attempted to offset any premium increase with lower deposit rates. Likewise, many borrowers, actual or potential, from large banks have alternative sources of funds—trade credit, loans from major finance companies and the securities market. Indeed, even consumer borrowers from the larger banks can easily obtain credit card loans directly from their retailers. The large banks, therefore, would risk losing lending business from these borrowers if they attempted to increase lending rates to offset any premium increase. Both of these effects apply as well to smaller banks, but probably to a lesser degree.

9. Calculated as the additional $2.5 billion gained in the first year divided by (0.10–0.05).

10. Leo T. Crowley, Statement in Hearings before the House Committee on Banking and Currency, *Banking Act of 1935*, pp. 10 and 49.

11. As with the NCUA contribution, banks under this option would be permitted to carry as much of the full 1 percent charge on their books as an asset (and thus as capital) as the FDIC has not drawn on to use for bank resolutions. For a description of the credit-union system, see James R. Barth and R. Dan Brumbaugh, Jr., "The Credit Union Industry: Financial Condition and Policy Issues," California Credit Union League, February 1991.

12. There is a model for a post-borrowing assessment. Recently, several earthquake insurance proposals have been introduced in the Congress that, among other things, would enable the property-casualty insurance industry to borrow from the U.S. Treasury Department in the event of a catastrophic earthquake to meet liquidity needs. A critical feature of most of these proposals is that they would require the industry thereafter to repay the Treasury. The situation facing the banking industry in the event of a substantial increase in bank failure costs would be analogous to a financial earthquake.

SIX

Reducing the Taxpayer's Risk From Deposit Insurance

As Chapters 2 and 3 fully demonstrate, the current condition of an important segment of the nation's commercial banks is dismal and if the *status quo* is maintained the prospect for the future is dim. Unless something is done soon to ameliorate this situation, the BIF will face excessively high costs of picking up the pieces of a significant number of bank failures and the taxpayers' risk exposure will increase.

Preventing an Explosion of Future Deposit-Insurance Costs

Federal policymakers have three main options for preventing an explosion of deposit-insurance costs in the future. First, they can raise bank capital standards even higher, as Federal Reserve Board Chairman Alan Greenspan has suggested.[1] The rationale is straightforward: if banks must, for whatever reasons, accept more risks, then they should have more capital to stand between them and the BIF.

The long-run deterioration in bank capital ratios certainly lends support to this view. Figure 5 illustrates that despite the apparent recent upward trend in the 1980s, the capital-to-asset ratio in the banking industry in

1990 (6.5 percent) was roughly half the level in 1934 during the Great Depression. As we have stressed throughout this report and as documented in Appendix Table A-5, the largest banks have the weakest capital ratios. Indeed, the average reported capital-to-asset ratio of the five largest banks stood at just 4.3 percent at year-end 1989. By comparison, the average capital-to-asset ratio of mutual savings banks was 7.1 percent, and for credit unions, 7.6 percent.

The dramatic decline in the capital-to-asset ratio indicates that deposit insurance has replaced capital as the depositor's major source of protection against banking losses. Moreover, the reported (nonrisk-weighted) capital-to-asset ratios overstate the degree of capital protection because many of the large banks have substantial off-balance-sheet commitments, as shown in Table 17.

Second, if banks are being driven to make riskier loans, then policymakers can prevent further risks to the deposit insurance fund by narrowing the list of eligible assets. One of us has advanced such a "narrow banking" proposal in the context of broader powers—that is, as the *quid pro quo* solely for those banking organizations that want to enter new nonbanking businesses or affiliate with firms so engaged.[2] Such enterprises would therefore be required to extend their risky, nonmarketable loans through nonbank affiliates, funded by uninsured debt and equity (as are finance companies today). Others, including former FDIC Chairman William Seidman, have discussed narrowing bank powers for all banks (in particular, prohibiting them from commercial real estate lending), whether or not they are affiliated with a broader range of activities.[3]

The third option to prevent future increases in desposit insurance costs is to keep the existing capital standards and bank powers but to provide a much more automatic system of regulatory intervention, ideally supplemented with market-like devices to impel regulators to act in a timely fashion to prevent weak banks from taking excessive risks. Below, we discuss and endorse such a plan.

The Problem with Higher Capital Requirements

There are several problems with simply increasing the capital requirement. For starters, there is no well-established basis for identifying the optimal capital standard. Although it is well-established in the literature that banks with thin capital margins have incentives to engage in excessive risk-taking at the expense of the federal insurance fund (since the owners do not bear all of the downside losses), it is not clear exactly how high the capital requirement needs to be set to balance the dangers of this moral hazard with the social costs of an excessively high standard.

In addition, there are special risks with raising capital standards still higher at this particular time when many banks cannot even meet the current standard (when fully phased-in in January 1993). There is anecdotal evidence that many banks are not currently lending to some credit-worthy customers.[4] Further increases in bank capital standards now could thus deepen the economic downturn that began in 1990 and prolong the recovery.

Though the need for capital is indisputable, the ability of many banks to raise capital relative to assets by any method but shrinkage is doubtful. In order to raise capital, a bank must demonstrate to investors that it can generate an expected present-value cash flow that will provide the investors with what they consider an acceptable risk-adjusted rate of return on their investment. The current incomes being reported by some of the largest banks in the country most desperately seeking capital provide rates of return on equity that are at unacceptably low levels. If these income flows are expected by investors to be permanent, then capital infusions are unlikely at banks with those income flows. Even improved income flows, moreover, may be inadequate to generate the required returns.

Finally, there would be less need for higher capital requirements if an effective system of more automatic, early regulatory intervention were implemented. As we have stressed throughout this report, capital measured by historical cost accounting (GAAP) can be seriously misleading. Accordingly, a GAAP-based capital requirement should be viewed as a mechanism providing the regulators with some margin for error in deciding when to close banks that are economically insolvent—or the only measurement standard of any relevance to the federal deposit insurer.

As we outline below, there are methods of supplementing GAAP accounting with other market indicators of actual or potential economic insolvency—specifically, the market for subordinated debt and deposit reinsurance—that can trigger automatic regulatory intervention without having to implement fully market-value accounting. If these steps are taken, then the market—rather than regulators—would decide whether banks need more capital.

In the end, whichever one or whatever combination of these options for containing risk in the banking system—more capital, narrow banking, or early intervention—is taken, the industry will continue to shrink relative to other types of financial institutions. As we have discussed, this trend has been a feature of the financial marketplace for at least the past four decades and almost certainly for the foreseeable future. Policymakers should not attempt to prop-up unhealthy banks against these market forces as was done with unhealthy savings and loans.

Indeed, if such action is taken in the banking industry, not only will the federal government face mounting losses for bank failures, but the economy will suffer from a severe misallocation of scarce investment capital. The major cost component of the savings and loan disaster is the $200 billion-plus dollars that were diverted toward the construction of now empty buildings and undeveloped real estate by open, unhealthy savings and loans. Clearly, these resources would have been far better used if they had been invested in productive plant and equipment. The past and future lending mistakes of banks have the same effect.

Discipline versus Opportunities

The foregoing discussion leads naturally into our recommending several proposals for reducing the federal government's potential deposit-insurance liabilities. The CBO recently has outlined many of the options in this area.[5] Each of us also has considered and proposed measures for reducing the government's deposit insurance costs.[6] And perhaps most important, in early 1991 the Bush Administration issued a comprehensive banking reform proposal that failed in 1991 but has been proposed again for congressional consideration in 1992. There are differences among us on the advantages and disadvantages of specific proposals in this area. Nevertheless, it is difficult to ignore the structural issues when discussing the BIF's current and projected future condition.

For the present purpose, we believe it is useful to classify reform suggestions into two categories: first, those that provide needed additional discipline against excessive risk-taking by the managers and owners of insured depositories that also put the federal government, as the deposit insurer, at risk; and second, those that provide banks with additional opportunities for enhancing profits and reducing costs that will help cure the long-term structural ills that threaten the continued viability of the United States banking industry, as it is presently configured.

Enhanced Discipline

Several suggestions would significantly enhance current discipline against excessive risk-taking, which has been substantially undermined in recent years by a combination of deposit insurance, the willingness of federal regulatory authorities to guarantee the deposits of even uninsured deposits (the so-called, but inappropriately named, "too-big-to-fail" doctrine), and regulatory forbearance.

Early Intervention

At the top of our list is a system of graduated, mandatory interventions by regulators, based on bank capital-to-asset ratios. Such an approach is embodied in the Administration's reform plan. In particular, under such a system, regulators would be required to suspend a bank's dividends if its capital ratio fell below some positive level and at a still lower, but positive level, to assume conservatorship over the institution. In addition, although we have strongly urged the FDIC to be provided with sufficient access to cash to implement a timely closure policy, in the event the FDIC is forced by a lack of cash to engage in regulatory forbearance, we also strongly urge that any bank otherwise meriting closure should have its dividends suspended, its growth limited, and conceivably its management significantly changed.

A recent example from the Bank of New England indicates the importance of early intervention in dividend policy. According to a GAO report, the dividends and management fees paid by the Bank of New England and two other subsidiary banks from their operating income to their holding company rose from $31 million in 1987 to $64 million in 1988, to $148 million in 1989.[7] The increasing upstream of income to the holding company, according to the report, was not questioned by federal regulators because the banks were still reporting income.

Our estimates presented in Chapter 2 indicated that the Bank of New England was insolvent by 1990. Ample evidence of distress was apparent long before 1990. Given the well-known use by deteriorated depositories of allowable accounting techniques, it is reasonable to conclude that reported income in the bank's last few years exceeded what would be considered true economic income. It is possible, indeed likely, that some of the dividends and fees which were paid to the Bank of New England holding company really came out of capital, if there was any in an economic sense, or from assets that would have otherwise been available to the FDIC.

Improved Financial Reporting

Timely intervention at any of the various points called for under any mandatory intervention scheme, however, depends on the accuracy of the financial data on which bank capital-to-asset ratios are computed. As we have noted, current GAAP accounting can significantly overstate the value of bank capital, especially for weak banks. In theory, market-value accounting (or "marked-to-market" accounting) eliminates this problem. However, a vigorous debate is now under way (for example, between Chairman of the Federal Reserve Board Alan Greenspan and Chairman of the Securities and Exchange Commission Richard Breeden) over the practical difficulties of valuing bank assets that are not readily traded and thus have no precise market value, as well as over the problems of valuing intangible bank assets such as franchise value (or, more generally, goodwill).[8] While we agree that bank accountants ultimately should aim toward adopting market-value principles for bank valuation, at the present time we also agree with those who charge that the practical problems with the technique render it difficult to replace current GAAP procedures.

Accordingly, we recommend that, until such time as market-value accounting is sufficiently well developed and accepted by the financial community and regulators to replace GAAP, regulators continue to use GAAP as the primary means for reporting banks' financial condition. However, at the same time, we believe that the investment community, depositors, regulators, and policymakers would be well served if banks were required to supplement their GAAP-based financial statements with statements resting more on market-oriented values. We understand that the Financial Accounting Standards Board (FASB) has made such a proposal and we believe it should be adopted.[9]

In essence, the debate over proper bank accounting standards boils down to when regulators should take various intervention measures. We believe it is possible to provide more automatic triggers of such actions without resolving this valuation debate.

The answer lies in introducing private market assessments of the condition of banks and then requiring regulators to use those assessments as the primary, if not exclusive, bases for taking such actions as suspending dividends or assuming conservatorships.

A Role for Subordinated Debt and Private Reinsurance

Two such methods are available, at least for larger institutions (those above, for example, $1 billion in assets): (1) requiring such banks to maintain some portion of their total capital in the form of subordinated debt, and (2) requiring the FDIC to obtain reinsurance from the private market on a small pro rata portion of its insurance risk for these banks.

Currently, banks are permitted to count subordinated debt toward their Tier 2 risk-adjusted capital standard. The first proposal would require that banks constantly maintain, perhaps on a quarterly basis, some fraction of Tier 2 capital as subordinated (uninsured) debt, with a maturity of at least one year. As numerous scholars have pointed out, unlike an equity capital requirement that banks can generally meet by continued earnings growth (rather than through new equity issues), a subordinated debt requirement, for at least the larger banks that are capable of accessing the debt market, would continually subject these banks to a market test. Regulators, in turn, could base their decisions to take various regulatory measures based on the spread between the interest rate on a bank's subordinated debt and Treasury securities of comparable maturity (the spread measuring the perceived riskiness of the bank). At the limit, if a bank could not sell its required issue of subordinated debt at any price, that would be a conclusive signal for regulators to place the bank in conservatorship (the regulators should perhaps also be required to do this if the interest rate spread on the subordinated debt exceeds a certain threshold, say 500 basis points).[10]

A mandatory reinsurance plan for the FDIC, such as the one proposed by Senator Alan Dixon (S. 3040), would accomplish the same objective. Briefly, Senator Dixon has proposed that the FDIC be required to obtain reinsurance on a small portion (10 percent) of its total risk in insuring the deposits of large banks, those with assets above $1 billion.[11] In principle, this plan would "kill two birds with one stone": it would both allow the private marketplace to set "risk-based" premiums and to determine when the regulators should close or place the bank in conservatorship.

There are competing advantages and disadvantages to the subordinated debt and mandatory reinsurance alternatives. The advantage of the mandatory reinsurance plan is that its market signals would be based on the collective decisions of actors whose principal business would consist of monitoring and assessing banks rather than on decisions by a diverse body of subordinated debtholders whose financial interests in the safety of banks generally would not be as strong. A mandatory reinsurance plan will only work, however, if sufficient capacity to provide that insurance is forthcoming to develop a competitive market, conditions that might not be met for some time. In addition, regulators would have to supervise and regulate the solvency of the reinsurers themselves. This degree of oversight would not be needed for a subordinated-debt requirement.

Since it is not clear at this point whether or how fast a competitive market in reinsurance would develop, we favor the immediate implementation of a subordinated debt requirement for large banks and a directive to the regulators that they monitor and supervise banks based on spreads between interest rates on bank subordinated debt and Treasury securities. We also believe that the FDIC ought to be encouraged to begin selling off portions of its risk so that it can get a private reinsurance market off the ground. Eventually, this market may mature sufficiently to serve as another source of automatic direction for regulatory intervention.

Automatic Regulatory Intervention Is Essential

Regardless of the mechanism used for triggering regulatory action, such action must be made more automatic than it has been in the past. At a minimum, for example, regulators must become more aggressive about compelling banks to cut or suspend dividends when earnings drop and capital is weak. Table 39 lists the number of large banks (those with assets above $1 billion) that have reported negative income yet paid dividends on their common stock during the years 1986–1989.[12]

This summary indicates that sizable numbers of large banks losing money paid dividends in 1987 and 1989, years in which most large banks made major additions to their loan loss reserves. In addition, most of the larger banks that paid dividends yet lost money in the years 1986–1989 had capital-to-asset ratios below 6 percent, or the threshold above which bank failure rates seem to be quite small (see Tables 20 and 21).

The Comptroller of the Currency intends to implement by year-end 1991 a complicated new system for calculating when banks may not pay dividends. As we understand it, however, even under this new system banks that lose money will still be able to pay dividends without regulatory approval if they pass a minimum capital test and as long as the dividend does not exceed the combined retained earnings of the current and previous two years.[13] Moreover, even if it flunks these tests, the bank may pay dividends if it obtains permission from the regulators.

Table 39 Number of Unprofitable Banks Paying Dividends		
Year	Total Number	Number With Capital/Asset Less Than 6 Percent
1989	37	29
1988	12	9
1987	41	39
1986	9	7

Source: FDIC.

We believe a more restrictive dividend policy is in order, especially at this time when so many banks need to shore up their capital positions. In brief, we believe that any bank losing money in the current year should simply be prohibited from paying dividends, regardless of its capital-to-asset ratio. In addition, regulators should curtail or even suspend dividend payments by banks showing a profit but nevertheless with capital-to-asset ratios below some threshold level.

Enhancing Profit Opportunities

The Administration's 1991 deposit-insurance reform package also included so-called "structural reform" provisions, specifically the removal of current interstate restrictions on bank branching and holding company expansion, as well as significant modification of the Bank Holding Company Act to permit banks to engage in broader activities and to affiliate with a broader range of financial (if not commercial) enterprises. Without delving deeply into these two issues, we wish here to make several points.

Nationwide Operations Are a Must

First, there is an overwhelming consensus among academic experts who have studied the matter that banks, not just bank holding companies, need the ability to operate nationwide. There is virtually no other business in the United States that is so geographically restricted as the banking business. These restrictions must be removed if the overall health of the banking system is to improve.

At a minimum, allowing banks to branch nationwide would permit them to diversify their risks and thus reduce the deposit-insurance liabilities of the federal government. It is difficult to believe that nine of the top ten banks in Texas that failed during the 1980s would also have failed had they been part of larger nationwide operations. Similarly, had Continental Illinois been able to branch beyond the confines of Chicago and thus diversify its funding sources, it is at least conceivable that the deposit run that helped trigger the bank's collapse would not have happened, or if it did, would have had the same disastrous effects.

Geographic diversification also would accelerate the much needed consolidation of the banking industry and the shedding of excess capacity. As discussed above, structural economic forces have been calling for the shrinkage of the banking industry over time, relative to other types of financial intermediaries. The current geographic restrictions, however, frustrate this shrinkage, preventing banks in different parts of the country from consolidating their back and front offices to cut costs.

The only real justification for the existing geographic restrictions, if one ever existed, was to prevent banks from amassing excessive economic and political power. Today, however, this concern is an anachronism now that no U.S. bank ranks even among the top twenty largest banks in the world.

Wider Asset Powers and Bank Affiliations with Other Firms Are a Must Too

Second, we believe that banks should have wider asset powers and the ability to affiliate with other types of enterprises in order to permit them to realize so-called economies of scope in delivering combinations of services. We recognize that there is limited evidence of how significant these economies are. But perhaps the best evidence that they exist is now being provided by many major European banks, which in preparing for so-called EC 1992 already have acquired or affiliated with major European insurers and securities firms.

An even better example, we think, is the substantial proliferation of ownership of nondepository financial service firms by commercial businesses in the United States. Forays into financial services are well under way by the General Motors Corporation, Ford Motor Company (which owns a savings and loan), American Express Company, General Electric Company, American Telegraph and Telephone Company, International Business Machines Corporation, and Sears, Roebuck and Company (which also owns a savings and loan) to name just a few. At this time it is almost impossible to name a financial service that is not in some way being provided by a firm ultimately owned by a nonfinancial commercial business. The complete absence of any evidence whatsoever that these structures present anything but efficient provision of services indicates that prohibition of depository ownership by commercial firms is both inefficient and unlikely to prevail over time.

As Table A-10 in the Appendix shows, moreover, more than 21 percent of all commercial-bank assets in the United States were in foreign-controlled banks. As is well known, many foreign countries allow nonbank ownership of banks and a wide range of nonbank activities by banks. Moreover, many state banks already have substantial access to nonbank powers. State authorization of selected expanded activities for state-chartered banks is substantial. Many states, for example, allow state banks to engage in securities brokerage, general securities underwriting, real estate equity participation, real estate brokerage, real estate development, insurance underwriting, and insurance brokerage.[14] Many of these states also allow entry into the home state by out-of-state banks on either a nationwide or regional reciprocity basis, some with triggers in 1992 to a nationwide entry. Only two states have no interstate statutes.

At the same time, however, it is critical that the government not extend the safety net—deposit insurance and the Federal Reserve's discount window—to nonbank activities. The last thing the federal government needs now is to socialize even more private-sector risk.

We see three broad approaches for preventing this outcome: (1) constructing so-called legal "firewalls" between banks and their affiliates; (2) requiring banks that want to broaden their affiliations to have additional capital (beyond the level already required); and (3) limiting the investments of banks that affiliate with a wider range of enterprises to "safe" assets (government and private securities with well-developed secondary markets), or "narrow" or "safe" banking, an approach that two of the authors of this book (Brumbaugh and Litan) have endorsed.[15]

We have different views among ourselves as to which of these various approaches is most desirable. Without engaging in an extensive discussion of this issue at this point, we note that the question has been complicated by the troubled condition of many of the nation's largest banks, a theme that runs throughout this book. As we discuss immediately below, the strongest argument for allowing banks to affiliate with or be owned by nonbanking concerns may be that to do so would minimize the immediate or short-run costs to the BIF for resolving these troubled institutions. If this is true, then policymakers must weigh the long-run risks of allowing such affiliations—perhaps without some of the protections outlined above in order to attract nonbank capital to the banking industry—against any short-run savings to the BIF.

Dealing with the Big Troubled Banks

We conclude by addressing perhaps the most challenging, yet most important, policy issue presented by the current and prospective condition of the banking industry: what to do with the many, troubled large banks. Four options short of liquidation—an uninviting prospect that few endorse—are available for dealing with the problem.

Hope and Pray, or Forbearance

The first approach, and the one most likely to be implemented, is simply to hope that the largest banks are really (if barely) solvent and that the economic downturn that began in 1990 will be sufficiently short and mild as not to tip these institutions over the edge. To be sure, this so-called forbearance policy was pursued in the savings and loan industry with disastrous results. The big banks are not expanding wildly, with the regulators' permission, as did the savings and loans; to the contrary, many are shrinking. Thus, a case can be made that like the forbearance policy pursued in the early 1980s after the LDC debt crisis first emerged, forbearance this time around could permit the large banks time to recover.

The flaw in this line of argument, of course, is that although the big banks reported recovery since the 1980s, their financial data have hidden substantial loan losses that they have begun to recognize only recently. In addition, as we have stressed throughout this book, many of these institutions face still additional losses from their high-risk lending. Everything we know about the trends in the banking industry point to new forms of risk-taking in the years ahead in which some banks may begin engaging. In short, the forbearance option carries with it big, probably unacceptable, risks.

Suspend Dividends

At the time of our original report, many of the larger banks had failed to raise loan loss reserves to realistic levels—close to the current levels of nonperforming loans. If this had been done, many of these banks would have had extremely thin capital margins measured at book value. This, of course, is why the stock market was pricing the shares of these institutions at well below book value.

With such thin margins for error, many large banks should not be paying dividends. Although some large banks recently have cut their dividends, the regulators should go even further. The only argument against doing so is that such a step will unsettle the markets. But to refrain from suspending dividends while banks also refrain from issuing new stock to shore up their capital is to permit these institutions to gamble with Hail Mary passes in the hope of recovery. Those that don't have been attempting to sell off their crown jewels, leaving behind little earning power for the future. At the very least, it is better to suspend dividends instead.

More Continentals

A third option is to repeat what was done when Continental Illinois Bank failed in 1984, but on a much larger scale, by having the government inject capital (in the form of preferred stock) into the larger troubled banks on the condition that they change management, cut costs, and streamline their operations. Although this option theoretically could lower costs to the BIF if the banks receiving these capital infusions actually recovered, it raises a series of troublesome issues. First, it might not work. Although Continental Illinois improved after the FDIC purchased preferred stock in its holding company, the bank is now laden with substantial volumes of high-risk loans that pose future risks (see Tables 6 and 10). In short, the verdict is not yet in on the Continental rescue.

Second, it would be highly ironic if the United States were to move toward more state involvement in its banking sector in an age when many developing countries are either thinking about or actually moving (in the case of Mexico) in the other direction. One of the major reasons our government has urged the governments of other countries to privatize their banks is to entrust the market, rather than the government, with the critical credit decisions that banks make. Yet effective nationalizations of our major banks could put our government in precisely this position. Third, the government will develop an inherent conflict of interest if it both acquires major ownership interests in a number of important banks, while simultaneously regulating and supervising all banks.

Finally, we fear that heavy government involvement in the banking industry could siphon off the needed political momentum for reforming the nation's banking laws. We suspect that Congress would not be too hospitable to removing geographic and product-line restrictions that hamper banks if the government at the same time is seen as being forced by events to rescue the major banks.

Aggressive Merger Policy Coupled with Financial Reform

If suspending dividends paid by banks will not sufficiently rebuild their capital, then policymakers ought to be aggressively pushing the larger banks into mergers with healthier partners as the principal way of protecting the BIF and ultimately the taxpaying public. The problem with this approach, however, is that there are only a few healthy U.S. banks with sufficient capital that could purchase most or all of the major troubled banks. To be sure, regulators could push the U.S. banks into the hands of the foreign banks (mostly European) healthy enough to make these acquisitions, but we suspect that this is hardly a preferred outcome for a nation that once prided itself on its financial prowess.

One minimum step that would make things easier for the healthy potential U.S. bank acquirers would be to eliminate the outmoded restrictions on interstate branching, which prevent banks from diversifying their deposit and lending risks and from efficiently shedding excess capacity. With interstate branching, a major regional bank would find it less costly to purchase part or all of another troubled regional or money center bank. There would be no need for duplicate management at the bank and holding company levels and the combined bank would have a larger lending limit that would better enable it to compete for borrowers against much larger foreign institutions.

A more ambitious step would be to permit commercial and industrial companies to invest heavily in, or even to own, commercial banks, as we have already discussed, with appropriate safeguards to protect the deposit insurance fund (such as some form of narrow banking or higher capitalization requirement). To put it bluntly, if commercial enterprises could be interested in purchasing troubled banks, they might be able to save the BIF down the road from paying for a much more costly bank-to-bank merger, or even a liquidation.

There is little doubt that many commercial firms already heavily engaged in financial activities have the wherewithal to make substantial investments in major banks. Table 40 lists the book- and market-value capital held by some of the largest of these enterprises, as well as their liquid assets. Compare those figures to the book-value capital in the top 10 banks, shown in Table 41, which for reasons we have already indicated, overstate the economic net worth of these institutions (in many cases, by considerable margins).

Table 40
Equity Capital and Liquidity of Major Non-Bank Companies
Already Engaged in Financial Services
($ Billions)

Name of Company	Book Value Equity Capital December 31, 1989	Cash and Investment Securities December 31, 1989
American Telegraph and Telephone Co.	12.74	1.18
Ford Motor Co.	22.73	5.73
General Electric Co.	20.89	1.75
General Motors Corp.	34.98	5.17
International Business Machines Corp.	38.51	3.70
Sears, Roebuck and Co.	13.62	2.31

Source: Moody's.

In combination, Tables 40 and 41 illustrate that the capital of the largest banks not only pales in comparison to that of the commercial companies already engaged in financial services, but that the commercial enterprises have liquid assets that equal or exceed the total capital in many of the major banks.

It is not clear, of course, to what extent commercial enterprises would help rescue part, or all, of the major troubled banks if allowed to do so. In addition, as we discussed immediately above, the mixing of banking and commerce threatens to broaden the federal safety net to commercial activities if at least one of the three mechanisms listed there for walling off the bank from its affiliates is not adopted. Nevertheless, given the serious situation in which many large banks do find themselves, coupled

Table 41 Equity Capital of 10 Largest U.S. Banks		
Name of Institution	Assets ($ Billions) June 30, 1990	Book Value-to- Equity Capital Ratio June 30, 1990
Citibank	164.20	7.91
Bank of America	90.68	4.66
The Chase Manhattan Bank	81.14	3.73
Morgan Guaranty Trust Co.	71.96	3.24
Security Pacific National Bank	64.13	2.73
Bankers Trust Co.	60.96	1.94
Manufacturers Hanover Trust Co.	56.49	2.63
Wells Fargo Bank	48.65	3.11
Chemical Bank	48.39	2.22
The Bank of New York	45.73	2.12

Source: *Bank Source*, W. C. Ferguson and Co.

with the risks they pose to the BIF, it is long past the appropriate time for policymakers to begin seriously considering whether and to what extent to permit entry into the banking business by commercial firms. At the very least, Congress should consider permitting commercial enterprises to buy or invest in troubled and failed banks just as was done with troubled and failed savings and loans.

Notes

1. Statement by Alan Greenspan, Chairman, Board of Governors of the Federal Reserve System, Before the Committee on Banking, Finance, and Urban Affairs, U.S. House of Representatives, September 13. 1990.

2. Robert E. Litan, *What Should Banks Do?* The Brookings Institution, 1987.

3. The objection that narrow banks invested only in safe assets could not earn acceptable returns for shareholders ignores that if a bank is truly invested in safe assets then regulators can afford to let it operate with a lower capital-to-asset ratio. Thus, even with a lower "spread" on its assets, the narrow bank could still earn a market return on invested equity.

4. Through August 1990, signs of a nationwide "credit crunch" were not apparent in the numbers: the loan-to-asset ratio in the banking industry was stable while the industry as a whole (measure by total assets) displayed steady growth. Nevertheless, it is possible that as more recent data are reported, evidence of a nationwide credit crunch may appear.

5. Congressional Budget Office, *Reforming Federal Deposit Insurance*, September 1990.

6. See, for example, James R. Barth, *The Great Savings and Loan Debacle*, American Enterprise Institute, 1991; R. Dan, Brumbaugh, Jr., *Thrifts Under Siege*, Ballinger, 1988; Robert E. Litan, *What Should Banks Do?*, The Brookings Institute, 1987; George J. Benston, et al., *A Blueprint for Restructuring America's Financial Institutions*, The Brookings Institution, 1989; and R. Dan Brumbaugh, Jr. and Kenneth E. Scott, "The Endless Banking Crisis: Prospects for Reform in 1992," *Challenge*, March/April 1992.

7. General Accounting Office, "OCC's Supervision of the Bank of New England Was Not Timely or Forceful," The General Accounting Office, Washington, D.C., September 1991.

8. A debate over market-value accounting can also be found between William H. Beaver, Srikant Datar, and Mark A. Wolfson, "The Role of Market Value Accounting in Regulation of Insured Depository Institutions," and George J. Benston, Mike Carhill, and Brian Olasov, "Market Value versus Historical Cost Accounting: Evidence from Southeastern Thrifts," in *The Reform of Federal Deposit Insurance: Disciplining the Government and Protecting Taxpayers*, James R. Barth and R. Dan Brumbaugh Jr., eds., HarperBusiness, New York, 1992.

9. Market-value data would also facilitate the implementation of either of the market-based mechanisms discussed below—a mandatory subordinated debt requirement or a private reinsurance system for a portion of the risks assumed by the FDIC—for triggering more automatic regulatory intervention.

10. One problem, however, with using the spread as a trigger for regulatory action is that the spread itself will reflect investors' probability that such an action might be taken.

11. The Senate Banking Committee version of the Administration's reform plan would require the FDIC to adopt Senator Dixon's plan on an experimental basis.

12. See Tables 1 through 4 of Appendix J in "Banks in Turmoil" for details.

13. In calculating earnings, however, banks would be required to deduct their total provisions for loan-loss reserves in the current period, rather than just their actual charge-offs for bad loans.

14. See The Conference of State Bank Supervisors, "State of the State Banking System," 1990.

15. Robert E. Litan, *What Should Banks Do?* The Brookings Institution, 1987; and George J. Benston, et al., *A Blueprint for Restructuring America's Financial Institutions*, The Brookings Institution, 1989.

Postscript

It is an old story. The government tends to react to well-publicized mishaps and calamities as they occur rather than fashioning what could be described as a longer-term comprehensive approach to a thoughtfully analyzed general problem. This statement surely describes each of the four savings and loan and banking bills passed by the Congress and signed into law in the 1980s, and the pattern was the same in 1991 when the Congress finished grappling with the fifth round of banking legislation. The spur to action is the continuing deterioration of the Bank Insurance Fund.

The BIF Revises Reserves Downward and Borrows From the Treasury

As we discussed in Chapter 2, the BIF's reported reserves declined from a peak of $18.3 billion in 1987 in annual increments to $14.1 billion in 1988 to $13.2 billion in 1989 to $8.5 billion in 1990. In each case the FDIC made significant errors in estimating its next year's reserves. Most recently, in 1991 the FDIC lowered its estimated year-end reserves to $4 billion. The adjustment was made as a result of a GAO audit of the FDIC in which the GAO found that the FDIC had not adequately written down its reserves to reflect expected losses in 1991.

In September 1991 the FDIC drew down on its $5 billion line of credit from the U.S. Treasury Department by borrowing $2.9 billion. This is a distinct break from the past in which all FDIC reserves were accumulated from the banks' insurance premium and income from invested reserves. For the first time taxpayer dollars now comprise part of the FDIC reserves. This is essentially parallel to the step taken by the FSLIC in 1987 when it first used taxpayer dollars through an elaborate borrowing mechanism established by Congress.[1] As with the savings and loan borrowing, the banks are responsible for paying back the $2.9 billion. Yet, for the first time the FDIC and the banks are in a position where the possibility of default exists on a specific borrowing of taxpayer dollars.

The banks and the FDIC contend that because the banks are responsible for paying back the borrowing (and the borrowing proposed in some legislation) there is no taxpayer expenditure unless the banks default on the loans. This is incorrect. By borrowing through the Treasury the banks are borrowing at a lower rate than they would otherwise. Thus, there is now a direct taxpayer subsidy to the banks equal to the interest-rate differential times the borrowed amount.

Not-So-Subtle Changes in the Legislative Focus

The focus of the early 1991 banking legislative proposal that came initially from the White House through the Treasury and subsequently evolved in Congress had two main parts: one, essentially to recapitalize the BIF; and a second to provide the banks with greater opportunities to compete. The emphasis was clearly on the latter category. The theme most frequently repeated was that with fewer regulatory constraints on bank ownership, allowable assets, and interstate branching, banks would be more profitable and thereby be in a position to (among other things) add to their capital.

In an economic sense benefits would accrue immediately with passage of legislation with these provisions because the future expected stream of bank income would increase. This is sometimes referred to as an increase in "franchise value." As we have discussed in many sections of this book, we agree that this would be the direction of the effects of such legislation. What was left vague by proponents, however, was the size of the effects and the distribution between healthy and unhealthy banks. The overall impression that proponents tended to convey was that the benefits would develop rather quickly, would be fairly well distributed to all kinds of banks, and would help alleviate the FDIC's acute problems.

As the decline in the BIF's reserves increased, accompanied by government reports primarily from the GAO that the BIF's reserves would be exhausted sooner than expected—now sometime in 1992—the focus of legislative concern changed. The focus became recapitalizing the

BIF with, in essence, a U.S. Treasury Department borrowing of approximately $70 billion. In what seems an echo of the 1987 Congressional debate over the savings and loan borrowing, the responsibility of the banks to pay back the borrowing has been emphasized and cited repeatedly as a protection against a "taxpayer bailout" of the BIF and of the FDIC.

The prospect of large taxpayer expenditures in part led Congress to defeat the bank ownership, assets power, and interstate branching proposals designed to be provided to healthy banks. The arguments opposing the proposals, ironically, tend to reflect apprehension about deregulation and to ignore how the inability of banks to adapt to competition got them into trouble. Although proposals for prompt closure of troubled banks were adopted, the process in general is lurching through another deposit-insurance funding crisis in which plugging the funding hole becomes a temporary preoccupation. As long as the chief motivation for legislation is emergency funding of the deposit-insurance agency, the needed structural changes in the banking industry will not receive the attention they deserve.

The Proposed Big-Bank Mergers of 1991: Cost Savings or Dangerous Gambles?

An example of an issue that is not getting the scrutiny it deserves arose in 1991 when several big banks announced their intentions to merge pending regulatory approval. The first was NCNB Corporation with C&S/Sovran Corporation followed by Chemical Bank and Manufacturers Hanover Bank and then by Bank America and Security Pacific. Each of these mergers raises issues for which there are both benign and troubling interpretations. Each of the mergers, for example, are justified by the firms involved as mergers that will result in substantial cost savings the result of which will make the combined firm more profitable.

Especially for noneconomists, this contention has great intuitive appeal in the latter two cases because they have substantial numbers of branches that overlap in the same geographic areas. Closing overlapping branches is an apparently straightforward cost saving. The cost-saving argument has less appeal in the first case because NCNB is headquartered in Charlotte, North Carolina and C&S/Sovran is headquartered in Atlanta, Georgia and Norfolk, Virginia. The potential cost savings are less clear in what is sometimes referred to as an "out-of-market" merger.

Yet, the economic analysis of these mergers can be harsh. As yet, there is no economic study that we know of that suggests that there are any economies of scale that cannot be fully achieved by banks of a size substantially below the size of these banks. A 1991 survey of the economic literature on economies of scale in banking done by economists at the Federal Reserve Bank of Chicago summarizes the studies of smaller banks as follows: "Basically, the results imply that scale advantages are fully exhausted once an institution achieves a size of approximately $100–200 million, a relatively small bank in the United States."[2] Regarding larger banks, the study reports: "the most typical conclusion the authors draw from these bank cost studies is that potential gains from altering scale via internal growth or merger activity are relatively minor."

In sum, the weakness and large size of the banks, the weakness of the BIF, the weakness of other large banks that could be acquirers, and the available evidence on the likely benefits of such mergers suggest that any proposed mergers should be viewed with skepticism and receive extremely close scrutiny. The relevant institutions face substantial moral hazard that may lead to great risks. Most important, by buying time with promised cost savings, mergers, if approved, may provide a large bank an opportunity to gamble for resurrection—protected even further from an assisted acquisition by its new size—while the bank regulators echo the themes of consolidation and cost savings and buy time for themselves as well. In other words, some of these (and other as yet unannounced) big mergers may turn out to be another manifestation of forbearance.

The Future of American Banking: Let the Banks Compete

The immediate future of American banking is grim because of the accelerating onslaught of competition. The government cannot halt this process beause other unregulated firms from around the world now offer traditional banking services and products. The government's current strategy of limiting banks' geographic location, allowable products, and ownership inhibits the banks from adapting to meet the competition. As a result, both the number of bank failures as well as their cost are greater than they would be otherwise. It is time for the government to change fundamentally its strategy. It must eliminate the regulatory carapace that limits banks' geographic location, allowable products, and ownership. The Congress must let the banks compete.

Notes

1. For a description of the savings and loan funding mechanism, see R. Dan Brumbaugh, Jr., Andrew S. Carron, and Robert E. Litan, "Cleaning Up the Depository Institutions' Mess," the *Brookings Papers on Economic Activity*, The Brookings Institution, June 1989.

2. Douglas E. Evanoff and Philip R. Israilevich, "Productive Efficiency in Banking," *Economic Perspectives*, Federal Reserve Bank of Chicago, July–August 1991.

Bibliography

Atkinson, Bill, "Texas Bust Tied to Lack of Exams," *American Banker*, November 5, 1990, p. 2.

Atkinson, Bill and Robert M. Garrson, "Bank Fund Loss Put at $3 Billion," *American Banker*, September 28, 1990, p. 2.

Barth, James R., Daniel E. Page, and R. Dan Brumbaugh, Jr., "Pitfalls in Using Market Prices to Assess the Financial Condition of Depository Institutions," *The Journal of Real Estate Finance and Economics*, June 1992.

Barth, James R., *The Great Savings and Loan Debacle*, American Enterprise Institute, University Press of America, 1991.

————.Testimony on Deposit Insurance Reform, Before the Senate Committee on Banking, Housing, and Urban Affairs, March 12, 1991.

Barth, James R., and R. Dan Brumbaugh, Jr., "The Credit Union Industry: Financial Condition and Policy Issues," California Credit Union League, February 1991.

————."Thrifts," in *The New Palgrave: The Dictionary of Banking and Finance*, Peter Newman, Murray Milgate, and John Eatwell, eds., New York: Stockton Press, June 1992.

————, eds., *The Reform of Federal Deposit Insurance: Disciplining the Government and Protecting Taxpayers*, New York: HarperBusiness, 1992.

Barth, James R., R. Dan Brumbaugh, Jr., and Robert E. Litan, "Bank Failures are Sinking the FDIC," *Challenge*, March–April 1991.

—————.“Banking Industry in Turmoil: A Report on the Condition of the U.S. Banking Industry and the Bank Insurance Fund,” Report of the Subcommittee on Financial Institutions Supervision, Regulation, and Insurance of the Committee on Banking, Finance, and Urban Affairs, House of Representatives, One Hundred First Congress, Second Session, Committee Print 101-8, Washington, D.C.: U.S. Government Printing Office, December 1990.

Barth, James R., R. Dan Brumbaugh, Jr., and Daniel Sauerhaft, “Failure Costs of Government-Regulated Financial Firms: The Case of Thrift Institutions,” Federal Home Loan Bank Board Working Paper 123, October 1986.

Barth, James R., R. Dan Brumbaugh, Jr., Daniel Sauerhaft, and George H.K. Wang, “Insolvency and Risk-Taking in the Thrift Industry: Implications for the Future,” *Contemporary Policy Issues*, Volume III, Number 8, Fall 1985.

Barth, James R. and Robert E. Keleher, “‘Financial Crises’ and the Role of the Lender of Last Resort,” *Economic Review*, Federal Reserve Board of Atlanta, January 1984.

Beaver, William H., Srikant Datar, and Mark A. Wolfson, “The Role of Market Value Accounting in Regulation of Insured Depository Institutions,” *The Reform of Federal Deposit Insurance: Disciplining the Government and Protecting Taxpayers*, James R. Barth and R. Dan Brumbaugh, Jr., eds., New York: HarperBusiness, 1992.

Benston, George J., et al., *A Blueprint for Restructuring America's Financial Institutions*, Brookings Institution, 1989.

Benston, George J. and George G. Kaufman, “Understanding the Savings and Loan Debacle,” *The Public Interest*, Spring, 1990.

Benston, George J., Mike Carhill, and Brian Olasov, “Market Value Versus Historical Cost Accounting: Evidence from Southeastern Thrifts,” *The Reform of Federal Deposit Insurance: Disciplining the Government and Protecting Taxpayers*, James R. Barth and R. Dan Brumbaugh, Jr., eds., New York: HarperBusiness, 1992.

Berger, Allen N., Kathleen A. Kuester, and James M. O'Brien, “The Limitations of Market Value Accounting and a More Realistic Alternative,” Federal Reserve Board, September 1990.

Brammer, Rhonda, “Good Banks, Bad Banks,” *Barron's*, September 9, 1991.

Bovenzi, John F. and Arthur J. Murton, “Resolution Costs and Bank Failures,” *FDIC Banking Review*, Fall 1988.

Brenner, Joel Glenn, "GAO: Closing of NBW Came Far Too Late," *Washington Post*, September 20, 1990, p. E1.

Brumbaugh, R. Dan, Jr., *The Demise of the Savings and Loan Industry: Explaining the Collapse and the Taxpayer Bailout*, New York: Garland Publishing Inc., 1992.

—————.*Thrifts Under Siege*, New York: Ballinger, 1988.

Brumbaugh, R. Dan, Jr., and Kenneth E. Scott, "The Endless Banking Crisis: Prospects for Reform in 1992," *Challenge*, March–April 1992.

Brumbaugh, R. Dan, Jr. and Robert E. Litan, "The Banks Are Worse Off Than You Think," *Challenge*, January-February 1990.

Carron, Andrew S. and R. Dan Brumbaugh, Jr., "The Viability of the Thrift Industry," *Housing Policy Debate*, Volume 2, Issue 1.

Clarke, Robert C., Testimony before the Senate Committee on Banking, Housing, and Urban Affairs, October 25, 1989.

Conference of State Bank Supervisors, "State of the State Banking System," 1990.

Congressional Budget Office, *Reforming Federal Deposit Insurance*, September 1990.

Cope, Debra and Robert M. Garrson, "Study Raises Doubts Fees Can Revive FDIC," *American Banker*, September 26, 1990, p. 1.

Crowley, Leo T., Statement in Hearings before the House Committee on Banking and Currency, *Banking Act of 1935*.

Federal Deposit Insurance Corporation, *Quarterly Banking Profile*, First Quarter, 1991.

Fromson, Brett Duval, "Will the FDIC Run Out of Money?" *Fortune*, October 8, 1990, pp. 119-27.

General Accounting Office, *Bank Insurance Fund: Additional Reserves and Reforms Needed to Strengthen the Fund*, September 1990.

Gorton, Gary and George Pennacchi,"Financial Innovation and the provision of Liquidity Services," *The Reform of Federal Deposit Insurance: Disciplining the Government and Protecting Taxpayers*, James R. Barth and R. Dan Brumbaugh, Jr., eds., New York: HarperBusiness, 1992.

—————."The Opening of New Markets For Bank Assets," paper presented to an October 1990 conference sponsored by the Federal Reserve Bank of St. Louis.

Gray, Edwin J., Chairman, Federal Home Loan Bank Board, Statement before the Committee on Banking, Housing, and Urban Affairs, U.S. Senate, March 13, 1986.

Greenspan, Alan, Statement before the Committee on Banking, Finance, and Urban Affairs, U.S. House of Representatives, September 13, 1990.

IBCA, Ltd., Report on U.S. Banking Industry [partially reprinted under "Apocalypse for U.S. Bank? Not Now, Says Credit Rater," *American Banker*, August 28, 1990].

Kane, Edward J., *The S&L Insurance Mess: How Did It Happen?* Washington D. C.: Urban Institute Press, 1989.

Leander, Tom, "New England's Banks Are Hurting," *American Banker*, November 15, 1990, p. 2.

Lipin, Steven, "Big Banks Slash HLT Exposure By Billions," *American Banker*, December 5, 1990, p. 1.

Litan, Robert E., "Remedy for S&L's: Operation 'Clean Sweep,'" *Challenge*, November-December 1990 (reprinted Testimony before the Senate Judiciary Committee, August 14, 1990).

————.*What Should Banks Do?* Brookings Institution, 1987.

Maloney, Eileen and George Gregorash, "Banking 1989: Not Quite A Twice Told Tale," *Economic Perspectives*, Federal Reserve Bank of Chicago, July–August 1990.

Meehan, John and Catherine Yang, "The Banks Are Running Out Of Running Room," *Business Week*, October 29, 1990, p. 88.

Pantalone, Coleen C. and Marjorie B. Platt, "Predicting Bank Failure Since Deregulation," *New England Economic Review*, Federal Reserve Bank of Boston, July–August 1987, pp. 37–47.

Rehm, Barbara, "New Pressure on FDIC Fund, Bank Capital," *American Banker*, December 11, 1990, p. 1.

Reischauer, Robert, Testimony before the House Committee on Banking, Currency, and Housing, September 12, 1990.

Romer, Thomas and Barry R. Weingast, "Political Foundations of the Thrift Debacle," in *The Reform of Federal Deposit Insurance: Disciplining the Government and Protecting Taxpayers*, James R. Barth and R. Dan Brumbaugh, Jr., eds., New York: HarperBusiness, 1992.

Ronn, Ehud I. and Avinash K. Verma, "Pricing Risk-Adjusted Deposit Insurance: An Options-Based Model," *Journal of Finance*, September 1986, pp. 871–95.

Roosevelt, Phil, "Home Loans Fall As Bulwarks for Bank Portfolios," *American Banker*, November 13, 1990, p. 1.

Rosenberg, James M., "The Big Bank Barbershop: Credit Risk Haircuts to Book Value," Shearson Lehman Brothers, June 10, 1991.

Rosenthal, James A. and Juan M. Ocampo, *Securitization of Credit: Inside the New Technology of Finance*, John Wiley & Sons, 1988.

Sinkey, Joseph F., Jr., *Problem and Failed Institutions in the Commercial Banking Industry*, Greenwich, CT: Jai Press, 1979.

Sinkey Joseph F., Jr., "Identifying 'Problem' Banks," *Journal of Money, Credit, and Banking*, May 1978, pp. 184–93.

Spellman, Lewis J., *The Depository Firm and Industry: Theory, History, and Regulation*, Academic Press, 1982.

Starobin, Paul, "Will the Banks Be Next?" *National Journal*, December 30, 1989, pp. 3090–3095.

Stiglitz, Joseph E., "S&L Bail-Out," *The Reform of Federal Deposit Insurance: Disciplining the Government and Protecting Taxpayers*, New York: HarperBusiness, 1992.

Suskind, Ton, "Some Banks Use Accounting Techniques That Conceal Loan Woes, Regulators Say," *Wall Street Journal*, November 29, 1990, p. 4.

White, Lawrence J., *The S&L Debacle: Public Policy Lessons for Bank and Thrift Regulation*, Oxford University Press, 1991.

Appendix

Table A-1: Assets and Liabilities of FDIC-Insured Savings Banks, 1980–1990

Table A-2: Income and Expense of FDIC-Insured Savings Banks, 1980–1990

Table A-3: Federally Insured Mutual Savings Bank Industry

Table A-4: Concentration Ratios for Federally Insured Mutual Savings Banks, 1984–1990

Table A-5: Selected Information for Federally Insured Commercial Banks

Table A-6: Selected Information For Federally Insured Commercial Banks

Table A-7: Total Banks Rated 4 or 5 As of Each Year-End, and Such Banks Failing in Each Subsequent Year

Table A-8: Total Banks Rated 4 or 5 As of Each Year-End, and Such Banks Failing in Each Subsequent Year

Table A-9: Top 100 Bank Resolution Losses, 1985–1990

Table A-10: Total U.S. Assets of Foreign-Controlled U.S. Banking Offices, 1972–1989

Table A-1

Assets and Liabilities of FDIC-Insured Savings Banks, 1980 - 1990 ($ Millions)

	1980	1981	1982	1983	1984	1985	1986	1987	1988	1989	1990
Total Assets	152,940	156,458	155,750	170,718	178,901	205,279	236,882	261,842	284,196	279,929	259,115
Cash and Due from Depository Inst.	3,928	5,065	5,986	5,630	4,501	5,162	7,480	7,086	8,291	6,719	N/A
Securities	44,544	43,876	42,637	53,632	53,911	56,400	66,837	68,942	64,576	53,702	N/A
Federal Bonds Sold & Securities Purchased Under Resale Agreements	5,186	4,287	3,945	3,755	3,096	4,124	4,461	3,450	3,633	5,583	N/A
Loans & Leases, Net	96,277	97,754	95,320	99,852	107,858	127,733	146,965	168,586	192,099	197,228	176,485
Plus: Allowance for Losses	181	176	179	191	267	381	573	819	1,134	1,988	4,073
Loans & Leases Total	96,458	97,924	95,499	100,043	106,125	128,114	147,538	169,405	195,233	199,216	181,558
Bank Premises & Fixed Assets (Includes Capitalized Leases)	1,466	1,572	1,516	1,563	1,577	1,813	2,113	2,521	2,945	3,029	N/A
Other Real Estate Owned	288	324	376	452	379	561	540	666	968	2,898	3,331
Intangible Assets	N/A	N/A	N/A	1,155	1,898	2,811	2,899	2,885	2,597	2,299	1,624
All Other Assets	2,876	3,245	5,453	4,880	5,681	6,676	7,587	7,709	9,086	8,474	N/A
Total Liabilities and Equity Capital	152,940	156,458	155,750	170,718	178,901	205,279	236,882	261,842	284,196	279,929	259,115
Total Deposits	137,314	138,906	139,460	153,796	160,059	178,785	193,560	206,800	220,936	223,884	212,631
Federal Funds Purchases & Securities Sold Under Repurchase Agreement	1,652	3,992	3,348	3,886.	2,220	3,026	5,033	7,445	8,970	7,307	N/A
Demand Notes Issues to U.S. Treasury & Other Liabilities for Borrowed Money	2,719	3,436	3,172	2,831	6,198	9,028	15,981	25,606	28,398	23,994	N/A
Mortgage In Debenture	68	88	62	84	85	103	106	150	173	177	N/A
Subordinated Notes & Debentures	374	337	515	512	459	609	939	995	996	757	683
All Other Liabilities	906	996	1,244	1,420	1,540	2,081	3,716	2,714	3,580	3,980	N/A
Total Liabilities	143,033	147,755	147,801	162,530	170,560	193,631	219,337	241,718	263,048	260,079	240,550

Table A-1 (continued) ($ Millions)

	1980	1981	1982	1983	1984	1985	1986	1987	1988	1989	1990
Total Equity Capital	9,533	8,366	7,434	8,188	9,341	11,646	17,345	20,124	21,146	19,850	17,256
Perpetual Preferred Stock	N/A	N/A	N/A	0	0	158	114	213	585	406	N/A
Common Stock	N/A	N/A	N/A	0	160	295	1,090	1,093	1,075	835	N/A
Surplus	4,398	4,165	3,734	4,184	5,820	4,955	7,918	9,570	9,776	10,299	N/A
Undivided Profits	4,065	3,183	2,767	2,942	5,757	5,508	7,846	8,898	9,379	8,074	N/A
Other Surplus Reserves	1,070	1,018	933	660	N/A	N/A	N/A	N/A	N/A	N/A	N/A
Net Worth Certificates	N/A	N/A	N/A	402	604	732	577	350	331	236	N/A
Number of Problem Institutions	N/A	N/A	N/A	N/A	N/A	N/A	27	16	12	17	34
Number of Failures	N/A	N/A	N/A	N/A	N/A	N/A	0	2	0	1	10
Return on Assets (%)	N/A	N/A	N/A	N/A	N/A	N/A	1.08	0.84	0.44	-0.27	-.094
Equity Capital-to-Asset Ratio (%)	N/A	N/A	N/A	N/A	N/A	N/A	7.41	7.69	7.44	7.06	6.66
Tangible Capital-to-Asset Ratio (%)	N/A	N/A	N/A	N/A	N/A	N/A	6.31	6.73	6.69	6.30	5.94
Noncurrent Real Estate Loans to Total Real Estate Loans (%)	N/A	N/A	N/A	N/A	N/A	N/A	1.02	1.01	1.07	3.14	5.32
Noncurrent Loans and Leases plus other Real Estate owned to Assets (%)	N/A	N/A	N/A	N/A	N/A	N/A	0.83	0.95	1.51	2.63	5.04
Number of Institutions	323	351	315	294	291	392	472	404	492	489	469

Source: FDIC Statistics on Banking Beginning 1982. Prior years were obtained from the FDIC Annual Report.

Note: Prior to 1983 data does not include Federal Charter Savings Banks.

Table A-2
Income and Expenses of FDIC-Insured Savings Banks, 1980 - 1990

	1980	1981	1982	1983	1984	1985	1986	1987	1988	1989	1990
Total Interest and Fee Income	12,445	13,852	13,952	14,577	16,540	18,804	21,064	22,624	24,652	26,457	24,522
Domestic Office Loans	8,386	9,334	9,478	9836	11,192	13,287	15,044	16,474	18,517	20,223	N/A
Lease Financing Receivables	N/A	N/A	N/A	0	56	82	98	35	7	76	N/A
Balance Due from Depository Institutions	N/A	N/A	N/A	N/A	N/A	N/A	200	184	219	269	N/A
Interest & Dividend Income on Securities	3,562	3,816	3,896	4276	5,078	5,078	5,288	5,553	5,323	5,312	N/A
Interest Income from Federal Funds Sold and Repurchase Agreements	497	702	578	465	375	357	434	378	386	577	N/A
Total Interest Expense	11,189	14,022	14,206	13,399	14,816	14,945	14,806	15,357	17,443	19,722	18,084
Interest on Domestic Office Deposits	10,635	13,169	13,256	12,827	13,932	13,963	13,418	12,955	14,351	16,414	N/A
Expense of Federal Funds Purchased and Reverse Repurchase Agreements	247	464	532	238	206	223	305	608	717	789	N/A
Interest on Demand Notes Issued to The U.S. Treasury and other Borrowed Money	271	356	369	288	569	712	1,004	1,683	2,250	2,399	N/A
Interest on Mortgage Indebtedness and Obligations Under Capitalized Leases	N/A	N/A	N/A	N/A	N/A	N/A	13	12	20	19	N/A
Interest on Subordinated Notes and Debentures	36	33	49	46	49	47	66	99	105	101	N/A
Net Interest Income	1,256	(170)	(254)	1,178	1,732	3,859	6,258	7,267	7,209	6,735	6,438
Provision for Loan and Lease Losses	49	28	38	51	251	265	416	482	792	2,168	3,487

Table A-2 (continued)

Total Noninterest Income	584	935	1,352	1,334	1,540	1,570	1,377	1,317	1,371	1,435	1,255
Service Charges on Deposit Accounts	100	132	150	183	215	274	152	174	203	229	N/A
Other Noninterest Income	484	803	1,202	1,151	1,325	1,296	1,225	1,143	1,168	1,206	N/A
Gains on Securities Not Held in Trading Account	19	57	188	114	130	319	591	297	200	(70)	(22)
Total Noninterest Expense	2,030	2,211	2,341	2,635	2,896	3,534	4,413	5,137	5,665	6,123	6,466
Salaries and Employee Benefits	926	1,025	1,032	1,144	1,248	1,535	1,937	2,310	2,466	2,513	N/A
Expense of Premises and Fixed Assets	352	396	417	460	516	602	717	843	946	991	N/A
Other Noninterest Expense	752	790	892	1,031	1,132	1,397	1,759	1,984	2,253	2,619	N/A
Pre-Tax Net Operating Income	(220)	(1,417)	(4,093)	(60)	255	1,949	3,397	3,262	(2,323)	(191)	1,227
Applicable Income Taxes	45	(134)	(24)	118	144	516	1173	1256	1080	514	196
Income Before Extraordinary Items	(265)	(1,283)	(1,069)	(178)	111	1,433	2,224	2,006	1,243	(705)	(2,457)
Extraordinary Items, Net	16	(165)	(160)	8	22	15	144	75	(5)	35	11
Net Income	(249)	(1,448)	(1,229)	(170)	133	1,448	2,368	2,081	1,238	(670)	(2,468)
Number of Banks	323	331	315	294	291	392	472	484	492	489	463

Source: FDIC Statistics on Banking Beginning 1982 Prior years were obtained from the FDIC Annual Report.

N/A - Not Available

Table A-3
Federally Insured Mutual Savings Bank Industry ($ Millions)

		1984	1985	1986	1987	1988	1989	June 1990
Less Than 0.0 Percent	Number	0	0	0	0	0	3	7
	Net Income	0	0	0	0	0	(247)	(406)
	Capital	0	0	0	0	0	(40)	(179)
	Total Assets	0	0	0	0	0	2,947	5,713
Between 0.0 Percent and 1.5 Percent	Number	5	3	2	1	2	5	6
	Net Income	(153)	(6)	(15)	4	(67)	(322)	(211)
	Capital	108	70	11	5	6	112	124
	Total Assets	12,293	6,041	1,574	419	1,261	12,681	13,158
Between 1.5 Percent and 3.0 Percent	Number	21	15	5	1	2	2	9
	Net Income	53	61	50	2	(119)	(119)	(314)
	Capital	2,452	468	242	4	343	20	222
	Total Assets	47,816	18,196	9,090	153	13,447	886	8,405
Between 3.0 Percent and 6.0 Percent	Number	87	68	51	32	31	36	57
	Net Income	53	275	321	210	(27)	(323)	(730)
	Capital	2,452	2,665	2,595	3,268	2,336	2,097	2,248
	Total Assets	47,816	51,928	52,122	71,437	49,842	44,165	45,404
Between 6.0 Percent and 8.0 Percent	Number	96	167	171	156	161	151	138
	Net Income	185	526	583	515	518	231	(97)
	Capital	2,594	4,002	4,136	4,572	6,017	6,348	5,401
	Total Assets	38,851	57,417	60,000	65,932	84,845	90,567	75,031
Greater Than 8.0 Percent	Number	60	113	217	273	273	271	236
	Net Income	82	266	865	934	755	558	141
	Capital	1,280	2,236	7,375	9,157	9,468	9,300	8,329
	Total Assets	13,819	23,031	60,969	79,455	88,492	89,156	82,402

Source: FDIC.

Note: Includes all FDIC-insured mutual savings banks reporting financial data to the FDIC.

Table A-4
Concentration Ratios for Federally Insured Mutual Savings Banks, 1984 to 1990

Year	Top 5		Top 10		Top 25		Top 50		Top 100		Total Number	Total Assets ($ Bil)
	% Number	% Assets	% Number	% Assets	% Number	% Assets	% Numbers	% Assets	% Number	% Assets		
1984	1.86	23.60	3.72	34.56	9.29	52.67	18.59	67.93	37.17	83.47	269	134.7
1985	1.37	22.24	2.73	32.01	6.83	48.43	13.66	62.57	27.32	77.05	366	156.6
1986	1.12	20.72	2.24	30.00	5.61	45.14	11.21	59.16	22.42	73.85	446	183.8
1987	1.08	22.45	2.16	31.76	5.40	46.98	10.80	60.46	21.60	74.68	463	217.4
1988	1.07	20.00	2.13	29.42	5.33	45.51	10.66	59.63	21.32	74.36	469	237.9
1989	1.06	17.53	2.14	27.21	5.34	44.62	10.68	58.84	21.37	74.02	468	240.4
June 1990	1.08	15.45	2.17	26.06	5.42	43.66	10.85	58.04	21.69	73.89	461	232.4

Source: FDIC.

Note: This table only includes savings banks that are supervised by and provide quarterly Call reports to the FDIC. As of June 30, 1990, there were an additional 18 federally chartered BIF-insured institutions supervised by and reporting to the OTS.

Table A-5
Selected Information for Federally Insured Commercial Banks
(By Asset-Size Category)

Assets < $100M

	1980	1981	1982	1983	1984	1985	1986	1987	1988	1989	June 1990
Number of banks in group	12,735	12,549	12,393	12,184	12,036	11,781	11,399	10,924	10,288	9,720	9,499
Total bank assets ($ millions)	356,165	372,450	385,177	397,025	403,974	404,946	404,459	393,728	378,661	365,606	362,624
Net income after taxes (%)	1.12	1.07	1	0.87	0.74	0.61	0.44	0.5	0.61	0.75	0.8
Net operating income before taxes (%)	1.14	1.12	1.01	0.86	0.75	0.52	0.27	0.44	0.59	0.72	0.78
Equity capital (%)	8.45	8.51	8.6	8.54	8.52	8.53	8.35	8.56	8.72	8.93	9.09
Subordinated debt (%)	0.19	0.16	0.12	0.09	0.08	0.06	0.05	0.05	0.04	0.04	0.03
Goodwill, other intangibles (%)	N/A	N/A	N/A	N/A	0	0.03	0.03	0.04	0.04	0.05	0.06
Mandatory convertible debt (%)	N/A	N/A	N/A	N/A	0	0.01	0.01	0.01	0.01	0.01	0.01
Minority interest in con. subsid. (%)	N/A	N/A	N/A	N/A	0	0	0	0	0	0	0
Primary capital (FDIC def.)(%)	N/A	N/A	N/A	N/A	9.15	9.25	9.15	9.41	9.58	9.77	9.93
Primary plus secondary capital (%)	N/A	N/A	N/A	N/A	9.23	9.3	9.19	9.44	9.6	9.79	9.95
Gross loans and leases (%)	54.44	52.86	52	51.63	54.1	53.49	51.59	52.57	53	53.24	53.73
Loans and leases past due > 90 days (%)	N/A	N/A	0.81	0.72	0.68	0.65	0.57	0.45	0.39	0.37	0.37
Nonaccural loans and leases (%)	N/A	N/A	0.42	0.53	0.72	0.96	1.03	0.93	0.82	0.73	0.72
Reserve for loan losses (%)	0.52	0.52	0.52	0.55	0.63	0.74	0.82	0.87	0.88	0.87	0.89

Table A-5 (continued)
(By Asset-Size Category)

$100M < Assets < $ 1B

	1980	1981	1982	1983	1984	1985	1986	1987	1988	1989	June 1990
Number of banks in group	1,508	1,658	1,828	2,026	2,158	2,297	2,448	2,418	2,469	2,607	2,630
Total bank assets ($ millions)	365,103	401,847	434,725	480,073	513,777	546,015	580,692	575,833	592,931	625,113	634,775
Net income after taxes (%)	0.92	0.87	0.8	0.79	0.84	0.77	0.62	0.65	0.71	0.85	0.89
Net operating income before taxes (%)	0.94	0.91	0.83	0.79	0.84	0.7	0.47	0.6	0.69	0.84	0.88
Equity capital (%)	7.06	7.09	7.06	7.01	7.05	7.19	6.97	7.22	7.23	7.47	7.76
Subordinated debt (%)	0.42	0.42	0.42	0.3	0.21	0.18	0.2	0.25	0.16	0.16	0.11
Goodwill, other intangibles (%)	N/A	N/A	N/A	N/A	0	0.12	0.1	0.11	0.09	0.11	0.15
Mandatory convertible debt (%)	N/A	N/A	N/A	N/A	0	0.01	0.01	0.02	0.02	0.03	0.02
Minority interest in con. subsid. (%)	N/A	N/A	N/A	N/A	0	0	0	0	0	0	0
Primary capital (FDIC def.)(%)	N/A	N/A	N/A	N/A	7.74	7.86	7.78	8.07	8.13	8.36	8.61
Primary plus secondary capital (%)	N/A	N/A	N/A	N/A	7.95	8.03	7.92	8.2	8.23	8.45	8.7
Gross loans and leases (%)	54.16	53.57	52.97	53.28	58.24	58.83	58.37	60.23	61.81	61.66	62.01
Loans and leases past due > 90 days (%)	N/A	N/A	N/A	0.52	0.46	0.45	0.44	0.35	0.33	0.36	0.36
Nonaccural loans and leases (%)	N/A	N/A	N/A	0.73	0.75	0.91	0.01	0.98	0.9	0.85	0.91
Reserve for loan losses (%)	0.58	0.58	0.61	0.63	0.69	0.78	0.89	0.95	0.97	0.97	0.99

Table A-5 (continued)
(By Asset-Size Category)

$1B < Assets < $10B

	1980	1981	1982	1983	1984	1985	1986	1987	1988	1989	June 1990
Number of banks in group	174	186	210	234	254	288	308	315	323	334	327
Total bank assets ($ millions)	445,825	474,663	552,602	629,878	725,947	831,436	900,335	921,492	996,890	1,056,012	1,049,622
Net income after taxes (%)	0.66	0.67	0.63	0.6	0.71	0.79	0.69	0.45	0.73	0.6	0.64
Net operating income before taxes (%)	0.72	0.73	0.68	0.6	0.71	0.75	0.58	0.41	0.71	0.57	0.64
Equity capital (%)	5.53	5.61	5.61	5.7	5.71	5.85	5.96	6.1	6.15	6.12	6.52
Subordinated debt (%)	0.65	0.53	0.54	0.41	0.38	0.46	0.45	0.42	0.36	0.36	0.38
Goodwill, other intangibles (%)	N/A	N/A	N/A	N/A	0	0.16	0.2	0.21	0.2	0.21	0.32
Mandatory convertible debt (%)	N/A	N/A	N/A	N/A	0	0.08	0.11	0.12	0.1	0.08	0.06
Minority interest in con. subsid. (%)	N/A	N/A	N/A	0.3	0	0	0	0	0	0	0
Primary capital (FDIC def.)(%)	N/A	N/A	N/A	N/A	6.49	6.61	6.76	7.27	7.19	7.28	7.61
Primary plus secondary capital (%)	N/A	N/A	N/A	N/A	6.89	6.99	7.1	7.57	7.44	7.56	7.94
Gross loans and leases (%)	52.76	52.52	52.44	53.46	60.93	61.77	61.91	64.53	65.5	66.13	65.51
Loans and leases past due > 90 days (%)	N/A	N/A	0.48	0.38	0.29	0.31	0.31	0.33	0.31	0.32	0.34
Nonaccural loans and leases (%)	N/A	N/A	1.19	1.13	1.17	0.98	0.94	1.21	0.94	1.17	1.39
Reserve for loan losses (%)	0.6	0.55	0.66	0.72	0.78	0.83	0.9	1.26	1.14	1.3	1.35

Table A-5 (continued)
(By Asset-Size Category)

Assets > $ 10B

	1980	1981	1982	1983	1984	1985	1986	1987	1988	1989	June 1990
Number of banks in group	18	22	22	23	24	27	33	37	40	44	45
Total bank assets ($ millions)	668,621	780,501	821,649	835,185	864,789	948,143	1,055,188	1,108,134	1,162,406	1,252,303	1,313,933
Net income after taxes (%)	0.54	0.52	0.5	0.47	0.35	0.49	0.55	-0.64	0.95	0.1	0.6
Net operating income before taxes (%)	0.55	0.54	0.52	0.46	0.34	0.42	0.4	-0.71	0.88	0.05	0.53
Equity capital (%)	3.93	4.03	4.13	4.43	4.84	4.91	5.14	4.43	5.1	4.86	4.99
Subordinated debt (%)	0.2	0.21	0.3	0.33	0.69	1.01	1.09	1.1	1.09	1.17	1.14
Goodwill, other intangibles (%)	N/A	N/A	N/A	N/A	0	0.01	0.09	0.11	0.12	0.16	0.23
Mandatory convertible debt (%)	N/A	N/A	N/A	N/A	0	0.58	0.53	0.58	0.55	0.51	0.48
Minority interest in con. subsid. (%)	N/A	N/A	N/A	N/A	0.01	0.01	0.01	0.02	0.02	0.02	0.02
Primary capital (FDIC def.)(%)	N/A	N/A	N/A	N/A	5.66	6.45	6.74	7.55	7.78	7.66	7.26
Primary plus secondary capital (%)	N/A	N/A	N/A	N/A	6.34	6.87	7.32	8.07	8.32	8.33	7.92
Gross loans and leases (%)	57.55	60.88	61.83	62.43	65.53	62.89	63.28	62.77	62.64	63.43	62.39
Loans and leases past due > 90 days (%)	N/A	N/A	0.39	0.45	0.24	0.18	0.21	0.18	0.2	0.21	0.25
Nonaccural loans and leases (%)	N/A	N/A	1.57	1.99	2.21	1.85	1.91	3.08	2.56	2.56	2.49
Reserve for loan losses (%)	0.5	0.55	0.6	0.69	0.8	0.95	1.15	2.63	2.24	2.43	2

Table A-6
Selected Information For Federally Insured Commercial Banks
(By Capital-to-Asset Ratios)

	1980	1981	1982	1983	1984	1985	1986	1987	1988	1989	June 1990
					Capital/Asset < 0						
Number of Institutions	1	2	4	13	11	28	72	76	103	80	35
Assets ($ Millions)	17	37	156	746	414	1,485	3,596	9,923	21,163	11,160	1,485
Net Income After Taxes (%)	(0.92)	(4.40)	(6.52)	(8.13)	(6.79)	(7.95)	(11.59)	(11.27)	(.81)	(.36)	(0.03)
Net Oper. Income Before Taxes (%)	(0.94)	(4.40)	(6.54)	(8.13)	(6.85)	(8.08)	(12.14)	(11.28)	(8.91)	(6.28)	(9.98)
Equity Capital (%)	(2.88)	(1.86)	(0.57)	(1.63)	(1.42)	(2.18)	(4.83)	(7.79)	(4.04)	(8.76)	(3.65)
Subordinated Debt (%)	9.86	5.30	0.23	0.83	0.52	0.14	0.12	1.24	0.50	0.29	0.07
Goodwill, Oth Intangibles (%)	N/A	N/A	N/A	N/A	0.00	0.01	0.28	0.11	0.36	0.06	0.04
Mandatory Convertible Debt (%)	N/A	N/A	N/A	N/A	0.00	0.07	0.01	0.00	0.16	0.26	0.00
Minority Interest in Con.Subsid (%)	N/A	N/A	N/A	N/A	0.00	0.00	0.00	0.00	0.02	0.01	0.02
Primary Capital (FDIC Def) (%)	N/A	N/A	N/A	N/A	2.23	2.03	1.11	0.02	1.42	(3.47)	(0.47)
Primary Plus Secondary Capital (%)	N/A	N/A	N/A	N/A	2.23	2.08	1.12	0.06	1.68	(3.28)	(0.41)
Gross Loans and Leases	53.49	49.22	75.27	62.95	68.66	72.84	68.88	68.79	68.47	65.27	61.22
Loans and Leases Past Due (%)	N/A	N/A	4.88	2.75	2.71	2.76	2.70	2.31	0.90	1.62	0.89
Nonaccrual Loans and Leases (%)	N/A	N/A	3.03	3.38	5.04	11.90	8.37	10.32	10.71	7.98	4.84
Reserve for Loan Losses (%)	1.07	1.57	4.72	3.13	3.65	4.22	6.21	7.91	5.68	5.26	3.20

Table A-6 (continued)
(By Capital-to-Asset Ratios)

	1980	1981	1982	1983	1984	1985	1986	1987	1988	1989	June 1990
				0 < Capital/Asset < 1.5 Percent							
Number of Institutions	2	5	13	22	23	37	88	108	97	70	56
Assets ($ Millions)	86	72	759	1,682	847	2,115	5,523	5,247	9,801	37,859	18,938
Net Income After Taxes (%)	(3.56)	(4.54)	(4.86)	(3.45)	(4.67)	(4.88)	(5.54)	(4.76)	(4.10)	(2.61)	(2.15)
Net Oper. Income Before Taxes (%)	(3.56)	(4.25)	(4.70)	(2.97)	(4.67)	(5.28)	(5.88)	(4.79)	(4.09)	(2.65)	(2.14)
Equity Capital (%)	0.68	0.41	0.62	0.60	0.87	0.78	0.86	0.73	0.79	0.72	1.28
Subordinated Debt (%)	2.56	0.69	0.79	2.32	0.52	0.14	0.14	0.01	0.14	0.67	1.51
Goodwill, Oth Intangibles (%)	N/A	N/A	N/A	N/A	0.00	0.24	0.01	0.02	0.09	0.05	0.04
Mandatory Convertible Debt (%)	N/A	N/A	N/A	N/A	0.00	0.00	0.05	0.00	0.00	0.16	0.49
Minority Interest in Con.Subsid (%)	N/A	N/A	N/A	N/A	0.00	0.00	0.00	0.00	0.31	0.00	0.00
Primary Capital (FDIC Def) (%)	N/A	N/A	N/A	N/A	3.16	3.00	4.03	3.77	4.33	4.64	7.81
Primary Plus Secondary Capital (%)	N/A	N/A	N/A	N/A	3.51	3.14	4.14	3.79	4.46	5.15	8.84
Gross Loans and Leases (%)	56.31	57.53	61.73	64.98	70.44	50.65	64.54	61.57	59.05	67.86	77.68
Loans and Leases Past Due[1] (%)	N/A	N/A	5.35	1.71	3.41	1.60	2.19	1.60	0.78	0.47	0.47
Nonaccrual Loans and Leases (%)	N/A	N/A	5.11	2.56	4.54	4.75	8.53	5.70	4.73	8.33	9.47
Reserve for Loan Losses (%)	1.55	1.89	2.25	1.41	2.29	2.45	3.14	2.83	3.28	3.82	6.0

Table A-6 (continued)
(By Capital-to-Asset Ratio)

	1980	1981	1982	1983	1984	1985	1986	1987	1988	1989	June 1990
			1.5 Percent < Capital/Asset < 3.0 Percent								
Number of Institutions	12	16	27	53	62	85	124	165	157	109	92
Assets ($ Millions)	1,583	3,982	3,204	3,778	7,279	6,970	14,137	111,474	38,607	75,610	9,747
Net Income After Taxes (%)	(0.74)	(0.65)	(1.65)	(2.30)	(2.33)	(3.06)	(4.35)	(2.40)	(1.32)	(2.47)	(3.41)
Net Oper. Income Before Taxes (%)	(0.78)	(0.46)	(1.68)	(2.34)	(2.41)	(3.19)	(4.51)	(2.37)	(1.36)	(2.24)	(3.37)
Equity Capital (%)	1.81	2.38	2.22	2.37	2.37	2.42	2.45	2.46	2.66	2.71	2.44
Subordinated Debt (%)	3.23	1.80	1.43	0.26	0.53	0.38	0.46	1.18	0.67	1.38	0.20
Goodwill, Oth Intangibles (%)	N/A	N/A	N/A	N/A	0.00	0.07	0.01	0.19	0.02	0.05	0.05
Mandatory Convertible Debt (%)	N/A	N/A	N/A	N/A	0.00	0.05	0.03	0.76	0.66	0.45	0.06
Minority Interest in Con.Subsid (%)	N/A	N/A	N/A	N/A	0.00	0.00	0.00	0.00	0.01	0.04	0.01
Primary Capital (FDIC Def) (%)	N/A	N/A	N/A	N/A	3.77	4.29	5.12	6.87	6.04	7.89	5.29
Primary Plus Secondary Capital (%)	N/A	N/A	N/A	N/A	4.59	4.62	5.56	7.29	6.06	8.82	5.45
Gross Loans and Leases (%)	66.03	40.46	57.34	57.34	56.43	55.16	65.58	68.53	61.64	48.54	64.66
Loans and Leases Past Due' (%)	N/A	N/A	0.93	0.93	1.51	1.24	1.50	0.29	0.25	0.13	0.56
Nonaccrual Loans and Leases (%)	N/A	N/A	1.56	1.56	3.10	3.43	5.70	4.85	2.86	3.08	4.94
Reserve for Loan Losses (%)	1.22	0.69	1.49	1.49	1.40	1.93	2.66	3.84	2.71	4.75	2.83

Table A-6 (continued)
(By Capital-to-Asset Ratio)

	1980	1981	1982	1983	1984	1985	1986	1987	1988	1989	June 1990
				3.0 Percent < Capital/Asset < 6.0 Percent							
Number of Institutions	1,038	1,041	1,141	1,426	1,508	1,569	2,030	1,604	1,402	1,289	1,138
Assets ($ Millions)	1,141,363	1,259,599	1,375,203	1,431,948	1,498,606	1,632,547	1,776,650	1,588,149	1,679,702	1,570,391	1,667,774
Net Income After Taxes (%)	0.57	0.55	0.51	0.46	0.51	0.53	0.50	-0.26	0.83	0.20	0.45
Net Oper. Income Before Taxes (%)	0.59	0.58	0.53	0.45	0.51	0.46	0.35	-0.32	0.79	0.13	0.39
Equity Capital (%)	4.40	4.45	4.53	4.73	4.96	5.02	5.11	4.76	5.16	4.91	4.89
Subordinated Debt (%)	0.43	0.38	0.42	0.38	0.59	0.79	0.83	0.84	0.86	0.90	0.90
Goodwill, Oth Intangibles (%)	N/A	N/A	N/A	N/A	0.00	0.05	0.10	0.11	0.10	0.11	0.13
Mandatory Convertible Debt (%)	N/A	N/A	N/A	N/A	0.00	0.38	0.37	0.41	0.41	0.40	0.37
Minority Interest in Con.Subsid (%)	N/A	N/A	N/A	0.02	0.01	0.01	0.01	0.01	0.01	0.01	0.01
Primary Capital (FDIC Def) (%)	N/A	N/A	N/A	N/A	5.75	6.26	6.43	7.12	7.36	7.29	7.02
Primary Plus Secondary Capital (%)	N/A	N/A	N/A	N/A	6.35	6.66	6.90	7.56	7.82	7.79	7.55
Gross Loans and Leases (%)	55.49	57.82	58.17	58.76	63.28	62.56	62.22	62.56	63.70	64.58	62.24
Loans and Leases Past Due' (%)	N/A	N/A	0.46	0.45	0.28	0.26	0.26	0.21	0.24	0.24	0.28
Nonaccrual Loans and Leases (%)	N/A	N/A	1.41	1.63	1.73	1.51	1.59	2.40	2.08	2.16	2.30
Reserve for Loan Losses (%)	0.53	0.57	0.62	0.70	0.79	0.90	1.05	2.05	1.89	2.09	1.88

Table A-6 (continued)
(By Capital-to-Asset Category)

	1980	1981	1982	1983	1984	1985	1986	1987	1988	1989	June 1990
					6.0 Percent < Capital < 8.0 Percent						
Number of Institutions	5,401	5,411	5,292	5,280	5,439	5,340	5,168	4,944	4,705	4,401	4,395
Assets ($ Millions)	434,181	465,971	494,451	560,480	647,749	709,610	755,911	846,055	994,191	1,114,623	1,107,011
Net Income After Taxes (%)	0.94	0.88	0.84	0.82	0.64	0.82	0.82	0.81	0.95	0.96	0.89
Net Oper. Income Before Taxes (%)	0.97	0.93	0.88	0.81	0.65	0.75	0.69	0.76	0.92	0.95	0.87
Equity Capital (%)	6.94	6.93	6.92	6.81	6.77	6.79	6.78	6.83	6.80	6.77	6.83
Subordinated Debt (%)	0.33	0.29	0.25	0.21	0.16	0.16	0.19	0.17	0.20	0.32	0.32
Goodwill, Oth Intangibles (%)	N/A	N/A	N/A	N/A	0.00	0.14	0.17	0.13	0.15	0.18	0.24
Mandatory Convertible Debt (%)	N/A	N/A	N/A	N/A	0.00	0.00	0.01	0.03	0.04	0.07	0.06
Minority Interest in Con.Subsid (%)	N/A	N/A	N/A	N/A	0.00	0.00	0.00	0.00	0.00	0.00	0.00
Primary Capital (FDIC Def) (%)	N/A	N/A	N/A	N/A	7.48	7.43	7.48	7.65	7.60	7.64	7.71
Primary Plus Secondary Capital (%)	N/A	N/A	N/A	N/A	7.58	7.58	7.65	7.79	7.74	7.88	7.97
Gross Loans and Leases (%)	55.39	54.10	53.06	53.89	59.96	59.66	60.12	62.55	64.26	64.51	64.53
Loans and Leases Past Due[1] (%)	N/A	N/A	0.63	0.50	0.46	0.41	0.40	0.35	0.31	0.34	0.31
Nonaccrual Loans and Leases (%)	N/A	N/A	0.69	0.72	0.93	0.97	0.82	0.78	0.66	0.81	1.00
Reserve for Loan Losses (%)	0.57	0.56	0.59	0.61	0.70	0.77	0.86	0.93	0.92	0.98	1.07

Table A-6 (continued)
(By Capital-to-Asset Ratio)

	1980	1981	1982	1983	1984	1985	1986	1987	1988	1989	June 1990
					Capital < 8.0 Percent						
Number of Institutions	7,981	7,940	7,976	7,673	7,429	7,334	6,706	6,797	6,656	6,756	6,785
Assets ($ Millions)	278,485	299,801	320,380	343,527	535,592	377,812	384,858	438,341	437,424	489,392	556,001
Net Income After Taxes (%)	1.24	1.24	1.20	1.17	1.10	1.05	0.96	0.94	1.07	1.10	1.21
Net Oper. Income Before Taxes (%)	1.26	1.29	1.21	1.17	1.10	0.99	0.82	0.88	1.05	1.07	1.23
Equity Capital (%)	9.75	9.94	10.05	10.07	10.08	10.29	10.39	10.32	10.39	10.43	10.57
Subordinated Debt (%)	0.06	0.10	0.10	0.13	0.07	0.18	0.19	0.30	0.13	0.14	0.17
Goodwill, Oth Intangibles (%)	N/A	N/A	N/A	N/A	0.00	0.09	0.12	0.21	0.20	0.25	0.48
Mandatory Convertible Debt (%)	N/A	N/A	N/A	N/A	0.00	0.00	0.00	0.00	0.01	0.00	0.02
Minority Interest in Con.Subsid (%)	N/A	N/A	N/A	N/A	0.00	0.00	0.00	0.00	0.00	0.00	0.00
Primary Capital (FDIC Def) (%)	N/A	N/A	N/A	N/A	10.70	10.90	11.02	11.04	11.00	11.00	11.05
Primary Plus Secondary Capital (%)	N/A	N/A	N/A	N/A	10.77	11.08	11.15	11.25	11.08	11.09	11.21
Gross Loans and Leases (%)	53.25	51.55	51.06	49.99	52.39	52.15	51.34	53.56	51.98	55.12	57.85
Loans and Leases Past Due[1] (%)	N/A	N/A	0.71	0.60	0.55	0.55	0.47	0.41	0.32	0.33	0.40
Nonaccrual Loans and Leases (%)	N/A	N/A	0.44	0.53	0.58	0.64	0.67	0.70	0.59	0.64	0.70
Reserve for Loan Losses (%)	0.06	0.55	0.55	0.57	0.61	0.71	0.76	0.93	0.79	0.82	0.94

Source: FDIC.

[1] Past due more than 90 days.

Table A-7
Total Banks Rated 4 or 5 As of Each Year-End, and Such Banks Failing in Each Subsequent Year, (By Deposit Size)

Failure Year	Deposit Size	Number of Banks Rated 4 or 5 as of Year-End:								
		1980	1981	1982	1983	1984	1985	1986	1987	1988
N/A	Total	165	240	484	682	938	1,322	1,553	1,425	1,246
	<$300m	*	*	*	*	873	1,252	1,484	1,368	1,177
	$300m+	*	*	*	*	65	70	69	57	69
1981	All	5								
	<$300m	*								
	$300m+	*								
1982	All	11	21							
	<$300m	*	*							
	$300m+	*	*							
1983	All	9	15	33						
	<$300m	*	*	*						
	$300m+	*	*	*						
1984	All	3	7	28	58					
	<$300m	*	*	*	*					
	$300m+	*	*	*	*					
1985	All	4	5	22	32	89				
	<$300m	*	*	*	*	89				
	$300m+	*	*	*	*					
1986	All	5	5	17	35	65	112			
	<$300m	*	*	*	*	63	110			
	$300m+	*	*	*	*	2	2			
1987	All	3	6	10	23	41	93	159		
	<$300m	*	*	*	*	40	90	155		
	$300m+	*	*	*	*	1	3	4		
1988	All	4		5	12	22	51	102	154	
	<$300m	*	*	*	*	21	48	100	149	
	$300m+	*	*	*	*	1	3	2	5	
1989	All	1	2	7	9	12	37	91	155	195
	<$300m	*	*	*	*	8	32	82	143	181
	$300m+	*	*	*	*	4	5	9	12	14.

* Sizes could not be determined because Call Report data are unavailable on FDIC data base.

Table A-8
Total Banks Rated 4 or 5 As of Each Year-end, and Such Banks Failing in Each Subsequent Year, (By Deposit Size)

Failure Year	Deposit Size	Deposits of Banks Rated 4 or 5 as of Year-end:								
		1980	1981	1982	1983	1984	1985	1986	1987	1988
N/A	Total	*	*	*	*	165,849	274,799	234,700	210,757	185,112
	<$300m	*	*	*	*	33,610	47,433	58,365	55,533	50,578
	$300m+	*	*	*	*	132,239	227,365	176,335	155,224	134,534
1981	All	92*								
	<$300m	*								
	$300m+	*								
1982	All	173*	541*							
	<$300m	*	*							
	$300m+	*	*							
1983	All	896*	2,797*	2,196*						
	<$300m	*	*	*						
	$300m+	*	*	*						
1984	All	35*	121*	1,162*	2,345*					
	<$300m	*	*	*	*					
	$300m+	*	*	*	*					
1985	All	80*	170*	783*	1,084*	2,419				
	<$300m	*	*	*	*	2,419				
	$300m+	*	*	*	*	*				
1986	All	174*	173*	999*	2,935*	4,787	6,285			
	<$300m	*	*	*	*	**	**			
	$300m+	*	*	*	*	**	**			
1987	All	44*	269*	661*	1,188*	2,231	4,851	6,636		
	<$300m	*	*	*	*	**	**	5,060		
	$300m+	*	*	*	*	**	**	1,576		
1988	All	163*	0	89*	520*	2,136	5,158	5,415	18,264	
	<$300m	*	0	*	*	**	2,047	4,179	5,111	
	$300m+	*	0	*	*	**	3,112	1,236	13,153	
1989	All	**	110*	3,169*	1,205*	5,215	6,955	18,500	23,805	24,073
	<$300m	*	*	*	*	772	1,669	4,083	6,854	9,552
	$300m+	*	*	*	*	4,442	5,286	14,416	16,950	14,521

* Call Report data before 1984 are not available on FDIC data base.
Deposits for "All" failed banks are from last exam preceeding year-end.

** Data are excluded for size category to prevent identification of individual banks.

Table A-9
Top 100 Bank Resolution Losses, 1985 - 1989

Name of Institution	State	Type	Year	Charter	Assets ($ Mil)	Est. Loss ($ Mil)	Loss/Asset (%)
First Republic Bank, Dallas	TX	PA	1988	N	18,124	1,666.82	9.20
Mbank- Dallas	TX	AT	1989	N	6,974	1,167.32	16.74
First City Bancorp.	TX	AT	1988	N	11,200	925.70	8.27
Mbank- Houston	TX	AT	1989	N	3,099	472.07	15.23
TAB / Ft. Worth	TX	AT	1989	N	1,991	390.60	19.62
First American Bank	FL	TA	1989	S	1,880	271.00	14.41
First Republic Bank	TX	PA	1988	N	2,875	260.01	9.04
First Service Bank	MA	DT	1989	S	888	230.09	25.92
Alliance Bank	AK	PA	1989	S	849	200.00	23.56
Bowery Savings Bank	NV	AT	1985	S	5,279	173.39	3.28
The First National Bank	OK	PA	1986	N	693	172.63	24.92
Guardian Bank	NY	PO	1989	N	420	172.25	41.05
First Republic Bank	TX	PA	1988	N	1,905	167.97	8.82
First Republic Bank	TX	PA	1988	N	1,731	161.29	9.32
MBank- Ft. Worth	TX	AT	1989	N	764	128.12	16.77
First National Bank	LA	DP	1988	N	272	127.18	46.75
First Interstate Bank	AK	PA	1987	S	368	117.86	32.06
The First State Bank	TX	DP	1989	S	262	113.36	43.19
United Bank- Houston	TX	DP	1987	S	217	108.89	50.20
MBank- Alamo, San Antonio	TX	AT	1989	N	688	107.59	15.65
MBank- Austin	TX	AT	1989	N	588	98.70	16.79
Western Bank-Westheimer	TX	DP	1987	S	292	98.07	33.60
Park BSNK	FL	PA	1986	S	602	93.00	15.44
Bossier Bank and Trust	LA	PA	1986	S	222	88.91	40.08
The Security National	OK	PA	1987	N	203	88.25	43.40
United Bank	TX	DP	1987	S	191	84.88	44.47
Louisiana Bank and Trust	LA	PA	1989	S	258	84.27	32.64
MBank- Wichita Falls	TX	AT	1989	N	455	76.19	16.74
The County Bank	FL	PA	1987	S	146	72.78	49.70
Bank of Dallas	TX	TA	1988	S	187	71.99	38.53
Yankee Bank for Finance	MA	DP	1987	N	464	70.32	15.14
Utica National Bank	OK	PA	1989	N	163	70.08	42.88
American Bank and Trust	LA	PA	1986	S	183	69.02	37.70

Table A-9 (continued)

Name of Institution	State	Type	Year	Charter	Assets ($ Mil)	Est. Loss ($ Mil)	Loss/Asset (%)
First Republic Bank, SA	TX	PA	1988	N	742	66.72	8.99
Banc Oklahoma Corp.	OK	AT	1986	N	468	65.00	13.88
Citizens National Bank	OK	DP	1986	N	166	61.84	37.27
MBank- Mid Cities	TX	AT	1989	N	369	61.80	16.75
First Republic Bank	TX	PA	1988	N	703	60.08	8.54
Central National Bank	NY	PO	1987	N	165	59.60	36.09
TAB/ Houston- Galleria	TX	AT	1989	N	300	58.87	19.62
The Jefferson Guaranty	LA	AT	1988	S	287	57.50	20.01
Sunshine State Bank	FL	PO	1986	S	104	56.51	54.25
Bank of Commerce	OK	PA	1986	S	166	56.39	33.88
Capital Bank & Trust Co	LA	PA	1987	S	387	56.13	14.49
MBank- Jefferson City	TX	AT	1989	N	324	54.35	16.80
MBank- Odessa	TX	AT	1989	N	322	53.94	16.77
United Oklahoma Bank	OK	PA	1987	S	147	52.88	36.01
Moncor Bank, N.A.	NM	PA	1985	N	238	52.74	22.17
First Republic Bank	TX	PA	1988	N	616	51.62	8.38
National Bank, Fort	TX	PA	1988	N	614	51.22	8.34
First Republic Bank	TX	PA	1988	N	600	50.22	8.37
MBank- Sherman	TX	PA	1989	N	275	45.89	16.70
American Exchange Bank	OK	PA	1987	S	92	44.64	48.33
TAB/ Dallas	TX	AT	1989	N	227	44.60	19.62
MBank- Longview	TX	AT	1989	N	260	43.67	16.77
First Republic Bank	TX	PA	1988	N	496	43.66	8.80
TAB/ Amarillo	TX	AT	1989	N	222	43.60	19.62
TAB/ Duncanville	TX	AT	1989	N	219	42.88	19.62
Rose Capital Bank	TX	PA	1989	S	56	42.62	76.12
Stockmens Bank	WY	DP	1987	S	118	40.93	34.69
Caribank	FL	TA	1988	S	533	39.59	7.43
TAB/ Levelland	TX	AT	1989	S	199	38.96	19.62
Northwest Bank & Trust	TX	TA	1988	S	97	38.63	40.00
MBank- Denton County	TX	AT	1989	N	230	38.50	16.76
First Bank and Trust Co.	TX	DP	1986	S	95	38.43	40.66
Alaska National Bank	AK	DP	1987	N	187	38.30	20.45
Union Bank and Trust	OK	PA	1988	S	115	38.22	33.38

Table A-9 (continued)

Name of Institution	State	Type	Year	Charter	Assets ($ Mil)	Est. Loss ($ Mil)	Loss/Asset (%)
Guaranty Bank	TX	TA	1988	S	82	37.89	46.31
Cordell National Bank	OK	DP	1986	N	77	36.90	47.94
La Salle State Bank	LA	TA	1989	S	38	36.71	97.65
MBank- Marshall	TX	AT	1989	N	218	36.45	16.74
The Farmers National	OK	PA	1987	N	64	35.31	55.58
Harris County Bank, NA	TX	DP	1988	N	74	33.58	45.33
TAB/ McKinney	TX	AT	1989	N	168	33.04	19.62
New Mexico National Bank	NM	PA	1986	N	152	32.93	21.63
Century Bank	AZ	PA	1989	S	119	32.62	27.34
The First National Bank	MO	PA	1985	N	180	32.56	18.09
First City Bank, N.A.	OK	PA	1985	N	66	32.24	49.04
MBank- Corsicana	TX	AT	1989	N	191	31.94	16.75
Forestwood National Bank	TX	DP	1989	N	55	31.81	57.62
MBank- Abilene	TX	AT	1989	N	189	31.70	16.74
Banker Trust of LA	LA	DT	1989	N	86	31.02	36.14
The National Bank	LA	PA	1989	N	78	30.47	39.22
The First National Bank	OK	DP	1986	N	67	30.47	45.46
The Citizens Bank	UT	PA	1985	S	46	30.43	66.87
Liberty National Bank	TX	PA	1989	N	63	30.30	48.19
The Bank of Commerce	LA	PA	1986	S	66	30.28	45.60
First National Bank	TX	PA	1986	N	77	29.75	38.45
United Mercantile Bank	LA	PA	1988	S	74	29.73	40.16
TAB/ Tyler	TX	AT	1989	N	148	29.10	19.62
Metropolitan Bank	LA	PA	1986	S	66	28.84	43.53
First Bank & Trust	TX	TA	1989	S	143	28.74	20.10
TAB/ Midland	TX	AT	1989	N	146	28.64	19362
TAB/ Fredricksburg	TX	AT	1989	N	145	28.48	19.62
TAB/ Austin	TX	AT	1989	N	144	28.33	19.62
Texas National Bank	TX	DP	1989	N	49	28.25	58.23
Western Bank	TX	PA	1986	S	63	27.90	43.94
MBank- Greenville	TX	AT	1989	N	166	27.81	16.76
MBank- Woodlands	TX	AT	1989	N	164	27.58	16.77
The First National Bank	OK	PO	1986	N	89	27.37	30.73

Source: FDIC.

Table A-10
Total U.S. Assets of Foreign-Controlled U.S. Banking Offices, 1972 - 1989
($ Billions)

	Foreign Banks					
Year	U.S. Branches and Agencies	Commercial Banks	Other[1]	U.S. Banks Owned By Foreign Individuals	Total	Foreign-Controlled U.S. Banking Assets/Total Domestic Banking Assets[2] (%)
1972	22.2	4.4	1.1	0.6	28.3	3.6
1973	25.2	5.4	1.5	1.0	33.1	3.7
1974	34.0	10.8	1.9	0.6	47.3	4.8
1975	38.2	11.8	2.0	2.1	54.1	5.3
1976	45.7	13.8	1.5	2.7	63.7	5.9
1977	59.1	16.2	1.6	4.9	81.8	6.7
1978	86.8	20.7	2.0	6.4	115.9	8.4
1979	113.5	34.6	2.4	7.7	158.2	10.3
1980	148.3	68.1	2.8	10.2	229.4	13.5
1981	172.6	78.5	3.2	11.5	265.8	14.2
1982	208.2	90.9	3.9	17.5	320.5	15.3
1983	229.0	99.3	4.2	19.7	352.2	15.4
1984	273.2	103.1	4.5	19.8	400.6	16.1
1985	312.4	111.3	5.4	23.0	452.1	16.5
1986	398.1	109.5	5.3	27.0	539.9	17.9
1987	462.7	112.8	6.1	28.7	610.3	19.8
1988	515.3	123.7	6.6	28.3	673.9	20.6
1989	581.3	134.1	6.5	29.1	751.0	21.4

Source: Report of the Subcommittee on Financial Institutions Supervision, Regulation, and Insurance, Task Force on the International Competitiveness of U.S. Financial Institutions of the Committee on Banking, Finance, and Urban Affairs, House of Representatives, One Hundred First Congress, Second Session, October 1990, Committee Print 101-7.

1. Includes N.Y. investment corporations and directly owned Edge corporations.
2. Total domestic banking assets include all assets of domestic offices of insured commercial banks plus those of U.S. branches and agencies of foreign banks. Consequently, in this table they also include balances booked in IBF's.

INDEX

Accounting practices 19
  and deteriorating depositories 13
  and exaggerated capital claims 8
  and misrepresentation of condition of banks 8
  obscuring deteriorating savings *and* loans with 4
Aggregate balance sheet
  risk in banking industry's 64
Aggregate measures
  and bank performance 19
Alternative cost estimates
  and recession 3
American Express Company 159
American Telegraph and Telephone Company 159
Annual deposit-insurance premiums 6
Asset values
  deterioration in 69
Asset-backed securities 64
Auburn University 45

Bad loans
  and big banks 29
Banc One of Texas 123
Bank call reports
  and baseline estimates 90
Bank capital ratios
  deterioration in 149
Bank capital standards
  and federal policymakers 149
Bank failure costs 3, 4
Bank failures 2, 19
  and taxpayer's risk exposure 149
Bank insolvencies 91
  and bank runs 5
Bank Insurance Fund (BIF) 1, 55
  baseline failure costs of 90
  and hidden costs to taxpayers 8

  and net cash reserves 117
  recapitalization of 139
Bank of Boston 37
Bank of New England 35, 44, 45, 77
  insolvency of 17
Bank of New York 32
Bank resolutions 93
Banking failures 87
Barnett Banks 37
Basel Accord standards 21
Baseline estimates 91
  of BIF 90
Bifurcation
  of savings bank industry 18
Book value 15
  capital 4
  insolvency 17
Breeden, Richard 154
Brookings Institution 15, 17
Building permits 37

Call reports 132
"CAMEL" system 110, 135
Capital
  at depository institutions 4
  inadequacy 21
Capital standards
  and federal regulators 21
Capital-to-asset categories
  and FDIC liquidation policies 92
Capital-to-asset ratio 18, 92
Cash Reserve Shortage
  and BIF 122
Cates, David 136
Charge-offs 29, 69
Chase Manhattan Bank 32, 41, 54
Chemical Bank 32, 41
  and Manufacturers Hanover proposed merger with 43

Citicorp 10, 32, 41, 54
Closure Costs 2
Commercial-bank assets
  domestic, foreign-controlled
    banks with 10
Commercial and industrial
  (C&I) loans 29, 65, 72
Commercial mortgage lending 37
Commercial paper market 9
Commercial real estate loans
  and big banks 29
Competition
  and government limits on
    banks 170
  and government policy 85
  and traditional bank functions 9
Comptroller of the Currency 21
Computer technology 62
Congress
  and BIF recapitalization 9
  and commercial firms 10
  asset restrictions imposed by 8
Congressional Budget Office (CBO)
  base-case projections of 123
Connecticut Savings Bank 35
Consolidation 9
  shedding of excess
    capacity and 158
Construction loans
  and big banks 29
Continental Illinois Bank 28, 37
  rescue of 161
Corporate paper market 65
Credit card loans 76
Credit contraction 144
Crowley, Leo 90, 144

Debt ratings 41
Demand deposits 77
Deposit-insurance
  agency, emergency funding
    of 169
  and excessive risk-taking 85
  cost estimate for 87
  funds 5
  liabilities, government's
    responsibility for 9

liabilities, baseline estimates of 88
  premium rate of 2, 6
  proposed "tax" 7
  system 15
Depositories 59
Desposit-insurance system 13
Dingell, Congressman John
  and New York Times article 54
Direct taxpayer subsidy 168
Disintermediation 61
Diversification
  geographic 158
Dixon, Senator Alan
  and mandatory reinsurance
    plan 155
Domestic deposits 77

Early intervention 11
"Economies of scope" 9
Equity capital 9
Equity capital-to-asset ratio 15
European American Bank 35

Failed banks
  acquirers of 2
  assets of 95, 114
Failure rates 110
Failure risks
  of individual banks 2
Federal Deposit Insurance
  Corporation (FDIC) 1
  losses of 114
  deposit-insurance funds of 5
  and insured depositories 13
Federal Home Loan Bank Board 28
Federal Home Loan Bank Board
  (FHLBB) 138
Federal Home Loan Mortgage
  Corporation (Freddie Mac) 62
Federal National Mortgage Association
  (Fannie Mae) 62
Federal Reserve Bank of Chicago 170
Federal Reserve Board 21
Federal Savings *and* Loan Insurance
  Corporation (FSLIC) 1
  bankruptcy through market-value
    losses of 13

Fee income 72
Finance companies 61
Financial Accounting Standards
  Board (FASB) 154
Financial Institutions Reform,
  Recovery, and Enforcement
    Act of 1989 (FIRREA) 117
"Firewalls" 159
First Republic Bank 28
First Union Bank 37
Fleet/Norstar 54
Forbearance 88, 111, 160
  and big banks 44
Ford Motor Company 10, 159
Foreign exchange contracts 72, 77
Foreign-controlled banks 10, 159
Former FDIC Chairman William
Seidman 150
Franchise value 56

General Accounting Office
  (GAO) 26, 88, 117
General Electric Company 159
General Motors Corporation 159
General revenues
  and recapitalization of BIF 7
General securities underwriting 10
Generally Accepted Accounting
  Principles (GAAP) 55
Goldome Savings Bank 134
Government National Mortgage
  Association (Ginnie Mae) 62
Government-sponsored enterprises 61
Great Depression 15, 28
Greenspan, Alan 149, 154

High-quality bank borrowers 9
"High-risk" lending 9, 33, 37
Highly leveraged transactions
  (HLT loans) 37, 57
Home equity loans 76
Home mortgages 37, 62
House Committee on Energy and
  Commerce 54
House Subcommittee on Financial
  Institutions, Supervision, Regula-
  tions, and Insurance 19, 43, 146

Housing starts 37
Howard Savings Bank (The)
  of Newark 35

Illiquidity 5, 63
Indices
  of bank decline 64
  of loan problems 64
Inflation 61
Information technology 9
Insolvency 5
  effective 131
  technical 131
Insolvent banks 5
  acquirers of 123
Insurance brokerage
  and state-chartered banks 10
Insurance underwriting
  and state banks 10
Intangible assets 56
Interest rates
  deregulation of 61
  double-digit 61
  swaps 72, 77
Intermediaries 63
Intermediation
  and competition in banking
    functions 9
International Business Machines
  Corporation (IBM) 159
Interstate branching 10
Interstate expansion
  restrictions against 9

Junk bonds 76

Large bank closure 28
Legislation banking
  1991 proposal 168
Letters of credit
  commercial 77
  standby 77
Liquid liablities 85
Loan charge-offs 65
Loan-loss reserves 29
Loans to Developing Countries
  (LDC) debt 15, 37

Maine Savings Bank 35
Mandatory reinsurance plan
    (S.3040) 155
Manufacturers Hanover 32. 41
    and proposed Chemical Bank
    merger with 43
Market-to-book valuations   41
Market-value capital   4
Market-value insolvency
    and additional bank failures 147
MCorp Banks of Texas 28
Mergers 10, 163
Money market deposit account
    (MMDA) 62
Money market mutual funds 60, 61
Moody's 41
Morgan Guaranty Bank 41
Mortgage-backed security 63
Mutual funds 60, 81
Mutual money market funds 9
Mutual savings banks 150

National banks
    and FDIC resolutions 95
National Credit Union Share
    Insurance Fund 6, 146
Nationalization
    of major banks 163
Nationwide Operations 158
NCNB Texas 123
"Negative spreads"
    and restructured loans   33
Net income
    volatility in 25
Net interest margins 9
New York Times
    and Congressman Dingell 54
1981–1982 recession 37
Nonaccrual loans 18, 28–29, 68
Nonbank commercial paper 65
Nonbanking organizations
    and affiliation with banks 9–10
Nondepositories 60
Nonfinancial companies
    acquisitions of banks by 10
Nonfinancial firms 10
Nonmarketable loans 150

Nontraditional activities 72

Off-balance-sheet activities 72, 77
Office building vacancy rate   35
Office of Thrift Supervision (OTS) 138
"Option-adjusted" value of capital 44
Option-price adjustment technique 58
"Option pricing" techniques 44
"Out-of-market" merger 170
Owner-contributed equity capital 7

Page, Dan 45
Pension funds 61, 81
Poorly performing loans
    and reduction of big-bank
        capital/income 29
Portfolio risk 18
Premium income
    and recapitalization of BIF 7
Present-value insolvency 131
Private reinsurance 155
Problem bank assets
    and ratings by bank examiners 19
Problem loans 68
    at New England banks 32
Problem-bank failures 113
Profitability
    and banks 8
Put option value 44
    of deposit insurance 44

Rates
    paid on subordinated debt 41
    paid on uninsured deposits 41
Real estate brokerage
    and state banks 10
Real estate development
    and state banks 10
Real estate equity participation
    and state banks 10
Real estate loans 35
Recapitalization
    of BIF 5, 137
    of FSLIC 138
Recession 3, 29
    and bank failures 129
    regional 129

Regional reciprocity 159
Regulators
   and bank and nonbank
      mergers 10
Regulatory Accounting Principles
   (RAP) 140
Regulatory forbearance 29, 89
   and troubled large banks 95
Reorganization policies 88
Representative Frank Annunzio 146
Reserves 167
   BIF revisions of 167
   and loan losses 18
Residential mortgage lending 37
Resolution costs 2, 4, 95
Resolution Trust Corporation
   (RTC) 35
Restrictions
   geographic 163
   product-line 163
Reischauer, Robert 134
River Bank America
   of New Rochelle 35
Rosenberg, James M.
   and New York Times article 54

Savings and loan industry
   bifurcation of 18
   debacle 4
Savings Association Insurance
   Fund (SAIF) 59
Sears, Roebuck and Company 10, 159
Securities markets 9
Securitization 9, 62, 76
   and depository revenue 63
Security Pacific 37
Shearson Lehman Brothers 54
Short-term Treasury securities 18
SNL Securities 54
Southeast Bank 54
Southeast Banking Corporation 45
Spread income 65
Standard and Poors 41
Standby letters of credit 72
State banks
   and insurance brokerage 10, 159
   and nonbank powers 10, 159

and real estate 10, 159
   and securities brokerage 10, 159
State-chartered banks
   and FDIC resolutions 95
Stock market 54
Stock prices
   and evaluating problem
      large banks 37
   of large banks 54
Subordinated debt 155

Tangible assets 56, 141
Tangible equity capital 55
"Taxpayer bailout" 169
Taxpayer protection 26
Taylor, William 5
Team Bank of Fort Worth 123
Technology
   and securitization of depository
      assets, 62
"Too-big-to-fail" doctrine 44, 153
Treasury securities 61
"Type 1" and "Type 2" errors 137

U.S. Treasury Department 6, 146
   and BIF line of credit from 6

Variable-rate mortgages 62

W.C. Ferguson
   database of 105
Wall Street Journal
   and Congressman John
      Dingell 54
Wells Fargo 37, 54